S0-AXR-408

COMIC BOOK COLLECTIONS FOR LIBRARIES

Bryan D. Fagan and Jody Condit Fagan

Foreword by Stan Sakai
Cover Art by Derek Steed

LIBRARIES UNLIMITED

AN IMPRINT OF ABC-CLIO, LLC
Santa Barbara, California • Denver, Colorado • Oxford, England

Copyright 2011 by Bryan D. Fagan and Jody Condit Fagan

All rights reserved. No part of this publication may be reproduced, stored in a
retrieval system, or transmitted, in any form or by any means, electronic, mechanical,
photocopying, recording, or otherwise, except for the inclusion of brief quotations in a
review or reproducibles, which may be copied for classroom and educational programs only,
without prior permission in writing from the publisher.

Library of Congress Cataloging-in-Publication Data

Fagan, Bryan D.
   Comic book collections for libraries / Bryan D. Fagan and Jody Condit Fagan ; foreword by Stan Sakai ;
cover art by Derek Steed.
      p. cm.
   Summary: "This book will help librarians extend literary graphic novel collections to attract a large,
untapped group of comic book readers with a sure-to-be-popular comic book collection"— Provided by
publisher.
   Includes bibliographical references and index.
   ISBN 978–1–59884–511–2 (pbk.) — ISBN 978–1–59884–512–9 (ebook)
1. Libraries—Special collections—Comic books, strips, etc. 2. Comic books, strips, etc.—Bibliography—
Methodology. 3. Libraries—Special collections—Graphic novels. 4. Graphic novels—Bibliography—
Methodology. I. Fagan, Jody Condit. II. Title.
Z688.C64F34   2011
025.2′77415—dc22   2010052532

ISBN: 978–1–59884–511–2
EISBN: 978–1–59884–512–9

15 14 13 12 11   1 2 3 4 5

This book is also available on the World Wide Web as an eBook.
Visit www.abc-clio.com for details.

Libraries Unlimited
An Imprint of ABC-CLIO, LLC

ABC-CLIO, LLC
130 Cremona Drive, P.O. Box 1911
Santa Barbara, California 93116-1911

This book is printed on acid-free paper ∞

Manufactured in the United States of America

COMIC BOOK COLLECTIONS
FOR LIBRARIES

Contents

Foreword

I grew up reading comic books. Comics gave me my love of reading in general. I wish I could say that my parents encouraged comics in our home, especially now that I am a professional in the field, but the truth is that they just tolerated it. Back then, comics were viewed as second-rate literature. It actually wasn't considered literature at all, but something kids read under the covers at night or your mother tossed in the trash. After all, what was the worth of seeing the Fantastic Four defeating Galactus the planet devourer or seeing Superman and the Flash racing around the world?

Today, comics have not only become accepted, but they are a learning tool. One of my greatest achievements was receiving an American Library Association Award for *Usagi Yojimbo, Book 12: Grasscutter*. That same book was used as a text book for Japanese history classes at the university level.

There was a wide gamut of genres when I started reading funny books—superheroes (of course), westerns, humor, science fiction, horror, illustrated classics, and even romance. They all shared something in common, though: they were meant to be read by all ages. Today's comics also span a wide range of genres but are much more sophisticated. Many creators write or draw with a specific readership in mind. It is often difficult to determine if a book is suitable for a reader.

Many young children enjoy the story hours and special reading programs geared for their age group. However, as they grow older, they are enticed by all the media now available, whether online or packaged as games. Librarians have found that comic books, or graphic novels, are a great tool for attracting youth and teens back into the libraries. I have spoken at a few library conferences and found that librarians are anxious to build a graphic novel section but do not know where to start or how to go about it. Comics in the library are not a recent innovation, nor is it limited to the United States. At a presentation in the Netherlands, I saw there were graphic novels in the adult as well as the children's sections of the library. Comics can be found throughout libraries in Europe.

Comic Book Collections for Libraries is Comics 101. It gives everything you need to know about assembling a collection of graphic novels. It tells the history of comics, an overview of the entire art form, and then focuses in on specific creators and titles. This book is helpful in creating and maintaining a graphic novel section and using comics effectively throughout the library.

I have been writing and drawing the adventures of Usagi Yojimbo the samurai rabbit for over 25 years. Usagi has been translated into a dozen languages. I still love to write and draw, and I still love to read.

Stan Sakai

Acknowledgments

Both authors would like to thank James Madison University Libraries and Educational Technologies for supporting our ideas and establishing a mainstream comic book collection. We also thank Mark Purington for reading Chapter 6 and Elizabeth Kline and Patrick Ragland for editorial assistance. Any mistakes are ours, not theirs. We also thank Carol Pinkus at Marvel Comics; Diana Schutz and Amy Huey at Dark Horse Comics; and DC Comics Legal Affairs. Finally, we thank Stan Sakai for honoring us with an introduction to this book.

I

Comic Books, Graphic Novels, and Popular Culture

The library profession is becoming accustomed to "graphic novels." Well-reviewed titles such as Alan Moore and Dave Gibbons's *Watchmen*—one of *Time*'s "All-Time 100 Greatest Novels" (Grossman and Lacayo 2005)—are now found in thousands of libraries. Exhibits dedicated to graphic novels at the American Library Association, at one point scattered throughout the exhibit hall, are now grouped on the exhibit floor in a "Graphic Novel Pavilion." There were 16 exhibits in 2004, the pavilion's first year, and at the 2010 conference, 35 publishers were listed in the "Graphic Novels/Comic Books" category (http://ala.cistems.net/product_locator.php). There seems to be a hesitation, however, to add mainstream "comic book" titles such as *Spider-Man* or *Wonder Woman* to library collections. Trade paperback titles such as *Batman Chronicles* are owned by only a few hundred libraries, and often only the first volume in a series is collected.[1]

This chapter will define comic books, graphic novels, and manga. It will provide an overall picture of the importance of mainstream comic books in American popular culture, including manga titles. If we are to follow the maxim "Every reader his book," then popular comic books—not just graphic novels—belong in today's libraries.

A BRIEF HISTORY OF COMIC BOOKS

The art form we know as "comic books" has been around in many forms for hundreds of years. Today, most people consider comic books to be brightly colored pamphlets that use a series of illustrations to tell stories, generally about men and women with powers far beyond those of mortal man. In actuality, comic books are more than that, from their artistic antecedents to a wide variety of modern fare.

Comic book scholar Scott McCloud defines comics as "juxtaposed pictorial and other images in a deliberate sequence" (1993). This adequately describes the comic books (and comic strips) we know today, but it also describes other precursors to the medium.

Sequences of art telling stories can be found in early Egyptian art and pre-Columbian works from Mexico. Although the Bayeaux Tapestry has none of the gutters and borders that separate the images in comic books today, it clearly tells the story of the Norman invasion of England using juxtaposed images in a deliberate sequence. In eighteenth-century England, artist William Hogarth painted a series of moralizing art works that told continuing stories over several canvases; these works, such as *A Rake's Progress* and *Marriage a-la-Mode*, would not be considered comic books today, but the resemblance of the techniques to modern comics are striking.

Newspaper comic strips began in the nineteenth century. Their beginnings led accidentally to the creation of comic books in America, which began sometime in the early twentieth century—scholars debate the exact date—with collections of comic strips, either reprinted from newspaper funny pages or written especially for the collections. The "comic" in comic books came from these strips, and the new medium kept the name even as it moved away from humor and into new genres. In 1938, Jerry Siegel and Joe Shuster began the Golden Age of comics when the company that would become DC Comics published the first adventures of Superman in *Action Comics* #1. From there, superheroes flourished, and despite their sharp decline in popularity during the late 1940s and 1950s, they returned to dominate comic books. Today, they are what most readers think of when they hear the term "comic book."

Comic books featuring a wide variety of stories gained an audience of both children and adults, although both tended to consider it cheap, disposable entertainment. In 1954, psychiatrist Fredric Wertham wrote *Seduction of the Innocent*, which accused comics, particularly horror and true crime stories, of corrupting youth. Wertham's hysterical crusade and the congressional hearings that followed caused the comics industry to censor themselves by setting up the Comics Code Authority (CCA).

The censorship, which removed many supernatural themes and mandated that good must always triumph, took the mature edge out of comic books, and the older readers left soon after, killing what little remained of horror and crime comics. By the 60s, the newly revived superhero genre began taking over the medium; sanitized by the CCA, superheroes were dismissed as youthful power fantasies. DC, with its original stable of superheroes anchored by Batman and Superman, were well equipped for this resurgence. Marvel Comics, however, created a new lineup of superheroes; writer/editor Stan Lee and a bullpen of talented artists such as Jack Kirby and Steve Ditko rose to prominence by creating a world filled with flawed heroes and villains.

A once-crowded comics field became less so as DC and Marvel survived when many others fell by the wayside in the 70s, 80s, and 90s. Comic books began retreating from the spinner racks in drugstores and grocery stores during the 80s and moving into the "direct market," a code word for comic book stores. The "Black-and-White Boom," an explosion of small, mostly black-and-white comic book publishers in the mid-80s, allowed many new creators, publishers, and ideas into the medium (Lavin 1999). Publishers popped up overnight, and some of them disappeared almost as quickly. Most of these creations left no impression, but some left their mark, such as Kevin Eastman and Peter Laird's ninja/funny animal series *Teenage Mutant Ninja Turtles*; *Zot!* which artist/writer Scott McCloud began as a science fiction/superhero story but turned into a coming-of-age story about a group of teenagers; and *Bone*, a humorous but epic fantasy-adventure story by Jeff Smith. Two new major publishers entered the market during this time: Dark Horse (1986) and Image (1992), the latter of which was originally created by disgruntled former artists from Marvel Comics. Today, there are still many smaller publishers, and imprints such as DC's Vertigo and Marvel's Icon give a greater scope to the medium.

Despite the greater visibility comics have gained through movies, television, and video games and through new imprints and publishers, comics' audience became more limited because of the decreased channels of distribution. Additionally, in the 90s, Diamond Comics gained a monopoly on comic book distribution to comic book shops, giving it a subtle control over which titles could and could not be sold. Online retailers and new electronic methods of distribution may help change that.

MEDIUM OR GENRE?

Many think of comic books as synonymous with superheroes, believing the genre stands for all comics. In fact, comic books come in every genre; comic books are a medium, not a story type. Comic books were once filled with genres such as romance, detective stories, Westerns, and monster stories. Although tales of superheroes dominate today, comics featuring crime, horror, alternative, humor, science fiction, fantasy, autobiography, and many other types of stories can still be found in comics shops. Additionally, there are a near-infinite number of mashups and crossbreeds between those genres: horror/crime, romance/superhero, humor/science fiction, etc. These stories are told in many languages and in many cultures throughout the world. In Japan, for instance, words and pictures have been used to tell stories for centuries, although the dominant form of today's Japanese comics market, manga, did not begin until after World War II.

THE VALUE OF COMIC BOOKS

Comic books have long been a derided medium, the hybrid of pictures and words being considered a bastard child that belongs neither to high art nor to worthy literature. But comic book protagonists are all around us. They are the foundations of blockbuster summer movies that dominate the box office; in 2008, *The Dark Knight* grossed nearly $1 billion (and won one acting award at the Academy Awards). They are also the basis of small films that are critical darlings; *Persepolis* won the Jury Prize at the 2007 Cannes Film Festival and was nominated for Best Animated Film at the Academy Awards and Best Foreign Film at the Golden Globes. They pop up on animated and live-action TV, as both direct licenses (*Smallville*) and as homages (*Heroes*). Comic book heroes are the subject of countless video games. They even are beginning to show up on Broadway, with Spider-Man swinging onto the Great White Way in January 2011. Via licensed goods, they have infiltrated the grocery, toy, and electronics aisles at Wal-Mart and Target. Through the graphic novel, they have sneaked out of the hobbyist ghettos of comic book shops and into mainstream bookstores.

The superhero genre has moved beyond being disposable action stories with science-fiction overtones. Today they are modern-day myths. Like other myths, they have been moral tales, such as during the Cold War when they were meant, if not to guide young peoples' minds to honor and virtue, at least to not tempt them into wickedness. Larger-than-life figures battled one another in conflicts over power, wealth, and justice. Figures from well-known pantheons, such as Hercules, Thor, and Ares, have been incorporated into superhero stories. Just like in myths, time is plastic, and a multitude of writers and artists collaborated over the years to make a sometimes-cohesive overall story, linking newer tales to older ones they believed gave the newer ones more resonance, credence, or detail. These stories, like myths, mirror what people believe in and shift their narrative to accommodate shifts in beliefs.

In short, comic books have a long reach in popular culture. People have a hunger for the stories they tell, even if they are not aware of that until the characters are transferred to a different medium.

Comic books are useful in reaching out to the young. Graphic novels have been cited as aiding reluctant readers and readers who either are visual learners or have trouble with visual learning (Hibbing and Rankin-Erickson 2003). Graphic nonfiction can add interest to otherwise dry topics. It does help that many young students already read comics; almost 60 percent of boys ages 9 to 11 claim to have read comic books, and 44 percent of girls in the same age bracket do as well; even very young readers, such as girls (39.5%) and boys (49.7%) between the ages of 6 and 8, read comics (Packaged Facts 2008). Although the average comic book reader is no longer a preteen or teenager, comics appeal to younger adults, with the average age of comics readers variously placed between 24 (Fetto 2001) and 30 (Brenner 2006) and female readers being slightly older (Emad 2006).

LIBRARIES, COMIC BOOKS, AND GRAPHIC NOVELS

A decade ago, a library would have had to subscribe to monthly comic books in order to satisfy the demand for these stories. The monthly issues—sometimes called "pamphlets" or "floppies" by fans—have many disadvantages for libraries; they are flimsy, difficult to store, and easily stolen. Their original, ephemeral design requires careful preservation or binding in order to last. But in the last decade, many comic book publishers have instituted graphic-novel programs, in which a large proportion of their current output and a smaller amount of their back catalog are reprinted in trade paperback and hardback forms.

Then what are graphic novels? That's a trickier question. Some use the term for works in the medium of comics that are originally published in book form rather than in individual issues. Sometimes the term is used only for works of artistic or literary quality, disparaging most of the medium while attempting to raise the object of the naming; others use it to denote a comic book story with a defined beginning, middle, and end. Strangely, the "novel" part of the term is rarely adhered to by the works it describes, as the term encompasses works that would not, if in text only, be termed as novels, such as nonfiction works or anthologies.

The term "graphic novel" was popularized after publisher Baronet Books used it to describe comics legend Will Eisner's *A Contract with God and Other Tenement Stories*. The book was a series of original short pieces about people in the real world, and "graphic novel" was used to differentiate it from the mass of comics. The term and form had been used before *A Contract with God*'s 1978 publication, but its use took off from there. By the 80s, publishers—notably DC Comics—occasionally repackaged popular stories from monthly comics into trade paperbacks and published them as "graphic novels." Two DC graphic novels, *Watchmen* by Alan Moore and Dave Gibbons and *The Dark Knight Returns* by Frank Miller, helped give prominence to the term and concept outside the comics world, as did Art Speigelman's Pulitzer-winning *Maus*. Some criticized the term as pretentious, dressing up the derided medium with a label that had not yet been associated with worthless pop culture ephemera.

Today, "graphic novel" is more often used for a collection of comic book material in book form. Other terms are used as well: collected editions; "phone books" for thick books published in black and white; trade paperbacks and hardcover editions, depending on whether the book is published with soft or hard covers; and digests, for books in the smaller 5½-x-8¼-inch size. Whatever they're called, they're big business. Nearly $400 million of graphic novels were sold in the direct market in 2008, up from $75 million in 2001. Of those, $175 million were manga titles (ICv2 2009). The sales of graphic novels in bookstores have become so prominent that the *New York Times* began a graphic-novel bestseller list in February 2009, listing the top 10 sellers in hardcover, softcover, and manga graphic novels.

Part of this growth lies in the explosion of available titles. In the 80s and 90s, most of the collections offered by DC and Marvel were either "best-of" or themed anthologies or titles deemed to be of extremely high quality—the aforementioned *Watchmen* and *The Dark Knight Returns*, for example, or Alan Moore and David Lloyd's *V for Vendetta*. These titles are examples of the graphic novels librarians initially embraced. Marvel published a line of "Marvel Graphic Novels" in the 80s, but it was more of an anthology comic series with unusual printed dimensions than "graphic novels" as we know them now. Some creators made the collected versions of their works part of their business model, such as Dave Sim with his series *Cerebus*, but by and large, graphic novels as we know them today were scarce and often unique.

In the early 90s, DC made the decision to group some of their edgier comic books, largely written by British writers new to the American market, under the Vertigo imprint. These books were for "mature readers," and the titles in the imprint were often sold as trade paperbacks after their original publication as comic books; both of these developments were rarities at the time. These new titles were sold not just in comics shops but in bookstores as well, and many of them—particularly writer Neil Gaiman's *The Sandman*—found audiences that never would have discovered them had they been sequestered in comics shops. Other publishers who had more general-interest output followed suit, although they rarely achieved the market penetration of the better-known Vertigo titles. A decade later, DC and Marvel decided to collect more of their titles; now, almost all their titles are reprinted in trade paperbacks, and many of them are available in hardback editions as well. Additionally, these companies have seen the potential profit available by reprinting titles from their back catalogs, and as such, affordable versions of their characters' earlier adventures have joined their new output on the shelves.

Although a recent entry into the American market from Japan, manga is now a large part of the graphic-novel market. Animated Japanese movies such as *Akira, Ghost in the Shell*, and *Vampire Hunter D* gained a cult following in the 80s, while anime (Japanese animation) programs such as *Pokémon* and *Dragon Ball Z* began to infiltrate television in the 90s. Manga began appearing in comics stores at the same time, but it was hit by the general slump in the comics industry in the early 90s. In the late 90s, American publisher Tokyopop had a hit with *Sailor Moon*, the story of a modern-day teenage girl who fights the forces of darkness, and Viz, a publisher with strong ties to Japanese manga companies, found success with *Dragon Ball Z*. The first mainstream success in manga was *Pokémon* in the late 90s. In 2002, Tokyopop began issuing their titles exclusively to bookstores in small trade paperbacks (Thompson 2007, 227). The audience followed them and brought its friends along with them. The wider audience manga commands in Japan, supported by its wide range of genres, has allowed it to appeal to a large audience in the United States; the lower prices of its less expensive, smaller, black-and-white digest format has also helped. Manga sales reached a high point of $210 million on 1,500 volumes (55% of all graphic novels) in 2007 (ICv2.com 2008). Some public libraries have added manga collections, primarily in the young adult section.

Marvel and DC dominate monthly sales of single comic book issues; in January 2010, only one of the top 25 selling comics in the direct market was from a publisher other than those two[2] (ICv2.com "Top 300 Comics" 2010). Marvel and DC also dominate the direct-market graphic-novel sales, although each issue of a title generally sells several times what it does when it's collected into a book. In January 2010, DC and Marvel combined to place 7 of the top 10 (and 18 of the top 25) graphic novels in sales (ICv2.com "Top 300 Graphic" 2010). The list is dominated by superhero (and supervillain) stories, but horror has a respectable showing; v. 11 of Image's zombie title *The Walking Dead* was the most popular volume, selling triple the second-place title, *Unwritten, v. 1: Tommy Taylor and the Bogus Identity*.[3] Other horror titles include *Creepy Archives*, v. 5, *House of Mystery, v. 3: The Space Between*, and the horror/crime *Goon: Rough Stuff*. Other genres represented include science fiction (*Star Wars: Knights of the Old Republic, v. 8: Destroyer*), crime (DC/Vertigo's *Young Liars, v. 3: Rock Life*), and fantasy (mangas *Immortal*, v. 22, and *Fullmetal Alchemist*, v. 22).[4]

Despite high commercial sales, some libraries continue to see mainstream and popular comic books as poor choices for their collections. Currently, many libraries that collect graphic novels focus on literary award-winners and juvenile literature. WorldCat shows about 4,500 libraries owning *Watchmen* and about 1,400 have holdings for Daniel Clowes's *Ghost World*, but only about 800 libraries report owning *Hellboy*, v. 1, and about 750 of *Wonder Woman: Love and Murder*, the most popular Wonder Woman title.[5] Although exact numbers are unreliable because of the numerous ways of cataloging comic book titles (see Chapter 6), this pattern holds for similar titles. Guides for librarians tend to emphasize the literary or highbrow entries in the graphic-novel market.[6] Titles such as *Maus, Clan Apis* by Jay Hosler, *Pedro and Me* by Judd Winick, and *Fax from Sarajevo* by Joe Kubert are all worthy works of literature, but they are not typical choices of comic book readers. As shown by the sales lists, when those who buy graphic novels vote with their money, their selections would rarely be seen as highbrow. Libraries are missing the meat of the graphic-novel market, and when they neglect that, the already established market of comic book readers—those who do not have to be convinced of the medium's value—will attempt to satisfy their comic book hunger elsewhere.

CONCLUSION

What are comic books? They are part of America's history; they offer myths of their own. They have been ridiculed and censored, but they have managed to maintain an avid readership. They are a vibrant part of today's popular culture, and the business of comics continues to grow. Libraries that have collections of well-reviewed graphic novels would do well to rethink their selection criteria. Why do they have *Watchmen* but not *Batman Chronicles*? Why do they have *Ghost World* but not Mike Mignola's *Hellboy*? Should public libraries have horror titles?

The answer is that all of these titles have a place in a comic book collection. However, since the object is to have books readers want to check out, an emphasis should be placed on popular titles. Satisfying the tastes of readers rather than including only "higher-quality" titles will result not only in increased circulation but potentially in new reader groups using the library.

NOTES

1. WorldCat was accessed using the FirstSearch interface (http://firstsearch.oclc.org) to search on the title, limiting the search to books in English. Libraries that had a record for the book series were considered to have the specific volume that was being searched for.

2. Dark Horse's *Buffy the Vampire Slayer* #31 was #25.

3. Although published by DC, *Unwritten* is a fantasy story released through the company's Vertigo imprint.

4. Because ICv2.com gets its data for most of these ranked lists from Diamond Comic Distributors, manga generally does not place very well on the lists unless "bookstores" are specifically mentioned on the list as a source. Other lists, such as the *New York Times* Bestseller rankings, are needed to get an idea of what's popular in bookstores.

5. See note #1 for an explanation of how WorldCat was searched. For these searches, only the series title was searched on, not the individual volume title. Libraries with either the specific volume or the series as a whole were considered to have the volume.

6. For instance, Francisca Goldsmith's *Graphic Novels Now: Building, Managing, and Marketing a Dynamic Collection* lists only one superhero title among 29 "selected graphic novels," and Alison and Barry Lyga's *Graphic Novels in Your Media Center: A Definitive Guide* intentionally has a lack of superhero stories for its list of graphic novels for school library collections. Although not specifically a library guide, *The Rough Guide to Graphic Novels* by Danny Fingeroth discusses only one superhero story among its "canon" of the top 60 graphic novels. Encouragingly, between one-fifth and one-quarter of Stephen Weiner's *The 101 Best Graphic Novels* are superhero titles, depending on how "superhero" is defined. This is a fair showing—unless sales are considered, which means essentially that more than two-thirds of the "best" graphic novels are low-selling hidden gems.

REFERENCES

Brenner, Robin. "FAQ." *Horn Book Magazine* 82, no. 2 (March–April 2006): 123–25.

Emad, Mitra C. "Reading Wonder Woman's Body: Mythologies of Gender and Nation." *Journal of Popular Culture* 39, no. 6 (December 2006): 954–84.

Fetto, John. "Funny Business." *American Demographics* 23, no. 4 (April 2001): 64.

Grossman, Lev, and Richard Lacayo. "All Time 100 Novels." *Time*, October 24, 2005. http://www.time.com/time/specials/packages/0,28757,1951793,00.html (accessed April 19, 2010).

Hibbing, Anne Nielsen, and Joan L. Rankin-Erickson. "A Picture Is Worth a Thousand Words: Using Visual Images to Improve Comprehension for Middle School Struggling Readers." *The Reading Teacher* 56, no. 8 (May 2003): 758–70.

ICv2.com. "Graphic Novels Hit $375 Million." April 18, 2008, http://www.icv2.com/articles/news/12416.html (accessed April 1, 2010).

ICv2.com. "Graphic Novels Up in 2008." February 5, 2009, http://www.icv2.com/articles/news/14239.html (accessed March 17, 2010).

ICv2.com. "Top 300 Comics Actual—January 2010." February 14, 2010, http://www.icv2.com/
        articles/news/16810.html (accessed April 1, 2010).

ICv2.com. "Top 300 Graphic Novels Actual—January 2010." February 14, 2010, http://www.icv2
        .com/articles/news/16811.html (accessed April 1, 2010).

Lavin, Michael R. "A Librarian's Guide to Independent Comics: Part One, Publisher Profiles."
        Serials Review 25, no. 1 (1999): 29–48.

McCloud, Scott. *Understanding Comics: The Invisible Art*. Northampton, MA: Kitchen Sink
        Press, 1993.

Packaged Facts. *The Kids and Tweens Market in the U.S.* 9th ed. Rockville, MD: Packaged Facts,
        2008.

Thompson, Jason, with art by Atsumisa Okura. "How Manga Conquered America: A Graphic
        Guide to Japan's Coolest Export." *Wired* 15, no. 11 (2007): 223–33. http://www.wired
        .com/images/pdf/Wired_1511_mangaamerica.pdf (accessed April 26, 2010).

Weiner, Stephen. *The 101 Best Graphic Novels*. New York: NBM, 2005.

2

The Structure of the Comic Book

Comic art has a grammar and structure that is unfamiliar to some readers. Some find staples of the medium, such as panels, transitions, gutters, and differing art styles, confusing at first glance. With practice, most people can master story structure; for those who have trouble, there are many excellent books on the subject, most notably *Understanding Comics* by Scott McCloud and *Comics and Sequential Art* by Will Eisner.

When dealing with collected editions, librarians must keep in mind that comic books as a whole have a structure they might be unfamiliar with, with quirks stemming from more than 75 years of history. To make sense of how comic books are collected into trade paperbacks and hardcover editions, it helps to know how comics companies initially package the adventures of their characters and how individual comic book issues are interrelated. Familiar concepts, such as titles, volumes, and issues, have different meanings in the world of comic books (see Chapter 6 for how these concepts affect cataloging). New structures and concepts, such as arcs, crossovers, and continuity, may seem peculiar, but plenty of guidance is available (see Chapter 9 for more on Web resources).

TITLES

A visit to a local comic book shop will reveal not just one *Superman* comic, but rather numerous titles with Superman's name and/or image. For new readers (and librarians) looking for the adventures of their favorite heroes, finding the right title—or, to be more accurate, titles—can be confusing. It seems logical that Superman's adventures should be found in a comic book titled *Superman*, but like many popular characters, his eponymous comic is not the only one he headlines, nor is it the flagship of his publisher's Superman offerings. *Action Comics*, which started with Superman's debut in 1938, is arguably the foremost Superman comic, and the hero also is usually the star of *Superman/Batman* as well as the expected *Superman*. In the past, he has also appeared in *Adventures of Superman*, *All-Star Superman*, *DC Comics Presents*, and many other titles.[1]

This may seem confusing, although fortunately most of the books featuring Superman do have "Superman" in the title. It is similar for other prominent heroes; for example, Spider-Man has starred in many comic book titles, and most of those do have "Spider-Man" in the name. But even that is not a foolproof rule. Spider-Man debuted in *Amazing Fantasy* and headlined *Marvel Team-Up* for more than a decade. Batman has starred in *Detective Comics* and *Brave and the Bold* in addition to *Batman*, *Batman Confidential*, *Batman: Shadow of the Bat*, and *Legends of the Dark Knight*. That's not even considering that the Batman with whom the public is familiar (Bruce Wayne) spent most of 2009 and 2010 not appearing in his own comics: during this time, *Batman* featured the first Robin filling in as Batman, and *Detective Comics*, the flagship Batman title, was given over to stories about Batwoman. Although this multiplicity of titles is common in American comics, manga rarely has this confusion; characters and plotlines are generally restricted to one title at a time.

The relationships between titles will be discussed in this and the "Continuity" section of this chapter. Appendix B provides a quick reference to some of the major characters and the titles in which they have appeared.

Titles can be divided into two types: ongoing and limited (also called miniseries). Ongoing titles are meant to run indefinitely; as noted above, *Action Comics* has been published continuously since 1938. DC's *Detective Comics* has been running even longer: the first issue is dated March 1937, and more than 850 issues have been published since then. DC even gets its eponymous abbreviation from this long-running title. Most famous superheroes who have been portrayed in successful movies appear in at least one ongoing title, as do many others who are unfamiliar to the public at large.

Limited series, on the other hand, are designed to run for a set number of issues, usually between 1 and 12.[2] Reasons for publishing limited series include testing the market for an unestablished character, taking advantage of a short time commitment from a writer or artist, or allowing a creator to work with a focused idea that cannot support an indefinite treatment. For instance, Marvel tried two miniseries featuring the Punisher in the late 90s (*Punisher: Purgatory* and *Wolverine/Punisher: Revelation*) that cast the violent vigilante as supernatural avenger before returning to the character's original, mundane war on crime in the 2000 *Punisher* limited series. Some characters or creators eschew ongoing series entirely in favor of linked limited series; stories featuring Hellboy, published by Dark Horse and created and written by Mike Mignola, are released in a series of limited series, with titles such as *Hellboy: Seed of Destruction* and *Hellboy: The Third Wish*.

When issues of a title are collected, publishers often use the hero's name at the beginning of the book's title, especially if the collection reprints issues from more than one comic title. For instance, DC tends to release collected editions of *Detective Comics* with titles that begin with "Batman," and issues of *Action Comics* usually are reprinted in book form with titles that begin with "Superman." The exception tends to be for editions that collect very old material or a large number of consecutive issues. DC's collections of *World's Finest Comics*, a comic that featured Batman, Superman, and Robin and began in the 40s, are issued under the name *World's Finest Archives*, and Marvel reprinted *Marvel Team-Up* in volumes titled *Essential Marvel Team-Up*. Manga reprints usually use the same name as the original title.

ISSUES

In this chapter, issues are discussed before volumes to illustrate one of the structural differences in comic books as series: Comic books are published as issues with little consideration to volumes, which are created and closed at the whim of the publishers. Unlike most magazines or journals, comic book volumes do not correspond to a year.

Issues are numbered consecutively and released at a rate of about one a month. Occasionally, a publisher will accelerate that schedule. For instance, Marvel cancelled two of its three Spider-Man titles in late 2007 and published the remaining title, *Amazing Spider-Man*, three times a month until October 2010. Other times, a publisher will release more than one issue of a title in a month, as Marvel did in the early 90s with certain popular titles during the summer, when young readers would presumably have more spare time. Miniseries are occasionally released weekly; DC's *52* used that as a gimmick, running once per week for an entire year.

Slower schedules are not uncommon. In the past, publishers released titles with lower sales once every two months, although bimonthly schedules are rare in the twenty-first century. Annuals, as their name implies, are original stories that are generally issued once a year.[3] Usually, however, the reason for slower-than-monthly publication is accident: either creators or companies fall behind schedule, or there is an editorial or printing problem. Despite the professional nature of the comic book industry, this happens more frequently than in other major entertainment media.

Occasionally, a comics publisher will play with numbering, releasing issues with improbable numbers: 0, -1, 1½, and 1,000,000 have all been seen in the past two decades. These numbers can be used to show an issue does not have to be read in sequence or to show that it should be seen as a prelude to a title (as with the -1) or far in its future (as with 1,000,000).

Collections usually reprint consecutive issues from a title or crossover (see below), but publishers will sometimes collect chronologically separated issues into "best of" compilations, with stories sometimes being separated by decades. Examples include *The Greatest Batman Stories Ever Told* and *The Complete Frank Miller Spider-Man*. Manga rarely has this sort of collection, although samplers with many short selections from stories from different titles may be released to get readers interested in more of a publisher's titles. Manga is also often published in thick, magazine compilations that are halfway between traditional American comic book issues and collections. These magazines, such as *Shōnen Jump*, have several serialized stories from different titles running at the same time. In the American market, these stories are often reprinted later in digest-sized collections.

The only effect the publication frequency of the individual issues has on collected editions is the collections' release date. Collected editions are released a few months after the final issue to be collected is published. If a hardcover version of the material is to be released—usually only for the more popular content—then it is usually released first, with a less-expensive paperback following later.

VOLUMES

In a technical sense, publishers have an infinite number of choices for the titles of their series. However, they sometimes wish to reuse titles of cancelled comics, and they therefore begin a new volume of a title. Comic book volumes, therefore, differ from the traditional library definition of a periodical volume.

Although volumes are easy to make sense of with journals, they are often difficult to determine for comic books. The biggest problem lies in determining if two titles had, in fact, the same name. Covers and indicia can disagree, and either might give a different title than advertising copy or the company's own Web site. This difficulty is most often encountered in miniseries; often the name of the miniseries's storyline can be seen as part of the comic series's title or part of the issue's title. For instance, the four-issue 1998–1999 miniseries starring the Punisher is sometimes referred to as *Punisher: Purgatory*, v. 1, and sometimes as *Punisher*, v. 4.

Some collectors and archivists try to avoid the confusion by avoiding using consecutively numbered volume numbers. The most popular method is to name the volume after the year it started; the above example would be referred to as *Punisher* (1998 series). This has the advantage of simplicity, but it also has some drawbacks. For example, in 1991, Marvel Comics released a second *X-Men* title. The first title featuring the X-Men had been called *Uncanny X-Men* for more than a decade at that point, although it had started out as just *X-Men* when issue #1 came out in 1963. For most collectors, the original series is known as *Uncanny X-Men* and the second as *X-Men*; for those delineating volumes by year, they are *X-Men* (1963 series) and *X-Men* (1991 series). This repetition of names and the unfamiliar notation could introduce confusion where most people familiar with comics had none.

At times, Marvel has seemed to be deliberately confusing in this regard. In the late 90s, they cancelled many of their longest-running titles and immediately relaunched them with new, second volumes.[4] More recently, Marvel has renumbered the issues in these second (or for some titles, third or later) volumes as if all the issues had been issued consecutively. Marvel released *Fantastic Four* #500, for example, after 416 issues of v. 1, 13 of v. 2, and 70 of v. 3. This new numbering could be referred to as v. 1 "continued" or "restarted," a continuation of v. 3, or the beginning of v. 4; there is no real consensus on which is correct.

Occasionally, a publisher will change the title of a series but not restart the issue numbering at #1. In the Silver Age, this was to give an aura of stability to a title— higher issue numbers meant a title had been around longer—and to save money on second-class mailing permits.[5] For example, the first volume of *Captain America* began its numbering with #100 because Marvel's *Tales of Suspense*, which starred Captain America in one of its features, was cancelled at #99 to clear room on the company's publishing schedule for the new title. In recent years, Marvel has returned to this practice, continuing the numbering of an old title on a new, similar title to convince readers of the old title of their similarities: *Incredible Hulk* (v. 2) #112 gave way to *Incredible Hercules* #113, and *Wolverine* (v. 3) #74 changed to *Dark Wolverine* #75 when the featured character's son took over the title.

Thankfully, the volume number of a title has little effect on its collection into a trade paperback. Consecutive issues are published in a single collection, bridging the two volumes if necessary for the story to make sense. The reader rarely notices. The volume number can give context to the comics being reprinted; *Wonder Woman*, v. 1 (1942) #1 is vastly different from *Wonder Woman*, v. 2 (1987) #1 or *Wonder Woman*, v. 3 (2006) #1, and although the latter two superficially resemble each other, they tell drastically different stories.

Keep in mind that collected editions will frequently have volume numbers of their own. These volume numbers indicate the order in which the reprinted issues were published or the order in which the reprints should be read and have no correlation to the volume number of the original comic issues. However, just as with comic book issues, this numbering of collected editions can be restarted at the publisher's whim. New numbering on a series of trade paperbacks might reflect a new writer, artist, or creative direction for the title or a desire to convince readers they do not need to read previous collected volumes. Publishers may also refrain from numbering collected editions for these same reasons.

ARCS/CROSSOVERS

In the Golden Age and the Silver Age, most stories were completed in one comic book—in fact, many comics had several complete stories in one book. As publishers began codifying the concept of "universes" (see "Continuity," below) in the 60s, they began producing stories that ran over several issues. These stories could either be loosely, implicitly connected by theme or recurring characters, or they might be explicitly connected by an overarching label that labeled each issue as part of the whole. These linked stories are called arcs.

Arcs, which usually encompass four to eight issues, are the basis of the modern comic book–collected edition, whether assembled into a trade paperback or hardcover. Many stories today are written with this subsequent collection in mind; in the past, some collections omitted pages and panels that did not directly pertain to the theme of the arc.

Crossovers are similar to arcs, in that they are stories spread out over two or more comic book issues. However, crossovers take place over at least two different comic titles; for example, *X-Tinction Agenda* was a crossover that happened in *Uncanny X-Men* #270–272, *New Mutants* (v. 1) #95–97, and *X-Factor* (v. 1) #60–62. Given the coordination needed to tell a story between two or more sets of writers and artists who create the stories that come out in their books, crossovers are usually bigger events than arcs—so big they affect the characters in other comics as well (see "Continuity," below). Crossovers may be planned to boost sales of a low-selling comic—the action from a higher-selling comic spills into the comic with lower sales. Sometimes the crossover is so large it affects a large portion of a publisher's output, and a majority of the titles will tell stories relating to the crossover for months at a time.[6] However, the name of the crossover story is sometimes attached to titles that have peripheral or even no connection to the crossover in the hopes that it will boost sales. In the mid-80s, DC advertised many titles as taking part in its "Crisis on Infinite Earths" story; however, some titles' only involvement included characters looking up at the sky, which had been turned red in the main story, and wondering at the color change (TVTropes.com).[7]

Crossovers made up the bulk of early trade paperbacks, as they were easily seen as a single story, received heavy promotion before their collection, and formed pivotal events other comics later referred to. In the twenty-first century, crossovers have often become so sprawling that it can take several books to cover the entirety of the story. For instance, Marvel released a collection of its "Civil War" crossover (in both hardcover and trade paperback) that reprinted the central story plus a *Civil War Companion* and 20 collections with "Civil War" in their titles. It can be difficult for librarians to know which crossover collections are significant, although reviews and comic book Web sites can be helpful (see Chapter 9). Usually, only the main crossover title is necessary to comprehend the crossover. Other titles can be added if they are part of a series the library is already collecting or if collection statistics reveal the main crossover's popularity.

CONTINUITY

What sets the superhero fiction of Marvel and DC apart from other comic book stories and from most other entertainment media are the concepts of continuity and universes. Continuity is the idea that nearly every comic book issue not only continues the character and plot developments that have been told so far in that title but also may continue (and should not contradict) character and plot developments in other titles published by that company. For instance, not only should the events in an issue of DC's *Green Lantern* further the story being told in that comic book, but if Batman or Superman appeared in the issue, they should look and act like they do in their own comics. Additionally, if the comic made more than superficial changes to the characters of Green Lantern, Batman, or Superman—such as scars, traumatic injuries, or loss of secret identity or memories—then that change should be reflected in other issues that feature that character. The importance of continuity and the stringency with which it has been enforced has fluctuated in the last 50 years, but it remains a core concept for superhero comics. Although non-superhero books usually do not have intertitle continuity, most do observe continuity within a single title.

Comics readers frequently refer to the "Marvel Universe" or "DC Universe," indicating the shared superhero world in which those companies set the bulk of their stories. Universes allow not only characters published by the same company to appear in other titles by the same company, but it also allows readers to be confident that the Invisible Woman who makes a guest appearance in *Avengers* is the same Invisible Woman who stars in *Fantastic Four*. In theory, this makes these comic book worlds richer and gives them more depth: these superheroes exist in a world that not only allows them to meet and work with other heroes (and fight against other heroes' villains) but also gives those characters the same narrative weight in other books as they receive in their own books. In a practical sense, it encourages readers to buy titles in which their favorite characters guest star. Some readers bristle at the interlinking concept, disliking the complexity and expense it entails.

"Universe" is also used in another sense: settings with mostly non-permeable boundaries that keep characters from other settings from interacting with the characters there. Just as the heroes in the Marvel and DC universes do not meet,[8] the characters in Marvel's "Heroes Reborn" universe (set on an artificially created Earth) and MC2 universe (set one generation in the future of the current Marvel Universe) do not meet, and they do not interact with the main Marvel Universe.[9]

Since DC has been publishing superhero comics since 1938 (and have had those characters meeting since 1940, in *All-Star Comics* #3) and Marvel has been publishing superhero comics since 1939,[10] creating new stories that agree with all the old stories is difficult, if not impossible. Each company has a different attitude toward continuity. DC has been more aggressive in altering its continuity. Originally, the company had several parallel universes, such as Earth-1, Earth-2, Earth-3, Earth-4, and Earth-S, where either the history of the universe was vastly different or the universe was populated by a different set of superheroes altogether.[11] In 1985, DC decided their dozens of alternate universes were too confusing and published *Crisis on Infinite Earths*, a 12-issue limited series; when it ended the next year, there was only one Earth, and all characters' histories were reset, to be retold in future issues. However, by 1994, DC and its readers had become troubled by continuity difficulties that had cropped up in the decade since *Crisis in Infinite Earths*, and another crossover miniseries, this one called *Zero Hour*, was written to patch the problems. More recently, *Infinite Crisis* in 2005–2006 and *Final Crisis* in 2008–2009 have altered continuity in minor ways and reestablished 52 parallel universes. Marvel has not ever tried such a drastic overhaul of their continuity, although they have ruled some of their Golden Age stories are not in continuity, and they have selectively excised certain events from their fictional history.[12] For such large changes in continuity, publishers may use large-scale events such as cosmic battles, the unraveling of space and/or time, powerful magic spells, or literal deals with the devil.

Publishers frequently rewrite their own continuities in different ways. The most drastic are reboots, in which everything that has happened to a character, title, or universe is thrown out.[13] Less drastic is a revamp, in which a character's history and design are picked over to create a new, more appealing continuity. For day-to-day continuity corrections, there are retcons (short for "retroactive continuity"). These changes may alter previous stories, or they may add new information to what was previously known about past events. Mechanisms for retcons can include false memories, time travel, or magic.

Certain issues (and titles) have been labeled as being out of continuity by publishers. In the Silver Age, DC explained such events as dreams, hoaxes, or imaginary stories. Today, both DC ("Elseworlds") and Marvel ("What If?") have labels for stories that feature their characters in alternate—and usually original—continuities. Other stories may not be explicitly said to be out of continuity but are held as such by readers, who note too many contradictions with established continuity to fit the events of the story into the fictional universe. Generally, stories set outside the main universes are lower sellers and attract less interest, as their inability to affect the main continuity gives readers the impression they are forgettable or fluff. However, there are exceptions, especially when well-known writers and artists are involved.

Often, knowledge of continuity is essential to understanding newer stories. Knowing the fate of the second Robin, who was murdered by the Joker, can help explain Batman's initially reluctant attitude toward having another boy take the role of his sidekick. Reading writer/artist Frank Miller's seminal work on *Daredevil* can enrich readers' experience with more recent *Daredevil* stories, as creators frequently echo themes and plots from Miller's work. Although many stories explain their fictional underpinnings, others leave readers to work out what has gone before, often to the stories' detriment. In any event, the original story brings more emotion to the current plot than a footnote or dry narration can convey. For example, readers who have read the story of Jean Grey's self-sacrifice on the moon[14] or Spider-Man's agony over the death of his girlfriend[15] will be more moved by later events that reference these tragedies.

Some readers can find this referential context off-putting. Others may simply ignore the accumulated library of stories and pick up what's needed as the story goes along. Still others may find the wealth of continuity an attractive part of the genre. No matter the readers' attitudes, however, dealing with continuity is an integral part of the DC and Marvel superhero universes.

Little to no continuity is typically necessary to understand stories from outside the main DC or Marvel universes. For example, in *Watchmen*, writer Alan Moore and artist

Dave Gibbons told a story deeply rooted in superhero myth without using any previous continuity. Still, knowledge of comics is helpful. Moore's story deconstructed the superhero genre, looking at its themes and characters and reconstructing them in a more "realistic" way that arrived at a different conclusion from those of contemporary comics. The structure of Gibbons's art mimicked earlier eras, and most of the major heroes were based on characters DC had just acquired from Charlton Comics. Knowing the genre gives readers a different and stronger idea of what the story is about.

CONCLUSION

Understanding the structure of comic books will help libraries identify graphic novels for acquisition. Generally speaking, collected editions group consecutively numbered issues of a title; the confusing volume numbers of comic book series usually can be ignored. Libraries may want to buy consecutive volumes of the collected editions of specific titles, at least to avoid a sudden end to stories. If a popular title is involved in a crossover, libraries may want to consider other major titles in that crossover event as well.

As with many aspects of comic books, the local comic book shop can be a great place to ask for clarification on issues of comic book structure, and the resources in Chapter 9 can also be of help.

NOTES

1. Strangely, Superman was absent from most of the core "Superman titles" in 2009. While Superman starred in the *Superman: World of New Krypton* miniseries, *Action Comics* and *Superman* were turned over to other, less famous heroes.

2. One-issue series are generally called "one-shots" rather than miniseries or limited series.

3. In the 60s and 70s, annuals were often used to reprint older stories, but that practice has become rare.

4. At the time, issues with #1 on them were considered friendlier to new readers and therefore more likely to gain a large audience. This is still the predominant thinking. In earlier decades, the opposite position ruled; larger issue numbers were seen as more desirable to readers since they indicated a title that was more stable and had been around for a long time.

5. Second-class mail, a less expensive mailing option, was the way publishers delivered issues to their subscribers. The new title would use the previous title's permit, and the publisher would hope the subterfuge would go unnoticed by postal inspectors.

6. Sometimes one crossover event will lead directly into the next, as with DC's "Darkest Night" leading into "Brightest Day."

7. The term "Red Skies Crossover" is given to issues deceptively advertised in this way.

8. That is, with certain exceptions. The two companies have cooperated to create intercompany crossovers, such as *Superman vs. the Amazing Spider-Man: The Battle of the Century* (1976), *Marvel and DC Present Uncanny X-Men and the New Teen Titans* (1982), and the four-issue miniseries *JLA/Avengers* (2003–2004). The out-of-continuity nature of these stories means the characters will not remember or refer to them in their regular DC or Marvel Universe titles after they happen.

9. Since superhero comics are, at their heart, speculative fiction, no one can say these characters "never" meet. Superhero comics show a great deal of imagination, and with comics being released monthly, unusual and outlandish plot ideas will be explored regularly. Breaking barriers the readers are told are inviolate is one of those ideas.

10. The first Marvel superhero was Namor the Sub-Mariner, who appeared in the unreleased (or extremely limited release) *Motion Pictures Funnies Weekly* #1 (April 1939). Since this comic was almost completely unknown until 1974 (Cronin 2007), many sources still list Namor's debut as *Marvel Comics* #1, which was dated October 1939 and also featured the debut of the original Human Torch and Ka Zar.

11. Earth-1 was the main DC universe. Earth-2 featured the heroes as if they had aged normally, and many heroes and villains had died or given way to another generation. In Earth-3, analogues of the heroes were villains, and the only hero was Alex Luthor Jr., son of Lex Luthor. Earth-4 and Earth-S were receptacles for characters DC had acquired from other companies. Earth-4 had the superheroes from Charlton Comics, such as Blue Beetle and Captain Atom; the characters were acquired in 1983. Earth-S had characters from Fawcett Comics, most notably Captain Marvel, whose title outsold Superman in the mid-1940s. DC began licensing those characters in 1972 and purchased them in 1991.

12. The most prominent excised event for Marvel was the marriage of Peter Parker (Spider-Man) and Mary Jane Watson in 2007's "One More Day" storyline. When Peter's Aunt May was mortally wounded, Mephisto—Marvel's chief Satanic stand-in—offered Peter and Mary Jane a deal: he would let Aunt May live if he could "take" their marriage; that is, after May was healed, history would be rewritten so that their marriage—but not their original romance—would never have occurred. Peter accepted. Understandably, this caused some confusion among readers who wondered how much of the stories that had happened while the couple had been married were still in continuity, especially when other events in Spider-Man's history were changed as well.

13. Because of the way it ignores and contradicts stories told in the various *Star Trek* series and movies, the 2009 *Star Trek* movie is a cinematic version of a reboot.

14. Jean Grey died on the moon in *Uncanny X-Men* #137 (September 1980).

15. Gwen Stacy died in *Amazing Spider-Man* #121 (June 1973).

REFERENCES

Cronin, Brian. "Comic Book Urban Legends Revealed #92," March 1, 2007. http://goodcomics .comicbookresources.com/2007/03/01/comic-book-urban-legends-revealed-92/ (accessed April 27, 2010).

TVTropes.com. "Red Skies Crossover." http://tvtropes.org/pmwiki/pmwiki.php/Main/RedSkies Crossover (accessed March 17, 2010).

3

The Players

To make sense of the world of comic books, it helps to know who's who. This chapter provides an alphabetical discussion of comics companies, writers, artists, and terms. This is not an exhaustive list of any of those elements, but it should help librarians get their feet wet. Figure 3.1 provides a brief timeline of comics history as a framework.

PUBLISHERS

Publishers have come and gone in the comics industry, with companies rising and falling, changing their names, and selling their characters to competitors. At one point, publishers such as Fawcett, Gold Key, and Charlton were major forces in the market, but today they and dozens of others have passed on. Marvel, one of the industry's leaders, changed its name twice before settling on the name it made famous, and it even filed for bankruptcy in 1996. Today, Marvel and DC dominate the medium, but dozens of other publishers are still in the field. Each one has its own niche, either in the genres they publish, their editorial philosophy, or the deals they offer creators. The following are some of the most prominent comics companies.

Archie

One of the oldest comics companies still publishing—it was founded as LMJ Comics in 1939—Archie Comics has a larger reputation outside the direct market than within it. The company's eponymous title and its spinoffs make up most of the company's output. These titles are drawn in a house style, making the identity of the artist hard to determine (and irrelevant, to a degree). The company tried a new style recently (2007–2010), which featured more realistic and less cartoony art. Archie Comics also publishes comics based on the *Sonic the Hedgehog* video game. Many times over the years, Archie has attempted a superhero line, but each time, the idea has failed.[1]

1933: *Famous Funnies*, the first American comic book, is published.

1935: *New Fun: The Big Comic Magazine* #1, DC's first comic book, is published.

1938: Superman, created by Jerry Siegel and Joe Shuster, makes his first appearance in *Action Comics* #1, ushering in the Golden Age of comics.

1939: Batman, created by Bob Kane, makes his first appearance in *Detective Comics* #27.

1939: Archie Comics (originally named LMJ Comics) founded.

1939: Marvel Comics (originally named Timely) publishes *Marvel Comics* #1, introducing its first superheroes.

1941: Captain America, created by Jack Kirby and Joe Simon, makes his first appearance in *Captain America Comics* #1.

1954: Publication of Fredric Wertham's *Seduction of the Innocent* leads to public hearings by the Senate Subcommittee on Juvenile Delinquency, chaired by Sen. Estes Kefauver; hearings lead comics publishers to form self-censorship group, the Comics Code Authority (CCA).

1956: Silver Age begins with the first appearance of the new Flash in DC's *Showcase* #4; DC revamps and reintroduces many of its superheroes over the next decade.

1961: Jack Kirby and Stan Lee cocreate *Fantastic Four*; over the next three years, Lee cocreates the Hulk, Thor, and the X-Men (with Kirby); Spider-Man and Dr. Strange (with Steve Ditko); Iron Man (with Don Heck); and Daredevil (with Bill Everett).

1969: The company that owns DC (then known as National Comics) merges with Time-Warner (then known as Warner Bros.–Seven Arts).

Around 1970: The beginning of the Bronze Age, which marked a maturing of superhero stories and a burst of fantasy titles.

1971: CCA revised for the first time, allowing classic movie monsters and more nuanced depictions of crime, criminals, and police.

Mid-1970s: The first "graphic novel" is published, although the identity of the first graphic novel is disputed.

1976: Fantagraphics is founded.

1979: DC publishes *World of Krypton*, the first miniseries (or limited series).

Mid-1980s: The Modern Age begins.

1985–1986: "Crisis on Infinite Earths" crossover reboots DC continuity.

1986: Dark Horse Comics is founded.

1992: Exodus of seven artists from Marvel leads to the founding of Image Comics.

1993: DC launches Vertigo imprint to tell more mature and non-superhero stories.

1999: IDW is founded.

2001: Marvel leaves the Comics Code Authority.

2009: Marvel is purchased by the Walt Disney Corporation.

Figure 3.1
A Brief Outline of Comics History

The company experienced a spike in attention in 2009 when it revealed it was releasing a story in which Archie married his long-time brunette sweetheart, Veronica, although the publicity did not go out of its way to reveal the story would not affect Archie continuity. Subsequently, a version in which Archie married his long-time blonde sweetheart, Betty, with as much impact on the rest of the publisher's stories, was also released.

Big Two

DC and Marvel are the Big Two comics companies, the largest publishers of American comic books.

Dark Horse Comics

Founded in 1986 in Portland, Oregon, Dark Horse Comics became one of the top five comic book companies on a diverse range of licensed and original comics. Dark Horse has few traditional superheroes or universes; an attempt at both (*Comics' Greatest World*, which ran from 1993 to 1996) was largely a failure, and few of the titles lasted past the line's end.

Dark Horse's output is diverse. The company is best known for original comics series based on movies and TV shows, including the *Star Wars* universe and the *Buffy the Vampire Slayer* TV series; the main *Buffy* title is a continuation of the TV show coordinated by Joss Whedon, the series' creator. Dark Horse also publishes original stories featuring Conan the Barbarian. Dark Horse also reprints Marvel's *Conan the Barbarian* (which ran from 1970 to 1993) and *Star Wars* (1977 to 1986) comics. A line of Japanese manga reprints, such as *Berserk*, *Oh My Goddess!*, and *Path of the Assassin*, help make Dark Horse the second-largest manga publisher in the direct market after Viz (Simba 2009, 15), although it fares worse in the bookstore market (19).

Dark Horse's strength, however, is creator-owned series. In addition to the modern folklore/military agent series *Hellboy* by Mike Mignola and Frank Miller's ultra-violent noir *Sin City*, both released in a series of miniseries, Dark Horse publishes Stan Sakai's *Usagi Yojimbo*, the adventures of a rabbit samurai in a medieval Japan populated by sentient, bipedal animals, and *Beasts of Burden*, a miniseries written by Evan Dorkin with painted art by Jill Thompson that features pets who battle supernatural threats in their neighborhood. Other creator-owned miniseries are published every year.

DC

At the moment, DC is the second-largest comics publisher in the direct market, although it has been the top publisher at various times in the past. Popular DC characters include the most iconic superheroes: Superman, Batman, and Wonder Woman.

The company started as National Allied Publications in 1934. By 1938, they had released *Action Comics* #1, which included the first appearance of Superman. Batman followed in *Detective Comics* #27, which hit newsstands the next year. In the years leading up to and through the United States' involvement in World War II, DC introduced other popular heroes, including the original Green Lantern, Flash, Wonder Woman, Hawkman, and Aquaman. The company also went through several small name changes, such as National Comics and National Periodical Publications, although it unofficially used the name "DC" (named after *Detective Comics*) long before the name's official adoption. Like the rest of the industry, their superheroes fell out of fashion after World War II, although Superman, Batman, and Wonder Woman stayed in print. Superman was so popular that he anchored both radio and television shows during this time.[2]

In the late 1950s, DC kicked off the Silver Age by revamping their superheroes under the direction of editor Julius Schwartz. New versions of old heroes were introduced, and these new superheroes proved to be quite popular. The old versions of the heroes returned as well, as DC introduced the first of their parallel worlds: Earth-2, in which the old heroes aged at a normal rate. The popularity of DC's heroes also received a boost in the 60s with the *Batman* TV show; the tone of many DC comics was changed to match the TV show's campy style. Similarly to Marvel, the superheroes largely overran the company's other output. However, unlike Marvel, DC developed other imprints that specialized in non-superhero fare, such as Vertigo (which publishes creator-owned stories, unrelated to their superhero stories), CMX (which imported Japanese manga), and Zuda (which published Web comics). DC also acquired the superhero characters of failed companies, such as Fawcett and Charlton, which were integrated into DC's superhero universe.

DC became part of the same company as Warner Bros. in 1969, when its owner, Kinney National, bought Warner Bros.–Seven Arts. The division with Warner Bros. and DC was split off from Kinney National in 1972; the new division was called Warner Communications (Cronin 2009). In 2009, DC was moved into a new division, titled DC Entertainment, presumably to allow it to work better with other divisions of Warner Bros.

Fantagraphics

Founded in 1976, Fantagraphics prides itself on high-quality work, going more for highbrow literature than commercially strong titles. They have published the critically acclaimed *Ghost World*, *Love and Rockets*, and *Hate*. They have no superhero titles to speak of. Fantagraphics also publishes *The Comics Journal*, one of the foremost magazines of comic book criticism; *The Comics Journal* has a reputation for first-rate commentary and reporting and for making critically negative remarks about mainstream comics. Fantagraphics also publishes reprints of Charles Schulz's *Peanuts*, E. C. Segar's *Popeye*, and other comic strips. Eros Comix, the company's "adult" imprint, prints pornographic comics.

IDW

Although IDW is not always considered a major publisher, its sales in the direct market frequently place it close to or above Dark Horse and Image. It relies mostly on licensed content, publishing comics based on entertainment properties such as *24*, *Angel*, *CSI*, *Transformers*, *Doctor Who*, and *G. I. Joe*. However, the company's first series was an original horror series, *30 Days of Night*, and IDW publishes other original series as well. The company also publishes reprints of Dick Tracy, Little Orphan Annie, and other classic comic strips under the Library of American Comics imprint.

Image

In 1992, Image Comics was founded by seven artists who wanted more creative and financial control of their creations. Tired of Marvel Comics' ownership of their art and creations, Rob Liefeld, Todd McFarlane, Jim Silvestri, Jim Lee, Erik Larsen, Jim Valentino, and Whilce Portacio formed Image under the proviso that the company would own none of the creator's work and that none of the founders could interfere with the work or finances of others (Dean 2000). In a sense, Image did not exist at all; it owned almost no intellectual property. The comics the company put out were published by each founder's "studio." As might be guessed from the company's previous experience, many of the original titles were superhero-based. The company's partners have changed over the years—Liefeld resigned, and Lee sold his studio to DC, where it became the company's Wildstorm imprint—but Image remains one of the top five American comic book companies.

Image's creative high point came soon after its founding, when its founders were bubbling with ideas they did not have to share with anyone else. It also published critically well-regarded titles from nonfounders, such as Kurt Busiek's *Astro City* (1995–2000) and Matt Wagner's *Mage* (1997–1998). The company has several long-running series: *Savage Dragon* by Larsen, *Spawn* and its spinoffs by McFarlane's studio, and *Witchblade* by Silvestri's studio. Eric Shanower's *Age of Bronze*, one of the few titles published by Image itself and not by one of the studios, is a retelling of the Trojan War. The most popular of Image's current offerings is *The Walking Dead*. This post-zombie apocalypse series, written by Robert Kirkman and drawn by Tony Moore and Charlie Adlard, routinely places highly in ICv2.com's direct market sales lists and in the *New York Times* graphic-novels bestseller list. Kirkman became the first nonartist partner at Image in 2008.

Marvel

With the largest share of the direct market and the majority of the most successful comic book movies of the last decade, Marvel is currently the larger of comic books' Big Two publishers. The company started as Timely Comics in 1939, and in its first years had a few successful characters: the original Human Torch, Namor the Sub-Mariner, and Captain America.[3] When the popularity of superheroes dropped after World War II, however, the company focused on other genres. The company changed its name to Atlas in the early 50s, and for the next decade, it followed whatever trends were popular at the time.

In 1961, the company became Marvel Comics, taking its name from the publication that had first published the Human Torch and the Sub-Mariner. Soon after, writer Stan Lee—the nephew of publisher Martin Goodman—followed the lead of DC, which had experienced success with their recent superhero revival. With artist Jack Kirby, who had cocreated Captain America for the company in the 40s, Lee created the *Fantastic Four*, a comic about a superhero team with more human foibles and troubles than other comic book heroes. The series' success soon inspired an entire universe of heroes, in which Lee cocreated heroes with a series of talented artists. Thor, the X-Men, Spider-Man, the Avengers, Iron Man, the Hulk, and Daredevil were the most prominent; Captain America was revived and given a new title. Lee was writing so many titles at the time that a new method for creating comics was developed; instead of giving the artist a script to draw from, Lee instead gave the artist an outline, which could vary greatly in complexity. The artist was given considerable leeway to draw the issue, so much so that Lee's involvement is sometimes denigrated in favor of the artists' contributions. After the art was finished, Lee then inserted the dialogue and narration. The method was called the "Marvel Method."

Marvel's output has become more and more focused on superheroes since that time, with almost all other content vanishing by the mid-90s. The publisher created the

Ultimate imprint in 2000 to publish titles based on its previous offerings but without the burden of continuity. Other imprints include Max, which can include explicit content, and Icon, which allows creators under exclusive contract to Marvel to publish creator-owned content. The company publishes some other genres, but they are mostly adaptations from other genres or licensed from other companies. In 2009, Marvel was purchased by the Walt Disney Corporation.

Tokyopop

Founded in 1997, Tokyopop is one of the largest publishers of manga in the North American market. Originally named Mixx, the company was a trailblazer in the sale of manga. In 2002, Tokyopop abandoned the newsstand market and targeted mainstream bookstores with a line of manga that was different from most other manga. The books were released in "unflopped" form, reprinting the pages to be read from right to left and back to the front (from the Western point of view). Tokyopop also decided not to translate the Japanese characters for sound effects, which are often integrated into the art. These more "authentic" manga volumes were also sold at a lower price: around $10 compared to their competitors' $15 to $25. The books' low price point and the "unfiltered" manga helped make Tokyopop the leader in manga in America (Thompson 2007, 225–27).

Building on its success, Tokyopop expanded greatly, opening branches in Germany and the United Kingdom in 2004. In 2006, Tokyopop signed an agreement that made publishing giant HarperCollins the company's North American distributor. In the deal, Tokyopop received the chance to adapt some of HarperCollins's books into manga originally published in the English language. Tokyopop is also a leader in the publishing manhwa, a Korean comics style influenced by Japanese manga, in the United States (Fingeroth 2008, 252–53). It also has licensed entertainment properties such as the *Kingdom Hearts* video game and the online game *World of Warcraft*. However, because of declining market share, Tokyopop cut its planned releases in half in 2008, and it has been passed by Viz in the manga market. Among the company's most popular titles are *Fruits Basket, Love Hina, Chibi Vampire*, and *Sailor Moon*.

Viz Media

Founded in 1986 as Viz Communications by Seiji Horibuchi, Viz had trouble breaking into the American comics market with its reprinted manga titles. Despite gaining a sizable amount of startup capital from Japanese manga publisher Shogakukan, Viz did not make much of an impact on the risk-averse American direct market. It was not until the 90s, when the company made a push into the bookstore market with their "graphic novels," that the company began to have success. The company moved into anime in the 90s as well. Japanese manga publisher Shueisha bought half of Viz in 2002; in 2004, Viz Communications merged with ShoPro Entertainment, an American branch of Shogakukan, to form Viz Media. Today, Shueisha and Shogakukan jointly own Viz, which publishes most of those companies' American products (Simba 2009).

Unlike American comics companies, Viz publishes few single-issue comic books, concentrating instead on digest-sized collections and the monthly anthology magazine *Shōnen Jump*. Started in 2002, each issue of *Shōnen Jump* serializes seven different continuing stories, printing one chapter each from titles such as *Bleach* and *Dragon*

Ball Z. The magazine is more than 300 pages of black-and-white shōnen manga—boys' manga, concentrating on action—for about $5, which compares favorably to American comics' 30 color pages for $3 or $4. As of 2008, the publisher claimed the magazine had a readership of more than 200,000, which is far above any ongoing American comics series, and Viz claims the majority of issues are purchased through subscriptions (Viz.com).[4] The publisher also uses "Shōnen Jump" and "Shōnen Jump Advanced" as imprints for shōnen manga. A sister title, *Shōjo Beat*, began in 2005, publishing shōjo (girls' manga, focusing on relationships and romance), but it was cancelled in 2009. The "Shōjo Beat" name is still used as an imprint at Viz for shōjo titles.

Today, Viz is the leader in the American manga market; according to ICv2.com, it published more than half of the top 25 manga lines in the direct market in each quarter of 2009 (ICv2.com "Top 25 Q1," "Top 25 Q2," and "Top 25 Q3," 2009; "Top 25 2009" 2010). Viz is also one of the leaders in the American graphic-novel market. According to BookScan, Viz published 10 of the top 20 graphic novels in American bookstore sales in February 2010, including the top three (ICv2.com "Naruto's" 2010). The publisher does not do as well in the larger direct market—it placed only 4 titles in the top 50 in graphic novels in February 2010, for instance (ICv2.com "Top 300" 2010)—but that's discouraging only when compared against Marvel and DC, who dominate the list.[5] Among Viz's prominent titles are *Naruto, Vampire Knight, Bleach, Death Note,* and *Fullmetal Alchemist.*

CREATORS (WRITERS, ARTISTS, EDITORS)

Although creators have, at times, been obscured or rendered anonymous by their publishers (see the entry for "Carl Barks"), today the identity of writers, artists, and editors are proudly published in every book.[6] Many readers will follow their favorites from project to project, regardless of the character, publisher, or genre. If a librarian reviewing circulation data discovers users are showing interest in a certain writer's or artist's works, then adding more titles by that person would be an excellent way to expand the graphic-novel collection.

Adams, Neal (Artist)

The detailed art of Adams was a sensation in the late Silver Age/early Bronze Age. His work helped DC inject dramatic action and seriousness into Batman after the camp TV series left the air, and his realistic art was an excellent complement to Denny O'Neil's socially conscious writing on *Green Lantern/Green Arrow.* Adams's work for DC and Marvel at the time drew critical support, but this rarely translated into sales, although it did influence other artists (Brancatelli, "Adams," 1999).

Barks, Carl (Writer, Artist)

Creating Scrooge McDuck for Disney was a major accomplishment, but it was merely part of Carl Barks's career. Known for his work with Disney's duck characters, Barks gained fame for the quality of his stories despite working in relatively anonymity (Walt Disney's name was frequently the only one on comics featuring Disney characters). Barks's stories ranged from humorous vignettes to adventure stories and combined humor with knowing irony, gaining admirers both young and old; his work set the tone for "funny animal" stories for years to come (Goulart, "Barks, Carl," 2004). Don Rosa is perhaps the biggest name to follow in his footsteps with Disney characters, with the artist/writer going so far as to use mostly the characters and settings Barks created and even writing sequels to Barks's stories.

Bendis, Brian Michael (Writer, Artist)

After starting out writing and drawing crime comics with small companies, Bendis came to prominence with his Image title *Powers*, in which detectives investigated crime in a world filled with superpowered criminals (Goulart, "Bendis, Brian," 2004). Bendis's handling of characters and trademark naturalistic dialogue—filled with stammers, slang, and overlapping speech—earned him a spot at Marvel, where he began a well-regarded run on *Daredevil*. Today, Bendis is Marvel's de facto chief writer, helping to organize and usually getting to write the most important parts of company-wide crossovers.

Bendis's writing is also seen as the most famous example of decompression, in which the plot advances at a slower rate than the previously frenetic rate comics fans were used to.[7] The slower pace is a deliberate choice, giving more space to characterization and dialogue; many fans, however, accused the decompression movement of padding issues to avoid coming up with new ideas and to make them fit trade paperbacks (Wesley Smith 2009).

Brubaker, Ed (Writer)

Although he has written far more superhero comics than anything else, Brubaker is one of the foremost writers of crime comics for the major companies. His *Sleeper* (DC/Wildstorm) and *Criminal* and *Incognito* (Marvel/Icon) are critically well-regarded crime stories. His superhero work often has a large crime component to it as well; DC's *Catwoman* is about a cat burglar, and *Gotham Central* explored the investigations of police detectives in Batman's Gotham City. As writer of *Captain America*, Brubaker killed and resurrected the title character, which gained some attention in the mainstream press (*Authors and Artists*).

Byrne, John (Writer, Artist)

Beginning as an artist with Marvel in the 70s, Byrne gained attention for his artistic and writing collaboration with writer Chris Claremont on *Uncanny X-Men* from 1977 to 1981 (#108–143). In the 80s, he became writer and artist for *Fantastic Four* and took the title to a creative height it had not seen since Stan Lee and Jack Kirby's days on the series. In 1986, DC lured Byrne from Marvel to rewrite Superman's origin after DC wiped the character (and its universe) clean of continuity. Byrne's work, which lowered Superman's power levels and tried to return Superman to his roots, gained publicity in the press and cast a long shadow on the character's development (Eury 2004).

Claremont, Chris (Writer)

Although Claremont is known mostly for his work on one title—*Uncanny X-Men*—it was an extremely influential run. Claremont wrote *Uncanny X-Men* from 1975 to

1991, during which time it became the most popular comics series in the American market. Claremont injected many soap-opera elements into the series and also added long-simmering subplots into issues. Both practices were widely imitated, and they changed the way superhero-team books were written. He is also famous for developing strong female characters at a time when women either were written as bland or fawning characters or were relegated to the background (Plowright 2004). In more recent years, his somewhat formulaic and peculiar dialogue[8] has fallen out of fashion, as have subplots that require a long time to come to fruition.

Eisner, Will (Writer, Artist)

One of the most influential comic creators, Eisner is best known for his series *The Spirit* (Horn, "Eisner, Will," 1999). Eisner and his studio told stories that gave almost as much detail to the setting and supporting characters as they did to their starring character; Eisner's Manhattan analogue, Central City, was gritty and detailed, and in some stories, the title character made only token appearances. The book featured a noir style that was frequently undercut with humor. Eisner is credited with popularizing the term "graphic novel" (Couch and Weiner 2004, 108)—although as mentioned in Chapter 1, no one is sure what that term means—and he published several highly praised examples, such as *A Contract with God and Other Tenement Stories*, *Fagin the Jew*, and *The Plot: The Secret Story of The Protocols of the Elders of Zion*.

Ellis, Warren (Writer)

An English writer with an uneasy relationship with superheroes, Ellis nevertheless seems to always return to the genre. Ellis saw work on superhero titles like *Wolverine* and *Ultimate Fantastic Four* as a necessity for his career, but he is better regarded for his work on science-fiction titles, which generally feature a cynical or dark outlook on human nature. His most famous work is *Transmetropolitan*, which follows gonzo journalist Spider Jerusalem in a near-future world that is tinged with both the familiar and dystopic. With artists Bryan Hitch and Paul Neary, Ellis created *The Authority*, a series about a superhero team that goes from protecting the world to remaking it. Other science fiction works Ellis has written include the graphic novel *Orbiter* (DC) and *Anna Mercury* (Avatar) (*Contemporary Authors Online*).

Ennis, Garth (Writer)

Starting with *Hellblazer* in 1991, Ennis, who is from Northern Ireland, has been a prominent writer in American comics while rarely writing a major title for the Big Two companies. With artist Steve Dillon, he created *Preacher*, an Eisner-award-winning Vertigo series about a Texas preacher who goes on a quest to confront God. His most famous non-Vertigo DC work, *Hitman*, is about a contract killer with low-level superpowers who takes on targets other hit men avoid. For Marvel, Ennis worked with Dillon again to revive the violent vigilante Punisher. Ennis is the major voice currently working in the small genre of war comics. Ennis's work is known for its combination of violence, profanity, and humor as well as Ennis's occasional antagonism toward superheroes and organized religion (*Contemporary Authors Online*).

Gaiman, Neil (Writer)

Best known for his best-selling and critically acclaimed 75-issue run on *The Sandman* for DC Comics, Gaiman epitomized two changes at the publisher. One was that he was part of the wave of British writers (along with Peter Milligan, Grant Morrison, and Jamie Delano) who followed Alan Moore to American comics, providing new perspectives on American comics and their characters. The second was the work Gaiman and these other writers did for DC, taking established characters, stripping them to their essential or most interesting characteristics, and writing stories about them with continuity and the comics universe being secondary concerns. These series, particularly *The Sandman*, became the foundation of DC's Vertigo line (Mangels, "Vertigo Heroes," 2004). Today, Gaiman mainly works as a novelist; comic books by him are a rarity.

Johns, Geoff (Writer)

After beginning his comics career around the turn of the century, Johns has become a major writer for DC. His work tends to be tinged with nostalgia, using characters readers of the 1980s are familiar with. He has helped push the hero Green Lantern back into the center of the DC Universe, widening the character's mythology and making a Green Lantern story, "Blackest Night," into a company-wide crossover in 2009. He also revived the second Flash and was one of the four cowriters for DC's weekly series *52* in 2006–2007. In 2010, he was named DC's chief creative officer, which gives him considerable control over DC's creative output (Hyde 2010).

Kirby, Jack (Artist, Writer)

An artist who worked in comics for more than half a century, Kirby is best known for his collaboration with writer Stan Lee as the Silver Age began at Marvel. He cocreated the Fantastic Four, Incredible Hulk, X-Men, and Thor with Lee. (He also cocreated Captain America in the Golden Age with writer Joe Simon, and his character designs were instrumental in the creation of Iron Man.) More importantly, he redefined how comic book art was drawn; previous illustrations had the reputation of featuring stiff characters, but Kirby's work was kinetic and explosive. His innovations and style are still dissected and imitated today, and many artists and comic book readers hail him as "King" Kirby. His imagination—both in his art and in his later stints as a writer for both Marvel and DC—displayed an unusual amount of creativity, with a boundless number of strange and fanciful ideas (Brancatelli, "Kirby, Jack," 1999) (see Figure 3.2).

Kubert, Joe (Artist)

Influenced by the detailed and precise art of adventure strip artists Hal Foster and Alex Raymond, Silver-Age artist Kubert is known for his adventure comics, including *Tor* and *Tarzan*, and his war comics, such as *Enemy Ace* and *Sgt. Rock*. The latter, about a battle-hardened sergeant who leads Easy Company in World War II, is probably his most famous creation. Although he has given most of his time since 1976 to his School of Cartoon and Graphic Art, which has produced several famous comics artists, in 1996 he also published the award-winning *Fax from Sarajevo*, a tale of the Yugoslavian Civil

Figure 3.2

A panel from page 15 of *Black Panther* #2 (March 1977), from *Black Panther by Jack Kirby, v. 1*; art and words by Jack Kirby. © 1977 Marvel Comics.

War (Brancatelli, "Kubert, Joe," 1999). His sons, Andy and Adam, are also prominent comic book artists.

Lee, Jim (Writer, Artist, Editor)

Rising to fame as the artist on *Uncanny X-Men* during the early 90s, Lee's clear, action-filled art and attention to detail drew many imitators. Lee, unsatisfied with just half the creative reins of *Uncanny X-Men*, was given the writer's position as well, taking over for Chris Claremont on *X-Men* #4 (January 1992). Soon after, however, he broke away from Marvel and became one of the founding members of Image Comics, starting the company's Wildstorm imprint (Horn, "Lee, Jim," 1999). Wildstorm's output is in many ways emblematic of 90s comics: flashy, violent, and well drawn, but with a reputation for a lack of depth. But Wildstorm did produce comics in a variety of genres during a time when superheroes were most firmly in control of the medium, and Lee emphasized the creative freedom he and the other Image founders were seeking by publishing critically praised comics by other creators, such as Terry Moore's *Strangers in Paradise*, Kurt Busiek's *Astro City*, and a whole line of Alan Moore comics. Lee later sold Wildstorm to DC, for which he frequently draws high-profile projects (Mangels, "Wildstorm Heroes," 2004). Lee was named copublisher of DC, along with Dan DiDio, in February 2010.

Lee, Stan (Writer, Editor)

Lee cocreated most of Marvel's enduring characters in the 60s. Working with talented artists like Jack Kirby and Steve Ditko, Lee gave outlines to the artists, who then drew the issues as they saw fit, with Lee adding the often-hyperbolic dialogue later. His characters were, unusually, more human than DC's popular superheroes, with Lee emphasizing that Marvel's heroes had the same sorts of problems as the readers did when the heroes were not in their heroic identities. Some critics believe the artists had a greater

Figure 3.3
Page 1 of *Amazing Spider-Man* #9 (February 1964); words by
Stan Lee and art by Steve Ditko. © 1964 Marvel Comics.

role in creating the characters than Lee, with Lee acting as much an editor as a writer.
Lee's flair for promotion—including self-promotion (see Figure 3.3)—has ensured that
his is the name most linked with Marvel's most popular characters ("Lee" World 1999).

In the 70s, Lee stepped away from writing, and by the 80s, he was rarely involved
with the day-to-day workings of Marvel, although he remained a figurehead, and most
Marvel issues were adorned with the banner "Stan Lee Presents." Today, his involvement with Marvel is mainly restricted to executive-producer credits and cameo roles
in movies based on their characters.

McFarlane, Todd (Writer, Artist)

At the same time Jim Lee came to prominence with *Uncanny X-Men*, McFarlane did
the same with his art on *Amazing Spider-Man*. His exaggerated style frequently
featured Spider-Man in positions that were far from realistic but were extremely
dynamic. His artistic popularity spurred Marvel to give him a new *Spider-Man* title to

write and draw, but like Lee, he was frustrated by the artistic, creative, and monetary limits that work for hire placed upon him. As a founder of Image Comics, McFarlane created Spawn, an antihero who struggles to hold on to his morality after being resurrected by a demon. *Spawn* was, for a time, as popular as comics from the Big Two, but its prominence has faded. Although McFarlane still works in comics, he's better known for his action-figure company, McFarlane Toys, and his penchant for collecting history-making baseballs (Goulart, "McFarlane, Todd," 2004).

Mignola, Mike (Writer, Artist)

Although Mignola started out drawing superhero stories with Marvel and DC with some success, Mignola's full potential did not become evident until he drew and plotted *Hellboy: Seed of Destruction* in 1994 for Dark Horse—with John Byrne scripting because Mignola had no experience writing (Arrant 2009). Mignola wrote later *Hellboy* miniseries himself. His stories of a demon who was raised by a human and later battled dark forces drawn from magic and folklore were well received for both the humanity he gave his characters (even when they were not human) and his distinctive blocky, shadowy art (Roach 2004) (see Figure 3.4).

Millar, Mark (Writer)

While this Scottish writer's early works for American comics often involved cowriting with Grant Morrison, Millar later grew a style completely different from Morrison's. Most of his early work was with DC; he took over the Wildstorm imprint's *Authority* from Warren Ellis and intensified the "widescreen" action style Ellis had given the team book. But friction with DC editors, who wanted to downplay violence following 9/11 and who were nervous about a kiss between two gay lead characters, led Millar to move to Marvel (Mangels, "Authority," 2004). There, he continued to display an over-the-top, violent, satirical style that has been criticized for lacking in subtlety; all those qualities are on display in his and John Romita Jr.'s *Kick Ass*, published by Marvel's Icon imprint. Still, he is one of the most prominent writers at Marvel; he was instrumental in the early success of the company's Ultimate line, and he has been given central roles in company-wide crossovers (Martin 2004).

Miller, Frank (Writer, Artist)

After his art on *Daredevil* became noticed for the noir style he injected into superheroics, Miller was given a chance to write the series as well as draw it. In his two years as writer, he helped transform a second-tier title into a top seller, and his *Daredevil* work is still extremely well regarded today. He also wrote and drew *The Dark Knight Returns* (1986), a story of an older Batman who returned from retirement to a confusing and violent world. Often hailed as one of the greatest comic book stories, Miller's popular tale, featuring violence and a darker viewpoint than its contemporaries, helped introduce more adult themes into the superhero genre. Since then, Miller's work has become even more violent while remaining popular, especially for a creator who does little work for the Big Two; he has written and drawn *300* and the *Sin City* miniseries. His art adds a gritty combination of violence and Japanese influences to American comic books (Goulart, "Miller, Frank," 2004).

Figure 3.4
A panel from Page 5 of "The Chained Coffin" in *Dark Horse Presents* #100 (August 1995), from *Hellboy: The Chained Coffin and Others*; art and words by Mike Mignola. Hellboy™ © 2010 Mike Mignola.

Moore, Alan (Writer)

Probably the most celebrated comic book writer still writing, Moore is known for his literary and adult themes as well as his deconstruction of the superhero genre. He is also known for the conflicts he has had with corporate entities who release his work: he refuses to work with either of the Big Two comics companies because of previous disagreements with them, mostly over creators' rights and royalties, and he had disavowed many of the cinematic adaptations of his creations—going so far as to refuse royalties and have his name taken off of movies based on his works ("Alan Moore Asks" 2005).

Moore, who is from England, first came to widespread attention with his work with Marvel UK (the company's British division) and *2000 A.D.* *V for Vendetta* and *Miracleman* were his first masterworks; in the former, Moore looked at a dystopic future England, while the latter showed his ability to work deeper meaning into the superhero genre for the first time. Working with DC in the mid-80s, he had a well-regarded run on *Swamp Thing*, and he cocreated *Watchmen*, which is considered one of the greatest graphic novels ever. *Watchmen* changed how creators and audiences looked at superheroes; more adult themes followed, mostly expressed as violence and sexual content without the complexity of Moore's vision. Moore has had several other celebrated creations since then, including *From Hell*, in which he "solves" the Jack the Ripper killings, and *The League of Extraordinary Gentlemen*, in which he uses a wide variety of public domain and popular characters to populate a world based on pulp stories (*Authors and Artists*).

Morrison, Grant (Writer)

Noted for his use of strange and big ideas, Morrison is not always an easy writer to read. Working for DC, he made second-tier hero Animal Man aware of his status as a comic book character, allowing him to discuss the nature of fiction with his creator. Morrison, who is from Scotland, was allowed to write titles with increasing visibility, including *Justice League of America* for DC and *New X-Men* for Marvel. Morrison injected counterculture thought, played with metafictional ideas, and added symbolism that was new to comics at the time (*Contemporary Authors Online*). Strangely, Morrison also showed a fondness for reusing Silver Age plots, looking past their simplicity and playing with the energy and inventiveness of their origins.

Perez, George (Artist, Writer)

Beginning in the 70s, Perez drew the adventures of prominent superheroes for both of the Big Two companies. His early work was influenced by Jack Kirby, but he became popular for his subtle yet energetic style. Also famous for the skill with which he drew crowd scenes, he is best known (mainly as an artist) for his work on team books: two separate stints on Marvel's *Avengers* and a fondly remembered run on DC's *New Teen Titans*. After DC reset the continuity of its universe—in its miniseries *Crisis on Infinite Earths*, which was drawn by Perez—he was given a chance to write and draw the new *Wonder Woman* series, where he tied her roots closer to Greek mythology than before (Goulart, "Perez, George," 2004).

Quesada, Joe (Artist, Editor)

Although Quesada's art allowed him to rise to the top of the profession, it was as an editor that he has had the greatest effect. After editing a successful revival of *Daredevil*—helped by his own beautiful, detailed art—Quesada became editor-in-chief at Marvel in 2000. Marvel's longest-termed editor since Stan Lee, Quesada presided over the launch of the Ultimate imprint, which retold the stories of Marvel characters freed from the decades of continuity, and authorized massive crossovers that have lasted for months, tying up the stories of many titles at once. In some ways, he has emphasized the history of Marvel titles, most prominently by restoring the old numbering of Marvel titles that had been relaunched with new #1s, but Quesada also retconned (see Chapter 2, under "Continuity") Spider-Man's nearly two-decade marriage out of existence. Quesada also helped guide Marvel into the collected editions market and its foray into making its own movies (Irving 2009).

Romita, John, Jr. (Artist)

The son of artist John Romita Sr., a prominent artist at Marvel in the 60s and 70s, Romita Jr. began working for Marvel in the late 70s. The younger Romita has worked mainly with Marvel during his career, drawing most of Marvel's major characters and enjoying repeat stints on some of the publisher's biggest titles. His style is detailed without skimping on action, and his art is clearly laid out. He remains one of the biggest names in comic art (Vaughan 2009).

Romita, John, Sr. (Artist)

An artist with a long career at Marvel, Romita drew romance comics for both the Big Two companies[9] before penciling *Daredevil* and then *Amazing Spider-Man*, where he took over for Spider-Man cocreator Steve Ditko with issue #39. Where Ditko's characters were plain or even homely, Romita made Peter Parker muscular and "dashing," and Spider-Man's world became populated with attractive people bursting with power, nobility, and life. Part of Spider-Man's popularity has to be attributed to Romita's work. In the 70s and 80s, Romita took less art work and became more involved with Marvel as a whole; in 1972, he became the publisher's art director, and in 1982, he was appointed to an executive position (Brancatelli, "Romita, John," 1999).

Ross, Alex (Artist)

Because of his photorealistic style (see Figure 3.5), Ross is sometimes called the "Norman Rockwell of comics." He came to prominence with two miniseries in the mid-90s. *Marvels*, on which he collaborated with Kurt Busiek for Marvel, retold the history of the early Marvel Universe in four issues through the eyes of a reporter; *Kingdom Come*, a four-issue miniseries in which he worked with Mark Waid, told of a possible cataclysmic future of the DC Universe. Ross's writing and art shy from darker depictions of heroes. Known for his painted art of superheroes, Ross uses real models, often dressed in costume, for his art; because of the detail put into each panel, his output is low, and he primarily works as a cover artist and as a plotter (*Contemporary Authors Online*). Librarians may be familiar with Ross from posters published by ALA Graphics.

Sakai, Stan (Writer, Artist)

Usagi Yojimbo, which features a samurai rabbit in a seventeenth-century Japan inhabited by humanoid animals, has been written and drawn by Sakai since he created the character in 1984. The series has had three publishers—Fantagraphics, Mirage Studios, and Dark Horse—but the series is owned by its creator. Sakai weaves Japanese folklore, religion, culture, and traditions into his stories while also making reference to Japanese cinema, especially samurai movies (*Authors and Artists*). Violence is stylized in a way that minimizes its shock without losing its impact (see Figure 3.6). Sakai's art

Figure 3.5
Panels from page 21 of *Kingdom Come* #1 (1996), from *Kingdom Come*; art by Alex Ross and words by Mark Waid. Kingdom Come © 1996 DC Comics. All rights reserved.

style is simple, with clean lines that sacrifice little emotional complexity ("Children's Book Reviews" 2009).

Schwartz, Julius (Editor)

A science-fiction agent who worked with Ray Bradbury and H. P. Lovecraft, Schwartz became an editor at DC in 1944. In 1956, he presided over the relaunch of the Flash, one of the company's superhero characters. The new Flash helped revive the superhero genre and lift the medium from the depths it had been battered into by moralistic hysteria. In 1964, Schwartz was tapped to revitalize Batman, and in 1970, he took over the Superman titles from Mort Weisinger; in both cases, he moved away from "gimmick" stories, adding more realism and character to the titles under his care. He was DC's senior editor from 1973 until 1986 (Brancatelli, "Schwartz, Julius," 1999).

Shooter, Jim (Writer, Editor)

A writer for both Marvel and DC before becoming Marvel's editor-in-chief in 1978, Shooter was a controversial figure during the 80s. He put an emphasis on getting issues out on time, ending frequently missed deadlines, and he managed to bring in new talent.

Figure 3.6
Panels from page 19 of *Usagi Yojimbo* (v. 3) #61 (2002), from *Usagi Yojimbo, v. 18: Travels with Jotaro*; art and words by Stan Sakai. Usagi Yojimbo™ © 2010 Stan Sakai.

Marvel had many successful runs with previously lackluster titles during his tenure, including Frank Miller's *Daredevil*, Chris Claremont and John Byrne's *Uncanny X-Men*, and Walter Simonson's *Thor*. He helped cement Marvel's commitment to the direct market and comic book specialty stores. Shooter also instituted creator royalties and creator-controlled material with the Epic imprint in 1982, and he introduced the lucrative company-wide crossovers as well.

Shooter's managerial style was sometimes seen as dictatorial, however, and many writers and artists left Marvel during this time to work at other companies. He also failed to attract any British talent—the kind that was revitalizing DC in the late 80s. The conflicts led to his firing in 1987 (Rhoades 2008, 111–19). Shooter founded Valiant and Defiant Comics, but neither made much of a lasting impression before folding.

Sim, Dave (Writer, Artist)

Cerebus the Aardvark, a 300-issue black-and-white series featuring a humanoid aardvark barbarian, seems an unlikely character to give a creator comic book fame.

But Sim's creation morphed from a parody sword-and-sorcery character to a vehicle for Sim to explore political, religious, and gender issues.[10] The sprawling epic, which began in 1974, took almost 30 years to complete and helped inspire the black-and-white boom of the 80s; Sim also used his reputation to campaign for creators' rights. However, his extreme views on women and feminism have earned him controversy and condemnation (Goulart, "Cerebus," 2004).

Takahashi, Rumiko (Writer, Artist)

Probably the best-known female manga artist and one of the richest women in Japan, Takahashi is known as the "Princess of Manga." Takahashi's writing and art generally combines romance with playful humor, regardless of whether she's working with fantasy or the modern world. Her most famous series include *Ranma ½*, a "slapstick martial arts romantic comedy" in which a boy changes sex when doused with water; *Maison Ikkoku*, a comic story of a love triangle in a modern Japanese apartment house; and *InuYasha*, in which a girl travels through an abandoned well into a feudal Japan filled with demons (*Authors and Artists*).

Tezuka, Osamu (Writer, Artist)

The creator of such seminal manga as *Astro Boy*, Tezuka is a giant figure in Japanese comics. Tezuka was influenced by Walt Disney and movies, bringing action and space to the formerly cramped Japanese comic page. Tezuka's style was cinematic, using angles and views to emulate movie views. In turn, he influenced countless other manga artists (Kato 1999). From World War II until his death in 1989, Tezuka wrote and drew more than 150,000 pages of manga in more than 700 series.

Waid, Mark (Writer)

In 1989, Waid left a short-lived career as an editor at DC to become a writer. In the 90s, his gift for characterization drew attention during his long runs on *Flash* for DC and *Captain America* for Marvel (*Authors and Artists*). Waid also wrote *Kingdom Come*, the story of a possible dark future for the DC Universe. The series was a reaction to the more morally ambiguous and violent stories of the late 80s and 90s that had been inspired by Alan Moore and Dave Gibbons's *Watchmen* and Frank Miller's *The Dark Knight Returns*; *Kingdom Come* features Superman returning to superheroics and having to right a world that has been devastated by less moral heroes. Waid's work is often steeped in continuity; in fact, he serves as the unofficial historian for DC stories (Beau Smith).

Weisinger, Mort (Editor)

Like Julius Schwartz, Weisinger was an editor at DC from World War II through its Silver Age resuscitation of superheroes. Weisinger, most famous for his editorship of the Superman titles, secured strong artists for the books and helped create many of the enduring trappings of Superman lore, such as the Fortress of Solitude and Supergirl. Weisinger, who claimed to talk to kids to get ideas and feedback, added humor and an element of slapstick comedy to Superman, often throwing bizarre villains and plots against the hero. He frequently gave his writers ideas to work with, rather than allowing the writers to come up with ideas on their own. Writers were also sometimes told to write a story based on a pre-drawn cover, an innovation Weisinger brought from pulp magazines (Lillian 1975). He stayed with DC until 1970.

OTHER INDUSTRY TERMS AND ORGANIZATIONS

The publishers own the most recognizable characters and control the methods of dissemination, and the writers and artists come up with the stories. Still, knowing about those groups does not cover all of the information necessary to understand how comics are created.

Artist

An artist is someone who draws comics. This can include penciling (see "Penciler") or inking (see "Inker"); some artists do both on a single comic, while others may serve in different roles for different comics or specialize in one role. For some graphic novels, the book's credits do not adequately distinguish between the two roles, listing two (or more) creators as "artist." This may mean more than one penciler worked on the book, or it may be a different way to credit the traditional penciling and inking roles. Reference sites can help untangle what role each artist took (see Chapter 9, under "Lists of Graphic Novels and Their Contents"); also, a critical eye can help discern differences in style that indicate that a title was penciled by two different artists.

Breakdowns

The process of placing characters, actions, and dialogue on the page is sometimes called "breakdowns" (or "layouts"). Usually, the role is taken by the penciler or by a writer who provides a detailed script. Breakdowns are generally not as complete as penciled art (see "Penciler"). This role is rarely credited separately, although an artist who provides pencils that are extremely "loose" (causing the inker to expend more creativity and effort) may be credited separately for breakdowns.

Bronze Age

The Bronze Age stretches from the end of the Silver Age—whenever that is placed (see "Silver Age")—to the beginning of the Modern Age in the mid-80s. The Bronze Age is marked by an increasing attempt for relevance, including more stories about drug abuse and the inclusion of more minority and female heroes and supporting characters.[11] Marvel and DC also published books that teamed up two heroes who previously had separate titles (Marvel's *Power Man & Iron Fist* and DC's *Superboy and the Legion of Super-Heroes*) or teamed a character with a rotating roster of costars (Marvel's *Marvel Team-Up* and *Marvel Two-in-One* and DC's *The Brave and the Bold* and *DC Comics Presents*). A brief burst of fantasy books also are a hallmark of the age, although only Marvel's *Conan the Barbarian* and DC's *Warlord* lasted beyond the Bronze Age. Romance, war, and western titles disappeared during this era.

Colorist

Colorists add color to the black-and-white art after the inker finishes with it. Color can be added by hand or, increasingly, by computer. Previously, colorists had to work with a limited palette, in part because some colors could not be reliably reproduced by previous printing processes on newsprint.[12] The colorist controls the entire color scheme of a book, which can give him or her a large role in the overall feel and tone of the book; like lettering, however, coloring is seen as more of a technical than artistic job.

Comics Code Authority

Faced with the specter of governmental oversight, the comics industry imposed a set of guidelines on itself in 1954 that was meant to reassure parents and legislators that their content would not corrupt children. The CCA, as originally imposed, was restrictive, virtually killing horror comics—even most classic movie monsters, such as vampires, zombies, and werewolves were forbidden—and the company Entertaining Comics (EC), which published many horror titles. The CCA prohibited excessive violence, sex, and drugs. Above all, it was important that "in every instance good shall triumph over evil" (Comics Magazine Association 1954). Nonparticipating comics companies were often barred from appearing at newsstands, the preferred distribution method of the time. Lower-circulation "underground" comics did not participate in the code and did not abide by their strictures.

In 1971, the U.S. Department of Health, Education, and Welfare asked Marvel to do a story about drug abuse. Marvel published the story in *Amazing Spider-Man* #96–98 (May–July 1971), showing drug use to be dangerous, but the CCA rejected the story, saying the context was irrelevant—it still showed drug abuse. The issues were published without the CCA seal, with little effect on sales. The code was revised soon after, loosening the restrictions,[13] and they were loosened again in 1989.

Marvel withdrew from the CCA in 2001, deciding to use its own rating system (Dean 2001). Other major publishers followed. Today, only DC and Archie participate in the CCA, although DC submits only its all-ages and mainstream superhero titles to the CCA, and they occasionally publish a superhero title without CCA approval.

Creator

Creators are the writers and artists who make a comic book.

Creator-Owned

A series in which one or more of the creators owns some or all of the intellectual property contained within the comics is referred to as creator-owned.

Diamond Comic Distributors

Although Diamond produces few comic books, it is a vital part of the comic book industry: it is the sole distributor of comic books to comic book shops and other non-bookstore retailers (see "Direct Market" for details on how Diamond gained this monopoly). Diamond also distributes collected editions for some publishers to bookstores, although both Marvel and DC use other distributors. This monopoly allows

Diamond to control the market in ways that are not immediately obvious: they can unilaterally set policies with publishers and comic book stores and decide which books they will or will not distribute. Libraries have the option to buy directly from Diamond, and the company offers promotional material like library-oriented reviews and *Bookshelf Magazine* to libraries at http://www.diamondbookshelf.com.

Diamond distributes comics not only in North America but also in the United Kingdom. DC has an option to buy Diamond outright, which it has not exercised (Dean 2002).

Direct Market

In the 70s, comic book publishers were facing declining sales at newsstands, their primary sales market. To counteract the slumping sales in drugstores, grocery stores, and other casual-magazine outlets, comics companies signed deals with distributors who sold their publications to stores that specialized in comics. This method managed to deliver their products to a focused market much more quickly. This new distribution deal was also more lucrative for comics companies because the copies sold through "direct" distributors were nonreturnable; newsstand distributors sold their comics based on an agreement that those not sold could be returned to the publisher or distributor. Before the direct market, vendors could order returnable copies and request far more than they would ever sell, leaving publishers with unsellable copies of months-old comics.

In the 80s, the direct market began to take over the comic book market. In the 90s, the comic book industry had one of its frequent bust periods, and distributors began failing. Marvel Comics, hoping to control its own distribution, bought the distributor Heroes World; Diamond Comics Distribution and its main competitor, Capital City Distributors, remained independent. With the loss of Marvel's business—a major amount of the market—other distributors sought exclusive deals with the major publishers. Diamond secured exclusives with DC, Dark Horse, Image, and others; Capital City and other competitors, unable to sell the products from the industry's biggest publishers, went out of business or were purchased by Diamond. When Heroes World proved inadequate for Marvel's purposes, Marvel also signed with Diamond. As the only remaining direct distributor and with the newsstand market for comics evaporating, Diamond was left with a near monopoly in the comic book distribution market.

The direct market, which deals mainly with specialty shops rather than vendors that appeal to the public at large, has been accused of making comic books harder for the average person to access and for choking diversity in the books, since the direct market caters to existing readers with already-set tastes.

Editor

There are many different levels of responsibility for editors. For work-for-hire projects, the editor may review pitches for series, hire the creative talent, critique the creators' ideas, and keep the project on deadline. Some editors may suggest plot or character ideas to writers or artists, but they are usually not credited in the comic books themselves for these contributions. Editors also make sure the stories fit in with the publisher's overall direction and policies. Although spotting potential continuity errors was a major part of the editor's role in the past, the more relaxed attitude toward continuity for some projects has caused that part of the job to be emphasized less. Editors for creator-owned books have much the same responsibilities but have less to do with dictating plot and hiring of creators.

Group editors oversee multiple titles that are related (although occasionally, the connections between titles are tenuous). The editor-in-chief serves as a public face for a publisher and either creates or appoints someone to set the overall direction for the company's stories.

Golden Age

The late 30s to the late 40s were the Golden Age of comics. During this decade, American comic books became popular, superheroes were created and codified, and some of the most popular heroes—including Batman, Superman, Wonder Woman, and Captain America—were created. Although the exact beginning of the era is disputed, many put the start of the Golden Age in 1938, when Superman made his first appearance in *Action Comics* #1.

During the Golden Age, Captain Marvel's adventures sold more than 1.3 million copies per issue (Rhoades 2008, 29); other popular protagonists included Plastic Man (Quality Comics) and Will Eisner's The Spirit. World War II provided fodder for stories and villains and supplied an audience in servicemen. The art in the Golden Age seems less refined by modern standards, and the stories range from more simplistic to insanely imaginative.

The end of the Golden Age is also fluid. The decrease in the popularity of superheroes and the rise of other genres, especially horror comics, in the late 40s and early 50s, ended the era.

Inker

Also known as a "finisher" or "embellisher," inkers are artists who take the penciler's drawings and use inks to make the drawing darker. This can be done with pens or brushes or digitally. The inker may simply trace the penciled art or may add to the art by correcting or emphasizing certain lines. A penciler's work can look dramatically different depending on the inker's interpretation of the pencils; however, the job of inking art is generally seen as a less creative job than penciling, and fairly or not, inkers generally get less credit than pencilers.

Letterer

The letterer draws and places the text in a comic book, including dialogue, sound effects, credits, and story titles. Some letterers design character logos as well. Letterers traditionally worked with pen (or brush) and ink, although the job today is performed with computers at the larger comics companies. Although the letterer's work may have a dramatic artistic impact, it is generally considered a more technical and less creative part of the process of creating comic books.

Modern Age

The Modern Age began in the mid-80s and stretches to the modern day. Its beginnings are debated, although DC's *Crisis on Infinite Earths* crossover miniseries (1985–1986), which rebooted the continuity of all their comics, certainly ushered in the Modern Age at that publisher. Frank Miller's *The Dark Knight Returns* (DC, 1986) and Alan Moore and Dave Gibbons's *Watchmen* (DC, 1986), both mature and violent comics that are often imitated, are also hallmarks of the era's beginning.

Stories in the Modern Age began taking a darker turn, with antiheroes becoming more common. These more amoral heroes, along with a rise in violence levels, led some readers to call those comics "grim and gritty" (Rhoades 2008, 125). Continuity, once the backbone of the Big Two's comic universes, became less prominent as reboots and reimaginings became more common. The concept of crossovers were created near the Modern Age's beginnings and became more common as the age went on (see Chapter 2). The direct market, which allowed publishers to sell their comics to comic book shops, became the dominant method of comics distribution. Independent, black-and-white publishers were able to survive, if not flourish. This, along with the creation of DC's Vertigo imprint, increased the variety of comic book genres available.

Penciler

A penciler takes the writer's script or outline and turns it into art, drawn in pencil. When the penciler is done, it is sent to the inker. Pencilers are the stars of comic book art, usually gaining the lion's share of credit and attention despite the inker's contributions. They are usually credited before inkers.

Plotter

A plotter is the writer who comes up with the plot for a comic book. This may be a simple or detailed telling of the story. Most writers come up with the plot of the stories as part of the overall writing process, so this credit is not common. Occasionally, an editor might suggest a plot to a writer, but editors are not often credited for that contribution.

Scripter

A scripter gives the penciler a breakdown of what happens during a comic book for the penciler to turn into art. Since this is part of the task of a writer, this role is not usually credited separately. The scripts can be as detailed as movie or television scripts ("full scripts"), or they can be breakdowns of the plot (see "Plotter"). The latter is often called the "Marvel Method" because during the Silver Age, Stan Lee wrote most of Marvel's comics and was pressed for time, so he gave his artists brief plot outlines. After the artist laid out and drew the comic, Lee added dialogue. Over the years, the Marvel style became more detailed, and today the full script is much more common.

Silver Age

The Silver Age of comics began in 1956 with the publication of DC's *Showcase* #4, in which a redesigned Flash made his first appearance. The new Flash was a different character from the Golden Age version but had some similarities; new versions of Green Lantern, Hawkman, and other heroes followed. Superheroes regained popularity, and Marvel Comics, headed by Stan Lee and a talented corps of artists (such as Jack Kirby, Steve Ditko, and John Romita) experienced a creative boom, creating most of the Marvel Universe's popular heroes. The art of the Silver Age was a leap forward from the Golden Age, although it may look dated to modern eyes. The characters and stories were more complex, with heroes—especially Marvel's—having real-world personal problems along with their heroic dilemmas.

Although the beginning of the Silver Age is well established, its end is not. Suggestions for the end of the Silver Age range from the end of 12-cent comics in 1969 to the death of Spider-Man's girlfriend, Gwen Stacy, in 1973. Whenever it ended, the decade and a half of the Silver Age has strongly influenced the shape of the comics that followed.

Work for Hire

In comics, "work for hire" refers to creative output that becomes the property of the company publishing it. Most of the Big Two's output—with some exceptions, such as DC's Vertigo and Marvel's Icon imprints—is work for hire, as were almost all the comics before the 80s.

Writer

The writer generally creates an idea and puts it into a form that a penciler can, in turn, put into art. The job of a writer includes the roles of plotter, scripter, and dialogue.

CONCLUSION

Knowing the major players in the world of mainstream comic books can help librarians make sense of a seemingly vast world. Understanding the history of comic book publishers, especially the Big Two, can help explain the current industry. Being aware of the important writers, artists, and editors can help libraries create a well-rounded collection of interest to comic book readers and justify the inclusion of collections of older comic books.

NOTES

1. Archie's first experience with superheroes was *Blue Ribbon Comics* (1940–1942), an anthology title that featured many genres of stories along with its superheroes. Other Archie Golden Age titles that had superheroes included *Zip Comics*, *Jackpot Comics*, *Hangman Comics*, *Shield-Wizard Comics*, and *Pep Comics*. The last had Archie's most famous superhero, the Shield, as a feature, but *Pep* introduced Archie Andrews in #22, and Archie took over the title in the following years. The Shield left *Pep* with #65 (1948).

In the Silver Age, Archie revived their superheroes in the "Archie Adventures" line, which lasted from 1959 to 1965. In 1965, the Archie Adventures line was replaced by a group of titles the publisher variously called "Radio Comics" and "Mighty Comics Group." None of the titles in this line survived past 1967. In the 1980s, Archie tried the "Red Circle Comics," which released the publisher's non-Archie offerings, but none of the superhero titles lasted past 1985. The Spectrum line, a 1989 attempt at superheroes, did not even make it to the newsstands because of its non–Comics Code–approved content (Offenberger). Archie licensed its heroes to DC after that, which published them as Impact Comics. Eight ongoing titles lasted from 1991 to 1993. DC's second attempt at publishing the Red Circle heroes began in 2009 and was cancelled the next year.

2. *The Adventures of Superman* aired on radio from 1940 to 1951 and on television from 1952 to 1958.

3. The Human Torch and Namor the Sub-Mariner made their first appearances on newsstands in *Marvel Comics* #1 (October 1939). The Human Torch, an android that burst into flame when in contact with oxygen, was created by Carl Burgos; Namor, an undersea prince with a grudge against the surface world that occasionally conflicted with his noble nature, was created by Bill Everett. Captain America, a patriotic super-hero, first appeared in *Captain America Comics* #1 (March 1941) and was created by writer Joe Simon and artist Jack Kirby.

4. However, this pales compared to the original Japanese version of the magazine, *Weekly Shōnen Jump*, which had a circulation of 27 million in 2007 (Ibaraki 2008).

5. Image placed only three in that top 50 and Dark Horse four.

6. As are other functions, such as inkers, letterers, and colorists. For a brief discussion on these other roles, see "Other Industry Terms and Organizations" later in this chapter or the glossary.

7. In 1962, it took Stan Lee and Steve Ditko 11 pages to tell the origin of Spider-Man in *Amazing Fantasy* #15. In 2000, it took Brian Michael Bendis and Mark Bagley seven issues (180 pages) to retell the same story in *Ultimate Spider-Man* #1–7.

8. Such as Wolverine's trademark phrase, "I'm the best there is at what I do. And what I do . . . isn't very nice" (as in *Wolverine*, v. 1, #1, September 1982) or Cannonball, a Southerner, explaining his powers by saying, "Ah'm pretty close to invulnerable when Ah'm blasting" (*New Mutants*, v. 1, #7, September 1983).

9. Although Marvel certainly was not that big at the time. When Romita first worked for the company just after World War II, Marvel was called "Atlas," and it had to release Romita because of market setbacks in 1957.

10. A collaborator, Gerhard, helped Sim with the art on the series from #65 to #300, drawing backgrounds.

11. However, few of these new, nonwhite male characters became stars, and comics titles headlined by women and minorities tended not to survive very long.

12. The Hulk was colored gray in his first appearance in 1962, but the printer advised Marvel it could not reliably reproduce the Hulk's shade of gray. Looking for a color that could be reproduced, Marvel changed the Hulk's color to green.

13. Although vampires and werewolves were allowed because of their distinguished literary and cinematic treatment, zombies were not. Marvel skirted this by having their heroes battle "zuvembies," as in *Avengers* #152 (October 1976).

REFERENCES

Arrant, Chris. "To Hellboy and Back: Mike Mignola—Full-Time Comics Creator," October 2, 2009. http://www.newsarama.com/comics/091002-mike-mignola.html (accessed April 1, 2010).

"Alan Moore Asks for an Alan Smithee." *Comics Reporter*, November 9, 2005, http://www.comicsreporter.com/index.php/alan_moore_asks_for_an_alan_smithee (accessed March 17, 2010).

Authors and Artists for Young Adults, s.vv. "Alan Moore," "Ed Brubaker," "Mark Waid,"
     "Rumiko Takahashi," "Stan Sakai," http://galenet.galegroup.com/servlet/BioRC
     (accessed April 26, 2010).

Brancatelli, Joe. "Adams, Neal." In Horn, *The World Encyclopedia of Comics*, 77.

Brancatelli, Joe. "Kirby, Jack." In Horn, *The World Encyclopedia of Comics*, 447–48.

Brancatelli, Joe. "Kubert, Joe." In Horn, *The World Encyclopedia of Comics*, 459–60.

Brancatelli, Joe. "Lee, Stan." In Horn, *The World Encyclopedia of Comics*, 472–73.

Brancatelli, Joe. "Romita, John." In Horn, *The World Encyclopedia of Comics*, 640.

Brancatelli, Joe. "Schwartz, Julius." In Horn, *The World Encyclopedia of Comics*, 683.

"Children's Book Reviews." Review of *Usagi Yojimbo: Yokai* by Stan Sakai. *Publisher's Weekly*
     256, no. 49 (2009): 41.

Comics Magazine Association of America. "Code of the Comics Magazine Association of America."
     October 26, 1954. http://historymatters.gmu.edu/d/6543 (accessed April 22, 2010).

Contemporary Authors Online, s.vv. "Alex Ross," "Garth Ennis," "Grant Morrison," "Warren
     Ellis," http://galenet.galegroup.com/servlet/BioRC (accessed April 26, 2010).

Cronin, Brian. "Comic Book Legends Revealed #223," September 2, 2009, http://goodcomics
     .comicbookresources.com/2009/09/03/comic-book-legends-revealed-223 (accessed
     April 1, 2010).

Dean, Michael. "The Image Story: Part 3." *Comics Journal* 224 (October 25, 2000). http://
     archives.tcj.com/3_online/n_image3.html (cited April 23, 2010).

Dean, Michael. "Marvel Drops Comics Code, Changes Book Distributor." *Comics Journal* 234
     (June 8, 2001). http://archives.tcj.com/234/n_marvel.html (accessed April 23, 2010).

Dean, Michael. "Will DC Buy Diamond?" *Comics Journal* 242 (April 8, 2002). http://
     archives.tcj.com/242/n_diamond.html (accessed April 23, 2010).

Eury, Michael. "Superman." In Misoroglu, *The Superhero Book*, 538–43.

Fingeroth, Danny. *The Rough Guide to Graphic Novels*. London: Rough Guide, 2008.

Goulart, Ron. *Comic Book Encyclopedia: The Ultimate Guide to Characters, Graphic Novels,
     Writers, and Artists in the Comic Book Universe*. New York: HarperEntertainment,
     2004. See particularly the entries on Carl Barks, Brian Bendis, Cerebus, Todd McFarlane,
     Frank Miller, and George Perez.

Horn, Maurice. "Eisner, Will." In Horn, *The World Encyclopedia of Comics*, 277–78.

Horn, Maurice. "Lee, Jim." In Horn, *The World Encyclopedia of Comics*, 471–72.

Horn, Maurice, ed. *The World Encyclopedia of Comics*. Philadelphia: Chelsea House,
     1999.Hyde, David. "DC Entertainment Names Executive Team," February 18, 2010.
     http://dcu.blog.dccomics.com/2010/02/18/for-immediate-release-dc-entertainment-
     names-executive-team (accessed April 1, 2010).

Ibaraki, Masahiko. "The Reminiscence of My 25 Years with Shonen Jump." Comipress.com,
     March 31, 2008, http://comipress.com/article/2008/03/31/3452 (accessed April 26, 2010).

ICv2.com. "Naruto's Back on Top: In Bookstores in February." March 4, 2010, http://www.icv2
     .com/articles/news/16976.html (accessed April 26, 2010).

ICv2.com. "Top 25 Manga Properties—2009." *ICv2 Insider's Guide* #70, March 17, 2010. http://
     www.icv2.com/articles/news/17082.html (cited October 26, 2010).

ICv2.com. "Top 25 Manga Properties Q1 2009: 'Naruto' Still Tops." *ICv2 Insider's Guide* #65,
     June 10, 2009. http://www.icv2.com/articles/news/15120.html (cited April 26, 2010).

ICv2.com. "Top 25 Manga Properties Q2 2009: Naruto Dominates Manga." *ICv2 Insider's Guide*
     #67, July 30, 2009. http://www.icv2.com/articles/news/15497.html (cited April 26, 2010).

ICv2.com. "Top 25 Manga Properties—Q3 2009." *ICv2 Insider's Guide* #69, November 6, 2009.
     http://www.icv2.com/articles/news/16212.html (cited April 26, 2010).

ICv2.com. "Top 300 Graphic Novels Actual—February 2010." March 11, 2010. http://www.icv
    2.com/articles/news/17021.html (cited April 26, 2010).

Irving, Christopher. "Joe Quesada: Marvel's Editor-in-Chief without Fear." GraphicNYC,
    November 2, 2009. http://graphicnyc.blogspot.com/2009/11/joe-quesada-marvels-editor
    -in-chief.html (accessed April 19, 2010).

Kato, Hisao. "Tezuka, Osamu." In Horn, *The World Encyclopedia of Comics*, 754–55.

Lillian, Guy H., III. "Mort Weisinger: The Man Who Wouldn't Be Superman." *Amazing World of
    DC Comics* #7 (July 1975): 2–8.

Mangels, Andy. "Authority." In Misoroglu, *The Superhero Book*, 43–45.

Mangels, Andy. "Vertigo Heroes." In Misoroglu, *The Superhero Book*, 613–15.

Mangels, Andy. "Wildstorm Heroes." In Misoroglu, *The Superhero Book*, 623–24.

Martin, Michael A. "Avengers." In Misoroglu, *The Superhero Book*, 45–48.

Misoroglu, Gina, ed., with David A. Roach. *The Superhero Book: The Ultimate Encyclopedia of
    Comic-Book Icons and Hollywood Heroes*. Detroit, MI: Visible Ink, 2004.

Offenberger, Rik. "Michael Silberkleit: Archie Andrews' Best Pal," Comics Bulletin, http://
    www.comicsbulletin.com/features/107048948896830.htm (accessed April 26, 2010).

Plowright, Frank. "X-Men." In Misoroglu, *The Superhero Book*, 641–45.

Rhoades, Shirrel. *A Complete History of American Comic Books*. New York: Peter Lang, 2008.

Roach, David A. "Hellboy." In Misoroglu, *The Superhero Book*, 254–56.

Simba Information. *Overview of the U.S. Comic Book and Graphic Novel Market 2008–2009.*
    Stamford, CT: Simba Information, 2009. http://www.academic.marketresearch.com
    (accessed April 27, 2010).

Smith, Beau. "Five Manly Questions with . . . Mark Waid." Comics Bulletin, http://www
    .comicsbulletin.com/busted/110478858298504.htm (accessed March 17, 2010).

Smith, Wesley. "Comics 101: What Is Decompression?" Examiner.com, August 27, 2009. http://
    www.examiner.com/x-19312-Columbus-Comic-Books-Examiner~y2009m8d27-Comics
    -101-What-is-decompression-Part-2-of-4 (accessed April 19, 2010).

Thompson, Jason, with art by Atsumisa Okura. "How Manga Conquered America: A Graphic
    Guide to Japan's Coolest Export." *Wired* 15, no. 11 (2007): 223–33. http://www
    .wired.com/images/pdf/Wired_1511_mangaamerica.pdf (cited April 26, 2010).

Vaughan, Owen. "Spider-Man Is Part of the Family: Marvel Artist John Romita Jr Opens His
    Heart." *Times Online*, October 30, 2009. http://entertainment.timesonline.co.uk/tol/arts
    _and_entertainment/film/article6893252.ece (accessed April 20, 2010).

Viz.com. "The Manga Entertainment Experience." http://shonenjump.viz.com/mediakit/images/
    SJ_MEDIAKIT_Web.pdf (accessed April 26, 2010).

4

Genres

"Comics are words and pictures," said Harvey Pekar, underground-comics creator and subject of the 2003 movie *American Splendor*. "You can do anything with words and pictures" (Walrus Comics 2008). To the general public and casual readers, this statement may seem optimistic at best. Superheroes have become the mainstream genre in the comics medium, so much so that superheroes and comic books are often conflated into a genre. But other genres flourished during comics' history, and most of them are still published today—if one knows where to look.

Although superheroes are by far the most popular comics genre, librarians can serve a variety of readers by delving into the medium's other genres. Just as it would seem foolhardy to stock the fiction section of a library's stacks with only literary or fantasy fiction, a popular graphic-novel collection needs more than just superheroes. Spicing the collection with other genres can lead to more opportunities to connect with different readers, and using circulation statistics can reveal in which genres the library should invest to grow the collection. Guides to graphic novels by genre include *500 Essential Graphic Novels: The Ultimate Guide* by Gene Kannenberg, Jr. and *Graphic Novels: A Genre Guide to Comic Books, Manga, and More* by Michael Pawuk;[1] more can be found in Appendix C.

SUPERHEROES

Except for the period from the end of World War II to about 1960, superheroes have almost continually dominated comics. The first superhero was Superman, who appeared in DC's *Action Comics* #1; his success spawned dozens of imitators, some of them produced by DC itself. Fawcett's Captain Marvel, a boy who became a superhero by saying a magic word, actually outsold Superman on the newsstands for a while in the 1940s, although DC sued Fawcett for infringement (Rhoades 2008, 30), and the resulting settlement caused Fawcett to cease publishing the hero's adventures in 1954.

Many stories from that era are considered crude, mostly interesting for their histori-cal value, although some efforts, like Will Eisner's *The Spirit*, were well ahead of their times. The art is less dynamic than modern examples, and the stories often lack well-rounded characters. In the Silver Age, the stories began to take on added complexity, and the heroes went from being pure idols of respectability to showing flaws, although the characters were still somewhat broadly drawn and the plots occasionally silly (at times, endearingly so). The idea of superhero universes, with the heroes of a given com-pany existing in the same world and meeting for adventures, gained popularity at about that time, as did the concept of continuity (see Chapter 2, under "Continuity"). These long-running narratives, which rewarded and in some cases required long-term followers, strangled other types of stories as the genre grew.

In the 80s, writers and artists such as Alan Moore and Frank Miller added a more complex and occasionally violent edge that took the genre away from its youth-oriented roots. In the 90s, the genre suffered through a glut of violent antiheroes, exac-erbated by a boom in the industry at the beginning of the decade; a bust later in the 90s curbed some of the excesses. Crossovers became more and more sensationalized, with increasingly dire situations: Superman's death, Batman's broken back, Spider-Man's replacement with a clone. These "event" storylines were out of favor at the beginning of the twenty-first century, although they made a strong comeback by the end of its first decade.

Picking out the most prominent superhero titles across the genre's history is, for the most part, a futile task. The genre is simultaneously wide and homogenized; there are dozens of titles, all offering slightly different flavors of the superhero experience. It is difficult to select "the best," as any list of "top superhero runs" quickly reveals personal tastes. Two DC books—*Watchmen*, Alan Moore and Dave Gibbons's brilliant decon-struction of the genre, and *The Dark Knight Returns*, Frank Miller's tale of an old Batman in a grim future—are among the high points of superhero stories, but there are more than a half-century of others to choose from. Older stories, like Silver Age comics, may seem simplistic by today's standards, but they are a foundation of the genre, and they laid the groundwork for superhero continuity, especially at Marvel. Event comics, such as the aforementioned *Death of Superman* and *Batman: Knightfall*, and more recent crossovers, like Marvel's *Secret Invasion* and *Civil War*, also attract a great deal of attention. Finally, well-received runs by star creators, like John Byrne's *Fantastic Four* or George Perez's *Wonder Woman*, are also popular.

MANGA

Japanese comics—called manga—have avoided the homogenization of genres that occurred in American comics. Although manga is not a genre per se, manga titles (and their Korean cousins, manhwa[2]) are often lumped together in the same way super-hero titles are. However, manga is an entire market in Japan, appealing to a wide cross-section of society with content that spans across all age levels and nearly all entertain-ment genres: in addition to the genres American comics have, it also features stories about sports, historical drama, business, and other topics (Gravett 2004). Although manga has its roots in pre–World War II culture (with perhaps some influence from American comics), it emerged as a publishing force during the American occupation after World War II.

Manga has several stylistic differences from its American counterpart, including:

1. It is meant to be read from right to left on the page, from the back of the book (from the Western perspective) to the front. American publishers may reverse (or "flop") the pages to make it easier for American audiences to read.
2. In Japan, manga is typically serialized in black-and-white magazines; each magazine can have several different serials going on at once.
3. The individual stories are collected and published in paperback form. In the United States, manga is released in digest-sized books.
4. Some series can run for thousands of pages in one continuous, epic story (Thompson 2007).

The variety of genres has helped make manga popular in the United States, particularly among young people. Mass-marketed manga entered the American marketplace in the 1980s, including *Lone Wolf and Cub*, republished by First Comics; *Appleseed*, republished by Eclipse; and *Akira*, published by Marvel under its Epic imprint. Still, manga remained a very small part of the comics market. In the early 90s, anime—Japanese animation—became more available to U.S. audiences on video, and later in the decade, anime such as *Dragon Ball Z* and *Pokémon* became popular on U.S. television. This popularity fueled interest in the original manga versions, spinoffs of the characters' adventures, and manga in general. Taking advantage of the Internet, fan pages that scanned and translated manga also appeared in the 90s (Thompson 2007).

In the twenty-first century, manga's growth in North America has been huge, fueled by a wide variety of offerings, a large back catalog of content, and a cheaper price per page of story than American comics. Prominent publishers include Viz, Tokyopop, and Dark Horse (see Chapter 3, under "Publishers"). Among the scores of prominent manga titles are *Naruto*, an action story starring a young ninja; *Inu Yasha*, a romance/adventure story about a half-demon from feudal Japan and a modern schoolgirl; and *Chibi Vampire*, in which a teenage vampire girl must inject blood into others rather than drink it.

For reference books about manga, please see Appendix C, under "Manga and Anime."

ROMANCE

The late 1940s and early 1950s were the heyday of romance comics, but today, the genre is all but moribund in American comics. The first romance comic, *Young Romance*, was written by Joe Simon and drawn by Jack Kirby—the cocreators of Captain America—in 1947 (Rhoades 2008, 52). The stories were designed to appeal to an older audience and took their inspiration from pulp magazines of the day. However, romance comics went into decline after the return of superheroes, and the titles that were once popular died away by the 1970s. Today, few American comics are devoted specifically to romantic relationships, and when the old titles from the 40s and 50s are republished, they are often looked upon as a source of humor. Terry Moore's *Strangers in Paradise*, which finished in 2007, is possibly the best-known modern romance comic, although the romance is strongly mixed with elements of crime comics. Dark Horse, in cooperation with the romance novel publisher Harlequin, has published a line of comics adapted from Harlequin titles and drawn in a manga style.

It is in manga that the romance genre has its strongest showing. Examples of the many manga romance series include *Fruits Basket*, in which a family is cursed to turn into animals of the Chinese zodiac when hugged by members of the opposite sex; *Love Hina*, which follows a young man trying to get accepted to Tokyo University and find a girl to whom he made a childhood promise; and *Skip Beat!*, the story of a girl who helps a young singer rise to the top and then vows to become a bigger star when he casts her aside.

WESTERNS

Westerns began their ascent at the same time as romance comics, but their decline began before the rise of superhero comics. It was a popular genre in the early 50s, with stories of historical, movie, and fictional cowboys all being featured. The genre declined in the mid-50s, just as the Silver Age began. DC and Marvel kept their original Western heroes around until the 70s. Charlton was a prominent publisher of Westerns before the company suspended publication in 1984. Today, most of the Western titles published are either revivals of Marvel's and DC's Western characters or "weird Western" comics—Western stories combined with supernatural elements, such as *High Moon* from DC's Zuda imprint, or some versions of DC's *Jonah Hex*. The Western genre is not a popular one in manga, although one famous manga series, *Trigun*, weds Westerns with science fiction by following Vash the Stampede, a nearly indestructible alien gunslinger.

HORROR

Like crime and romance comics, horror comic creators in the 1950s were trying to capture adult readers, especially former soldiers who had read comics during the war. To this end, publishers such as EC made their art and stories vivid and memorable, not skimping on the gore when the story called for it. This sparked a backlash: comics, especially horror and crime comics, were charged in the popular press with undermining the morals of youth. Congressional hearings and the Comics Code Authority (CCA), which the comics companies instituted to avoid federal legislation, followed. The code was so draconian that it proscribed the use of "Horror" and "Terror" in comics titles and the use of classic monsters such as vampires and werewolves. Entertaining Comics (EC) cancelled all its comics except for *Mad*, which they converted into a magazine outside of the CCA's reach (Rhoades 2008, 64).

Even after the institution of the code, monster comics were popular. The monsters—often massive creatures with a vaguely science-based origin, such as "alien races" or "radioactivity"—managed to skirt the edges of the code, and the subgenre lasted into the era of superheroes. In fact, those monsters occasionally served as the punching bags for early Silver Age heroes. These non-supernatural monsters occasionally popped up in later comics but rarely had titles of their own.

Horror comics made a slight comeback when the Comics Code was revised in 1971; classic monsters were once more in play, and references to or adaptations of literary horror, such as Edgar Allen Poe's tales, could be used. Marvel published comics such as *Tomb of Dracula* and black and white magazines (which were, as magazines instead of comics, outside of the control of the CCA) such as *Tales of the Zombie*. A few years before the revision, DC had revamped *House of Secrets* and *House of Mystery* to contain more of the frightening content the titles had included before the Code, and after the revision, they issued new horror titles such as *Secrets of Sinister House*. Unfortunately for horror fans, the genre fell out of favor in the 80s and 90s.

The twenty-first century has brought a resurgence of horror comics, with zombies leading the shambling charge. Robert Kirkman, Tony Moore, and Charlie Adlard's *The Walking Dead*, published by Image, is probably the most popular horror title, dealing with a world after the zombie apocalypse. *30 Days of Night* and its spinoffs by Steve Niles at IDW deal with vampires. Marvel's horror offerings are usually crossed with superheroes; its most popular horror stories, the series of *Marvel Zombies* miniseries, features a world filled with superheroes who have been turned into zombies. Additionally, Marvel heroes such as Ghost Rider and Blade have always been close to the horror genre. Many of DC's Vertigo titles, such as *Hellblazer*, which features an occult detective, have horror elements to them; DC also revived *House of Mystery* under its Vertigo imprint. Manga has an impressive array of horror titles, such as *Death Note*, in which a student finds a notebook that can kill people whose names are written in it, and *Uzumaki*, which is set in a cursed, fog-bound town haunted by a spiral pattern.

CRIME

Crime comics began in 1942 with *Crime Does Not Pay*, which was published by Lev Gleason Productions. The genre flourished, especially in the years after World War II, but crime stories were knocked out by the one-two punch of the CCA and the rise of superheroes. The Code limited violence and specified that criminals could be neither sympathetic nor victorious, and the watered-down leftovers of the genre were rolled over by superheroes. However, crime comics fared better than most other genres, as the superhero genre dealt with many similar themes and incorporated some of the genre's trappings—the most notable example being Batman, the "World's Greatest Detective," who stars in *Detective Comics*.

Like many other genres, crime comics have made a resurgence in the twenty-first century. DC and Marvel generally release crime comics through their various imprints. DC, for example, published editions of Max Allan Collins's 1930s gangster story *Road to Perdition* through its Paradox Press label,[3] Brian Azzarello and Eduardo Risso's *100 Bullets* through Vertigo, and Ed Brubaker and Sean Phillips's *Sleeper* through Wildstorm. As part of its DC Universe offerings, DC also published Brubaker, Greg Rucka, and Michael Lark's *Gotham Central*, which follows the police in Batman's home city as they deal with heroes and psychotic villains. Marvel publishes crime comics through its Icon imprint—although not by design, since it is an outlet for creators who work exclusively for Marvel and want to make creator-owned comics. Brubaker's *Criminal* and *Incognito* bear the Icon imprint, as does Brian Michael Bendis and Michael Avon Oeming's *Powers*, which follows a pair of cops who investigate superhero crimes. Bendis also restored Marvel's *Daredevil* to a noir-influenced narrative, and Brubaker continued this idea when succeeding him as writer for the title.

For Image Comics, Bendis also created *Jinx*, the story of a bounty hunter, and *Torso*, in which he and Marc Andreyko retold Elliot Ness's attempts to find the Torso serial killer in Cleveland in the 30s.[4] Frank Miller has written and drawn the violent, noir *Sin City* miniseries for Dark Horse since 1990. David Lapham has produced the award-winning crime comic *Stray Bullets* through his own company, El Capitan, since

1995. At Oni Press, Rucka has written *Whiteout*, which follows a U.S. marshal investigating murders in Antarctica; its sequel, *Whiteout: Melt*; and *Stumptown*, a story about a Portland, Oregon, private investigator.

Crime crosses over with other genres in manga. Some of the most prominent crime manga are *Lone Wolf and Cub*, an influential manga about a Shogunate assassin and his young son; *Case Closed*, in which a young detective transformed into a 7-year-old investigates crime; *Cowboy Bebop* (see "Science Fiction"); and *Ghost in the Shell*, which follows a cyborg police officer in a cyberpunk future.

SCIENCE FICTION

Science-fiction comics are nearly as old as superhero comics—just as old, to those who consider superheroes stories a branch of science fiction. Certainly the two genres are intertwined; mad scientists, space travel, and time travel are staples of superhero stories, while advanced or powerful humanoids are part of the science fiction landscape, and both were influenced by pulp stories. In the 30s and 40s, the adventures of heroes like Flash Gordon were staples of comic book racks, and in Britain, outerspace hero Dan Dare debuted in 1950. Although many science fiction titles were canceled in the wake of the comics scare in the mid-50s, the genre was not specifically targeted by the attack—indeed, the subgenre of monster comics (see "Horror," above) gained in popularity. After the advent of superheroes, science fiction comics' popularity was not unduly harmed, although they never seriously challenged superheroes' popularity in the United States. The best they could do was to merge with the superhero genre; an example of this is DC's *Legion of Super-Heroes*, which began in 1958 and featured teenage superheroes protecting the thirtieth century throughout the galaxy.

There have been several well-known science fiction titles in the intervening years. The British anthology series *2000 A.D.*, which features the character Judge Dredd, is probably the most prominent English-language science-fiction title, having been published continuously since 1977. Alan Moore set his 1980s story *V for Vendetta* in a dystopian future United Kingdom, with an anonymous rebel fighting the totalitarian government. From 1992 to 1997, Marvel published the 2099 line of comics, which featured superheroes in a bleak, corporate-controlled future. More recently, DC published *Y: The Last Man* through its Vertigo imprint. *Y*, which ran from 2002 to 2008 and was produced by Brian K. Vaughn and Pia Guerra, followed the only survivors (a man and his monkey) of a mysterious plague that killed all mammals with a Y chromosome. Paul Pope's *100 Percent*, which has romantic elements, is set in a 2038 Manhattan after the United States and United Nations have merged. Matt Fraction's *Casanova* (published by Image and Marvel's Icon imprint) tells the adventures of a superspy who is drawn into an alternate universe and has weird science plots continually thrown at him. Warren Ellis's work is known for its science-fiction themes, which he weaves into his superhero work as well. His straight science-fiction titles include *Transmetropolitan* (published by Vertigo), *Anna Mercury* (Avatar), and *Global Frequency* (DC's Wildstorm imprint).

Science fiction is a popular genre in manga. Among the many science-fiction manga are *Maximum Ride*, an original English-language adaptation of James Patterson's young adult novels about human-avian hybrids; *Cowboy Bebop*, which features bounty hunters chasing criminals throughout the solar system; *Ghost in the Shell* (see "Crime"); and

Neon Genesis Evangelion, several series about teenagers piloting giant robots to fight against apocalyptic monsters.

Comics featuring characters and settings from science-fiction television shows and movies, such as *X-Files* and *Star Wars*, are discussed in the "Licensed Comics" section.

FANTASY

Fantasy comics—at least in the genre's sword-and-sorcery or epic forms—have rarely made much of an impact upon the American comics landscape, except in the 1970s. The medium lacks a prominent example of this genre in the Golden Age; DC introduced sorcerer Dr. Fate in *More Fun Comics* #55, but he acted more like a traditional superhero than a fantasy hero, battling mobsters, thugs, and a few supernatural threats. In the Silver Age, Stan Lee and Steve Ditko created sorcerer supreme Dr. Strange for Marvel, although his adventures also had the strong flavor of the superhero, with not much to separate his adversaries from the supervillains featured in other Marvel comics.

In 1970, Marvel acquired the rights to publish a comic based on fantasy hero Conan the Barbarian; the title and its spinoffs lasted at Marvel until the mid-90s. Now Dark Horse publishes both new Conan books and reprints Marvel's *Conan* comics. The success of Conan inspired other sword-and-sorcery and fantasy titles, a hallmark of the Bronze Age. DC published Mike Grell's *Warlord* from 1976 to 1989; *Warlord* followed an Air Force pilot who fell into a magical kingdom beneath the earth. Richard and Wendy Pini's *Elfquest*, published by WaRP Graphics until 2003 and now published by DC, began telling the stories of the Wolfrider elves in 1978. However, most other fantasy series were short-lived.

Most popular fantasy comics have dispensed with the overt sword-and-sorcery trappings, incorporating elements of folklore and magic into a modern setting. DC's *Fables* and its spinoffs, published by Vertigo and created by Bill Willingham, take characters from fairytales and integrate them into the modern world, where they battle against fairytale adversaries. Dark Horse publishes Mike Mignola's *Hellboy* and its spinoffs, which show Hellboy, a good-hearted demon, and his colleagues fighting against evil monsters from folklore around the world; the series has many horror elements as well. DC's *Books of Magic* recount the adventures of Timothy Hunter, a boy magician in the modern world. Through its Vertigo imprint, DC also publishes *Hellblazer*, the adventures of foul-mouthed occult investigator and magician John Constantine, and collections of the extremely popular *Sandman*. The latter series, written by Neil Gaiman in the 90s, features Morpheus, the Lord of Dreams, who escapes into the modern world after being held prisoner for 70 years and sets about reconstructing his domain. Dark Horse publishes Stan Sakai's *Usagi Yojimbo*, which combines Japanese myths and history in a seventeenth-century Japan populated by anthropomorphized animals.

Epic and sword-and-sorcery fantasy stories, other than *Conan*, are harder to find in recent comics, but some examples exist. Jeff Smith's *Bone*, published from 1991 to 2004, is a beautifully drawn epic, with the hidden heir to a throne and a former queen fighting the Lord of Locusts and his twisted legions. The publisher CrossGen, which operated from 1998 to 2004, featured several titles that were influenced by fantasy, including *Mystic, Scion*, and *Sojourn*. The bankrupt company's titles may be reprinted through a partnership between Disney, who bought the rights to the CrossGen's properties, and Marvel Comics, which Disney also owns.

Fantasy manga titles include *Fullmetal Alchemist*, the story of two brothers crippled by forbidden alchemy searching for the Philosopher's Stone; *Bleach*, which shows a teenager who accidentally gains the power to defend humans from evil spirits; *Vampire Knight*, in which vampires and humans try to coexist in a special school; *Yu-Gi-Oh!* several series of manga that uses a fantasy-based holographic card game as a background; *Naruto* (see "Manga"); and *Berserk*, a tale of medieval mercenaries.

NONFICTION

Nonfiction comics cover the same spectrum as nonfiction books, although autobiographical titles are probably the most prominent branch of this comics genre. With the rise of underground comics in the late 60s and 70s, more creators could use their comics to tell true stories. One of the most famous graphic novels of all time, Art Spiegelman's *Maus*, recounts the author's relationship with his father and his father's experiences as a Jew in World War II Eastern Europe. However, although occasionally some other nonfiction titles gain prominence, this is not as popular a genre among comic book fans.

Still, many well-regarded titles represent this genre. Harvey Pekar's *American Splendor*, which began in 1976 and ended in 2008, tells about Pekar's everyday life in Cleveland, where he worked as a clerk in a Veteran's Health Administration hospital. Marjane Satrapi's *Persepolis* tells of Satrapi's life growing up in Iran during and after the Islamic Revolution. Other nonbiographical, nonfiction graphic novels include Will Eisner's *The Plot: The Secret Story of The Protocols of the Elders of Zion*, which recounts the history of that anti-Semitic hoax; *Safe Area Goražde*, Joe Sacco's story of his four months in Bosnia during 1994–1995; and *The 9/11 Report: A Graphic Adaptation*, in which Sid Jacobson and Ernie Colon give an abridged, graphic version of the 9/11 Commission's final report on the September 11 attacks.

ALTERNATIVE

The term "alternative" describes a category that is wider than a genre: it is a miscellaneous grouping of comics whose topics roughly correspond to the mainstream genre in novel fiction.[5] These comics came out of the underground- and independent-comics movements of the 60s, 70s, and 80s; their comics generally sell in small numbers, although their critical reception can be much better. The number of alternative comics are legion. Prominent alternative comics include *Love and Rockets*, a series of related series about primarily Latino characters, produced by brothers Gilbert, Jaime, and Mario Hernandez and published by Fantagraphics; *Scott Pilgrim*, a humorous book about a young Canadian slacker, written and drawn by Bryan Lee O'Malley; David Clowes's *Ghost World*, which follows a pair of girls who have just graduated from high school; and *Weirdo*, an anthology created by underground-comics pioneer Robert Crumb. Will Eisner's *A Contract with God*, which tells the stories of families in a Bronx tenement in the 1930s, can also be classed as alternative. In the medium and in mainstream conversations, the term "alternative comics" can also be used as a term for comics from small publishers rather than denoting any real genre; in this use, titles that might fall into a specific genre—Jeff Smith's *Bone*, for instance—might be termed "alternative," and Eisner's *Contract* might be excluded because it was published by a major book publisher.

WAR

War comics were another genre that gained popularity after World War II, but they managed to fight off the encroaching superheroes longer than other genres. Charlton was the most prolific publisher of war comics, but the genre as a whole sold to an audience who had grown up hearing about war. America's wars in Korea and Vietnam kept the stories vital and evergreen. Titles such as DC's *Sgt. Rock*, drawn by Joe Kubert, and Marvel's *Sgt. Fury and His Howling Commandos* lasted until the 80s, despite growing distaste for the Vietnam War. As a final gasp for the genre, Marvel published *The 'Nam*, based on writer Doug Murray's experiences in the Vietnam War, from 1986 to 1993. Today, the war genre is almost nonexistent in comics except for occasional titles by writer Garth Ennis. Among his war miniseries are *Adventures in the Rifle Brigade* (DC), *Battlefields* (Dynamite!), *War Is Hell: The First Flight of the Phantom Eagle* (Marvel's Max imprint), and *War Story* (DC's Vertigo imprint).

LICENSED COMICS

Although most comic books licensed from an already-established intellectual property will fall within the above genres, they are often treated as their own type. Readers are more likely to lump an *X-Files* comic book with *CSI* or *Indiana Jones* comics than with science-fiction titles. These comics resemble each other by trying to replicate TV or movie actors' likenesses into comic art, which they do with varying success. Also, these series often have a reputation for being creatively lacking; because the TV series or movie they are licensed from does not want anything important to happen in a medium with a fraction of the viewership (and profitability), licensed comics stories often have little dramatic impact.

However, some licensed titles have escaped this reputation; unsurprisingly, the two most prominent examples are from Dark Horse, which has a strong history of publishing licensed comics. The latest *Buffy the Vampire Slayer* series (called "Season 8," taking up where the TV show left off after it was canceled following its seventh season) is produced by series creator Joss Whedon, and the series has sold very well. Dark Horse's many *Star Wars* series have long survived (and occasionally thrived) by publishing stories on the fringes of movies' universe: before, after, and on the edges of the *Star Wars* movies. Dark Horse also reprints Marvel's original *Star Wars* comics—published from 1977 to 1986, and chronicling the characters in the original movies—in large, black-and-white collections.

CHILDREN'S COMICS

Children's comics also can cross over with other genres, but the main hybridization occurs with superheroes and licensed titles. Comics have been aimed at children since the beginning of the genre, and much of its output—save for the comics that caused the uproar in the 50s and some more modern titles—is suitable for children.[6] In more recent years, the comic book market has changed, diversifying slightly and aiming major comics at an older audience. For this reason, both DC and Marvel have lines of comics specifically aimed at audiences of all ages. Marvel's "Marvel Adventures" comics essentially recasts their heroes into kid-friendlier stories, while DC's "Johnny DC" line has superhero stories as well as titles based on various Warner Bros. properties, such as *Scooby-Doo* and *Looney Tunes*.

Jeff Smith's *Bone*, also mentioned in the fantasy section, is an excellent title for older children. Archie Comics' line is a mainstay of humor aimed at children; various Disney comics, most prominently *Uncle Scrooge*, have also been around for decades, with the Disney license being held by many companies: Western (under its Dell, Gold Key, and Whitman labels), Gladstone, Disney itself, Gemstone, and the current publisher, Boom Studios. Other acclaimed children's comics include *Owly*, Andy Runton's series aimed at very young audiences that features the eponymous owl (Top Shelf); *Amelia Rules!*, written by Jimmy Gownley , which follows a fourth-grader who deals with her parents' divorce and moving from New York (Simon and Schuster); and *Castle Waiting*, Linda Medley's recasting of folk tales and mythology with a slightly modern sensibility.

The closest analog to children's comics in Japan is kodomo (or "kodomomuke"), which is manga aimed at children. Its purpose is frequently to teach children how to behave or to educate them. Examples include *Yotsuba&!*, the misadventures of a five-year-old girl who is ignorant of the world around her; *Doraemon*, which focuses on the eponymous robot cat who travels back in time from the twenty-second century; and *Big Adventures of Majoko*, in which a young girl meets a young witch from another world and goes on adventures. Recently, two manga publishers started children's imprints (Udon Kids, http://www.mangaforkids.com, and VizKids, http://www.vizkids.com) with material suitable for younger audiences.

Two other types of manga are aimed at younger readers: shōjo (girls' manga, such as *Fruits Basket*, *Vampire Knight*, and *Sailor Moon*) and shōnen (boys' manga, such as *Naruto*, *Fullmetal Alchemist*, and *Bleach*). Both are aimed at preteens and adolescents and are roughly analogous to the American young-adult market. Shōnen is the most popular type of manga in Japan and is disproportionately represented in Western reprints and exported anime; it tends to emphasize adventure, comedy, and teamwork (Gravett 2004, 55–56). Shōjo focuses more on emotions, relationships, and expressing individuality (77–80).

For resources on children's comics, both American and manga, see Chapter 9, under "Age-Appropriate Material."

CONCLUSION

Libraries' comic book collections should feature some titles in each of the genres presented in this chapter. By tracking circulation reports (see Chapter 5, "Monitoring and Maintaining the Collection"), libraries can grow the collection according to readers' demonstrated interests. By having at least the most popular and most significant titles in each genre, libraries can ensure the comic book collection is a well-rounded reflection of the medium.

NOTES

1. Kanneberg's book gives a "top 10" for each genre and then lists several other titles as "best of the rest." Pawuk does not rank the titles, but he lists more titles and also breaks down genres into subgenres; for instance, the "Fantasy" chapter has entries on sword and sorcery, fairy tales and folklore, mythology, parallel worlds, contemporary fantasy, and dark fantasy. Since genre divisions are somewhat arbitrary, there are slight disagreements between both authors and this book about genre names and classifications.

2. Manhwa is heavily influenced by Japanese manga and is in many ways similar to it. There are two major differences: manhwa is read left to right, just as Western comics are, and manhwa tends to have less exaggeration and more realistic backgrounds than manga (Fingeroth 2008, 247).

3. The original graphic novel was published by Pocket Books. Paradox Press has been the first publisher of the book's sequels.

4. The first seven issues of *Jinx* were published by Caliber Press.

5. What is alternative in comics is mainstream in novels; what is mainstream in comics is marginal in novel fiction.

6. Modern comics run the gamut of age level, however. Although the CCA is weakened, some publishers have ratings on their covers or on their Web sites. See Chapter 5, under "Determining Age-Appropriateness and Creating Selection Guidelines," for details.

REFERENCES

Fingeroth, Danny. *The Rough Guide to Graphic Novels*. London: Rough Guide, 2008.

Gravett, Paul. *Manga: Sixty Years of Japanese Comics*. London: Lawrence King, 2004.

Kannenberg, Gene, Jr. *500 Essential Graphic Novels: The Ultimate Guide*. New York: Collins Design, 2008.

Pawuk, Michael. *Graphic Novels: A Genre Guide to Comic Books, Manga, and More*. Westport, CT: Libraries Unlimited, 2007.

Rhoades, Shirrel. *A Complete History of American Comic Books*. New York: Peter Lang, 2008.

Thompson, Jason, with art by Atsumisa Okura. "How Manga Conquered America: A Graphic Guide to Japan's Coolest Export." *Wired* 15, no. 11 (2007): 223–33. http://www.wired.com/images/pdf/Wired_1511_mangaamerica.pdf (accessed April 26, 2010).

Walrus Comics. "Harvey Pekar—Living Legend." 2008. http://www.walruscomix.com/pekarinterview.html (accessed April 26, 2010).

5

Creating and Maintaining a Core Comic Book Collection

As discussed in Chapter 1, libraries have been collecting literary graphic novels for some time, but mainstream comic books—even those collected into book form—have received short shrift. Yet mainstream comic book characters saturate popular culture, spurring interest in the original books. At the academic library where the authors created a core comic book collection, 72 percent of the collection circulated in its first six months. Any library with a popular reading collection needs to include core comic titles in their collections. For academic libraries, the medium's long history and visual imagery have additional value: a wealth of primary sources for social science, media, art, design, writing, and communications research.

The core comic book collection proposed in this book is designed to meet the expectations of adult mainstream comic book readers. Grouped together, some might think the collection's colorful book covers with spandex-clad heroes, monsters, and fantastic imagery looks a little out of place, but to a comic book reader, its discovery would be an immediate identification of a familiar, welcoming environment. Unlike a comic book shop, however, the library would not have cardboard boxes of newsprint back issues. The title selection would be smaller. But the library would have a few advantages over the typical comic book shop: quickly searchable information about the collection in the library catalog, the ability to check out items, and a comfortable place to browse and read through titles without being asked to pay.

This chapter presents information about new formats for comic books, where to buy graphic novels, and suggestions for binding and processing. It looks at collection development considerations, including issues related to age appropriateness, and proposes an initial title list and an outline of needed policies for the collection. The chapter offers several ideas for funding an initial effort, and concludes with information about how to evaluate and maintain the collection.

FORMATS FOR LIBRARY COLLECTIONS

Gone are the days when comics were available only in fragile newsprint. Compilations of individual comic book issues are published frequently and are available on Amazon.com in trade paperback or hardcover bindings. Most library purchases will be in these formats. Some publishers, such as Marvel and DC, offer hardcover and trade paperback versions of the same collected titles; the hardback versions are more expensive but are more durable and are released earlier, while libraries buying the paperback version may have to wait months or even a year for the cheaper version. Despite nearly a decade of serious collected edition programs, neither Marvel nor DC has a fraction of their company's output available in graphic-novel form, although most comic books released in the last five to eight years have been collected in some format.[1] Marvel and DC also publish large amounts of their back catalog in black-and-white series (Marvel Essentials and DC Showcases). DVD-ROMs are available for some comic books, including some that provide decades of issues of titles with long histories, such as *Amazing Spider-Man*.

Like other print formats, comics are slowly expanding online. Marvel Comics offers more than 5,000 of its stories, ranging from the beginning of the Silver Age to the present day, in its "Digital Comics Unlimited" database (http://marvel.com/digital_comics/unlimited); unfortunately, the program does not allow institutional subscriptions. For libraries, Marvel offers around 300 issues of mostly all-ages titles from OverDrive Digital Library Reserve (http://www.overdrive.com/resources/ContentWireArchive.asp?CW=20100413).[2] Archie Comics offers access to "hundreds" of comics via. Archie Digital Comics (http://www.archiedigital.com) but currently has no institutional pricing (Archie Digital). H. W. Wilson offers a "Graphic Novels Core Collection," which grants an institution access to about 2,000 graphic novels in a variety of genres and age levels for $225 a year (H. W. Wilson). Several small publishers also release comics through Wowio—some free and some for a fee (http://www.wowio.com/users/categorypage.asp?cbBrowse=4).

Digital downloads of comics are increasing, especially for devices such as the iPad and iPhone. Several companies, such as ComiXology, Panelfly, Genus, Verse, and UClick, have released applications for the iPhone and iPad to view comics; Image, Dark Horse, Archie, and many smaller publishers are using this distribution model to sell some comics, and IDW claimed to sell as many copies of *Star Trek: Countdown* via download as it did physical copies (ICv2.com 2010). ComiXology has also released an app for Marvel allowing iPad/iPhone users to read Marvel comics on those devices (Ihnatko 2010). But the selection of comics that can be bought and viewed electronically is limited; also, buying comics this way leads to licensing and equipment concerns for libraries, which makes this an unappealing way to buy comics, at least until the technology matures. Libraries may also prefer some of print comics' benefits, such as attracting new users into the library's physical building.

Although a library could develop a collection entirely composed of trade paperbacks and hardbacks, binding newsprint titles is also an option and may be a way to expand the collection through gifts.

WHERE TO BUY COMIC BOOKS

Libraries have several options for buying comic books, each with their own advantages. For most libraries, the easiest way to buy graphic novels might be to use the library's usual book jobber or wholesaler. Diamond Comics Distributors lists Baker &

Taylor, Booksource, Brodart, BWI, Follett, Ingram, and Partners West as possible options for librarians, although that list is not exhaustive (Diamond Bookshelf). If the library has a relationship with one of these vendors, a discount is likely available. However, these vendors likely will not have the expertise that other, comics-focused vendors will have, and they might not be able to help libraries with out-of-print books. The latter can be important, given the rapidity with which many collected editions go out of print.

Because comics are serials, timeliness can be important, and local comic shops will have the most recent issues before other retailers. They are also excellent resources not just for expert information but for potential discounts. Compared to most of their clientele, the library would be a big customer, and most comic shops would offer volume discounts. This is an excellent option for libraries concerned with timeliness; comic shops get collected editions the day they are released and usually can handle large orders with ease. Many shops allow customers to set up criteria for new purchases or lists of desired titles that can then be picked up regularly. There are several ways to find nearby comic book shops, such as http://www.comicshoplocator.com.[3] Libraries can also buy straight from the direct-market distributor, Diamond.[4]

Some comic book stores have branched out to the online retailing world in a large way. Retailers such as Tales of Wonder (http://talesofwonder.com), Mail Order Comics (http://www.mailordercomics.com), Mile High Comics (http://milehighcomics.com), and My Comicshop.com (http://www.mycomicshop.com) allow customers to order and preorder comic book collections, usually giving the greatest discount for titles ordered the month they are solicited (that is, about three months before they are released). The amount of the discount varies widely, and shipping charges can increase the cost enough to make this option less competitive than other options. However, many of these vendors offer used copies of books for less and have copies of out-of-print titles.

Another option for out-of-print titles is eBay. However, as eBay is the largest online auction site, it is where other comic book fans go to find out-of-print collections as well, driving up the prices for the hardest-to-find titles. The selection is both diverse and unpredictable, and the condition of the books can range from excellent to awful. Although most sellers will respond quickly to concerns, watch out for sellers who are uncommunicative or evasive. eBay can also be a good place to sell gift comics that are not kept for the library collection.

For librarians, Alibris (http://www.alibris.com) is a more familiar option for out-of-print titles. Unlike eBay, which can be searched only for seller-supplied auction titles and descriptions, Alibris allows for searching by titles, creators, keywords, and ISBNs; users can also browse by book category, which can be very useful. Each title generally has several copies available, varying in price and condition. For titles that are not listed, Alibris offers its Book Fetch service (http://www.alibris.com/bookfetch), which allows users to specify a title, binding, and the price range the user is willing to pay for a book. When items that match the user's criteria become available, Alibris sends the user an e-mail.

Other online vendors are also a possibility. Amazon.com is the largest and best known of these options, and although their discounts will be greater than most other vendors, Amazon generally sells trade paperbacks two weeks to two months after comic book shops get access to them. Also, keep in mind that less expensive comics, such as digests, will have a smaller-percentage discount or no discount. Third-party sellers also sell new, used, and out-of-print books through Amazon Marketplace; the warnings that apply to eBay apply there as well. Many other online booksellers can be used to buy trade paperbacks and hardcovers as well. The Web site The Cheapest

Book (http://www.thecheapestbook.com/) can be used to quickly search across major online bookseller sites.

BINDING CONSIDERATIONS FOR COMICS

Although some graphic novels are available in hardcover editions, most comic book collections come in paperback. Libraries will have to balance the cost with the potential benefits of binding, which may reduce the chance of theft or defacement and increase durability. Paperback books can be rebound in hardcover using a digital scan of the original cover to provide an attractive hardback for about $8 to $10 per title. Obviously, binding every acquisition in this way will reduce the number of titles that can be added to the collection, and binding paperback titles that are available in hardcover can be more expensive than buying the hardcover in the first place. After tracking circulation statistics (and wear and tear on the books) for a year, libraries will have a track record of which titles tend to circulate the most and therefore deserve hardback treatment.

Newsprint comics can be bound in a traditional periodical binding for $10 to $20 per volume.[5] A cover image from one of the issues can be mounted on the bound cover to add visual interest. If the library is given a series of newsprint comics, this can be an inexpensive way to grow the collection and add original (color newsprint) material. Theft may be less likely with this kind of binding, since the comics lose their value as collectibles, and library bindings are not typically as attractive or as suitable for resale.

DETERMINING AGE APPROPRIATENESS AND CREATING SELECTION GUIDELINES

Deciding what titles to buy should be based on a library's users and mission. Public libraries, with readers of all ages, will need to pay special attention to the age appropriateness of material. Most academic libraries can focus on comic books written for adult readers, although they may well have a juvenile book collection for use by education majors and users' children. By developing selection guidelines, libraries can review different users' interests and try to divide resources fairly.

Determining age appropriateness is extremely important when developing a comic book collection. In the past, the Comics Code Authority (CCA) has been, if not a guarantor that material would be suitable for younger readers, at least a good general guide. But since most publishers opted out of the CCA—only DC and Archie submit comics to the CCA, and DC submits only its young readers and mainstream superhero titles—readers and buyers are left with differing standards.

Most superhero comics from DC and Marvel are suitable for younger readers. Marvel has a five-tier system:

- "All ages" titles are appropriate for everyone and include its young readers' titles, such as Marvel Adventures
- "A" titles, which include some Marvel Universe comics, are suitable for readers age 9 and up
- "T" comics are recommended for readers age 13 and up, although parental guidance may be recommended; this category includes the rest of the Marvel Universe comics
- "Parental advisory" Marvel suggests for readers age 15 and above (Marvel.com)
- "Max" or "Explicit Content" comics are for adults only and mainly contains the publisher's Max imprint

The rating for each collected edition is printed on the back cover, and it is on the front cover of the single-issue comics. Additionally, ratings for individual comics and collections can be found at Marvel.com. However, these ratings are assigned by Marvel and may not match local standards.

Although DC places a tiny CCA symbol on its Code-approved comics, the symbol is absent from the collected editions. DC does not have an internal rating system, although its imprints are a general guide: its Johnny DC line is suitable for all ages, DC Universe titles are for younger to teen readers, and Vertigo is suitable for more mature readers.

Of the other major publishers, only Dark Horse appears to have detailed age-related guides. In the "Libraries" section (http://libraries.darkhorse.com) of its Web site, under the "Backlist" tab, it gives links for titles appropriate for readers older than 8, 10, 12, 14, 16, and 18 as well as for titles for "all ages." The lists are not inclusive; titles are listed only in the youngest appropriate age range. Image and IDW do not appear to have consistent age recommendations, although one Image studio, Shadowline, has an all-ages imprint, Silverline Books. Manga publishers Udon and Viz have children's manga lines (Udon Kids, http://www.mangaforkids.com, and VizKids, http://www.vizkids.com).

ALA's Young Adult Library Services Association can be helpful for those looking for titles geared toward young adults. Every year, the division releases a list of graphic novels suitable for teenagers. The list is lengthy and includes fiction and nonfiction and American-style and manga titles. YALSA also has a top 10 list for librarians who want only the highlights. The archive of the division's "Great Graphic Novels for Teens" recommendations can be found at http://www.ala.org/yalsa/ggnt. For more resources on age-appropriate materials, see Chapter 9, under "Age-Appropriate Material."

Even after grappling with the issue of age appropriateness, libraries need to consider other questions related to the collection. Developing guidelines for selection will help guide the initial selection process, although these should be revised as necessary in response to use. Some questions to aid libraries in developing initial guidelines include:

- To what extent will the collection's title list be based on popularity in the bookstore or direct market?
- Will an effort be made to include some independent titles, rather than focus on DC and Marvel?
- Will an effort be made to include titles with a leading female character or character of color, even if they are not among the most popular?
- Which genres will be included in the collection? (See Chapter 4.)
- How much emphasis will be given to collecting consecutive volumes of titles?
- Do titles need to be available in a bound or DVD-ROM format to facilitate preservation?
- Will historical comics, such as those from the Golden Age (1930s–1940s) and Silver Age (1956–1970), be included, or will the focus be on recent comics?
- To what extent will the collection include manga?

See Table 5.1 for examples of criteria for a comic book collection.

Chapter 9 provides useful Web resources that can help libraries make specific title decisions once general collecting guidelines are determined. Six months to a year after an initial title list is acquired, libraries can review circulation statistics to determine which choices have been most popular with readers (see "Monitoring and Maintaining the Collection" in this chapter), and revise the selection guidelines accordingly.

Appendix A provides an example of the initial title list used at the authors' library for a mainstream comic book collection, along with a brief rationale for each title's

Table 5.1
Example Criteria for a Comic Book Collection

Criteria Type	Criteria Example
What formats will be collected	"Titles are available in a bound or DVD format to facilitate preservation."
Guidance for which characters and/or titles should be collected	"Titles are either one of the major comic titles or feature a leading female character or character of color." "The collection should include comics from the Golden Age (1930s–1940s), Silver Age (1956–1970), and modern day to facilitate time-series research."
What age levels are targeted	"Most comics titles will be appropriate for adult readers, but some high school–level titles will be included to gauge use"
Whether manga will be included	"The collection should include a few major manga titles."
About how many titles are envisioned for the collection	"The collection will initially contain about 10 percent of the number of total titles in the pleasure-reading collection."

inclusion. A list of the additional 140 new items added the following year (after circulation demonstrated the collection's use) is also included.

POLICIES FOR COMIC BOOKS

Policies related to the use of comic book collections in libraries will likely parallel those already in place in your library. Libraries should consider the following areas:

- Circulation periods
- Location of comic books
- Gift policy related to comic books
- Replacement policy for stolen, lost, or damaged comic books

Ideally, circulation periods will be the same as they are for other popular reading items. As discussed in "Determining Age Appropriateness and Creating Selection Guidelines" earlier in the chapter, some titles will be for adult audiences only, so if a library has policies related to younger readers, they will come into play for comic books as well.

The location of comic titles within the library is important for the collection's success. A surefire way to limit circulation is to shelve them by classification number (see Chapter 6, "Collection Location"). The best place for a new collection is a highly visible display where all the comic titles are located together for easy browsing. Readers will not automatically expect their local library to have comic books, so they may not try to look up titles or authors in the online catalog. Once they see the library

The JMU Comic Books Collection

is getting 140+ new titles!

Currently, these titles are located HERE, in Carrier Library's browsing area.

All can be checked out.

You will find the latest ...

- Hellboy
- Essential Wolverine
- Batman Chronicles
- Promethea
- Fables
- And much, much more!
- Strangers in Paradise
- Queen and Country
- New Avengers
- Kabuki
- Runaways

Visit http://www.lib.jmu.edu/resources/comics for more info!

Questions? Email librarian@library.jmu.edu

Figure 5.1
Example of an Informational Handout. The actual handout featured a header graphic composed of a collage of licensed images (not included here for copyright reasons).

has a sizeable collection, however, they will begin to search for them as for other titles. Be sure to have informational handouts in the comic book display area that explain how to search by title. Figure 5.1 shows an example informational handout.

Libraries that launch and market a comic book collection should not be surprised to hear from enthusiastic comic book readers who are eager to donate some or all of their collection to the local library. Be prepared with an appropriate gift policy. Considerations include:

- Who donors should contact with a title list
- Whether gift items can be bound and under what circumstances
- Whether incomplete runs or random issues will be accepted
- Whether to insert a book plate in bound items to honor the donor
- Whether the donor will receive an official letter of thanks for the library

Even though bound comic books are durable, titles contain attractive art that may tempt patrons to help themselves to a favorite page, cover, or panel. Will the comics collection fall under the library's regular repair and replacement policy? Thankfully, because of the number of fans always willing to sell comics on eBay, lost or defaced copies may be relatively easy to replace.

FUNDING FOR A COMIC BOOK COLLECTION

Although a comic book collection need not be expensive, it takes some initial effort to find room in the budget for new collections. To begin the process, prepare a proposal for decision makers regarding the library's collection budget. The decision makers may be a committee, a person, or even the library director. First, be sure to review your library's collection development policy, strategic plan, and similar documents. Think about how a comics collection supports the library's goals. While writing the proposal, use the language from these existing library documents. Consider also whether your library has any existing "niche" collections that could be used for comparison purposes. This may be especially important in academic libraries, where most titles need to support the college curriculum. However, most academic libraries have some type of popular reading collection (sometimes called a "browsing collection"), and librarians may be able to find money for comic books within this budgetary line. Comic books deserve to be at least a small proportion of popular reading titles.

Some libraries may already use subscription services, such as McNaughton (http://www.books.brodart.com), to lease popular collections. The list of titles likely includes at least a handful of "graphic novels" each month. Try including these in several months' selections, then track circulation statistics to demonstrate interest.

Gathering information from other libraries can be another way to strengthen the proposal. Search WorldCat for the latest holdings information for comic titles, and write to a few libraries that seem to have larger comics collections. Say you are impressed with their collection and seek to start one at your own library. Ask about the collection, their circulation, and any challenges they've encountered. Even a few anecdotal quotes from a library that has created a collection will provide some support.

Along with the proposal narrative, create a tiered title list with prices, showing how even a modest expenditure can create a well-rounded if small collection, with options for medium-sized and larger collections. Provide brief summaries about what each level offers the library.

Be sure the proposal also describes a plan to promote and assess the collection (see Chapter 7). It's likely that decision makers will have some doubts about comics in the library, but if an assessment plan is lined up, those doubts may be relieved. Include any ideas about comic-related events or exhibits in the proposal. It may be easier for some people to warm to comic books if they think of them as a strategy for drawing people into the library building.

If the proposal does not meet with success, consider refining and submitting it again next year. Library budgets are different every year. Also, after reading the proposal, decision makers may be more sensitive to the existence of comic books in everyday life and be more receptive the next time it is submitted. Comic books are only growing in popularity in libraries, so you may be able to provide additional evidence of the success of comic books in other libraries.

MONITORING AND MAINTAINING THE COLLECTION

Because most comic books are serials, libraries will want to review use data regularly to determine which serial runs to continue. Which titles have circulated the most and the least? What are their characteristics? By examining circulation reports yearly, libraries can make sure they are collecting in the areas in which patrons are most interested.

Circulation reports can provide a wealth of information for growing any comics collection. Start by finding out what reports are available. The circulation manager or integrated library system expert may already be running circulation reports for the rest of the library. A parameter limiting a report to comic books can be added to generate comic book–specific data. This parameter might be a call number range, a unique note field value, or a specific location.

The report manager may ask which fields are desired in the report. Fields related to circulation counts may include total checkouts, year-to-date checkouts, and renewals. Common bibliographic elements such as title, author, and publisher can be helpful for sorting. Also ask for the date on which the item was added to the library's collections— this might be the record-creation date, an order date, or another cataloging-related date. Obviously, it is unfair to compare circulation numbers for brand-new items with items that have been in the collection for years.

Specific views of the report and related calculations will provide valuable information:

- For existing collections (items owned for at least a year), sort by year-to-date circulations in order to determine the most popular titles and suggest new or continued directions for future acquisitions.
- If the library purchased a batch of new items during the last year, sort by the record-creation date, then by year-to-date circulations, to show the relative success of these titles.
- If the report can be grouped by publisher, it might be interesting to see which comic publisher has the greatest circulation. Be sure to divide the year-to-date circulation total for each publisher by the number of items in each publisher's category in order to normalize the data.
- Total circulation, as opposed to year-to-date circulation, can be a good number to brag about. For example: "Although the City Library has only 30 comic book titles so far, these have circulated more than 100 times since the collection was added early last year." Consider adding renewals into the total circulation.
- Consider comparing the circulation rate (year-to-date circulations divided by number of items) for the comics collection to other parts of the collection. In academic libraries, compare with the rest of the browsing or "pleasure reading" collection; in public libraries, compare with the fiction collection.

Another type of report that might be available is circulation by patron type. Patron type can be very useful in an academic library, where different categories of users (i.e., faculty and students) are more central to the institutional mission. Alternately, a library might be trying to reach out to a specific user population (community patrons). School libraries may be interested in whether older or younger students are checking out graphic novels. Patron-type reports might actually be a set of reports similar to the ones mentioned previously, with each report limited to each specific type of patron. By charting the circulation counts from these reports on a graph, one can see which patron group is using the collection.

Any kind of report can be run regularly in order to show trends over time. Yearly or twice-per-year reports should be sufficient. The integrated library system expert should be able to suggest the ideal time of year to run the reports. If the system tracks "year-to-date" information, the report should be run shortly before the year ends to get the most information. The report should be run at a similar time each year so year-to-date information can be compared from year to year.

If the circulation data shows little use compared to the rest of the library collections, consider the promotion strategies discussed in Chapter 7, and run the reports again after wrapping up a promotional effort. Look carefully to see which comic books are circulating the most, and consider making more purchases from that genre (see Chapter 4) or publisher (see Chapter 3, under "Publishers").

Review the results from such reports with a colleague to check assumptions and preliminary conclusions. A second look at the numbers might suggest additional views of the data, different interpretations, or different conclusions. For example, the report excerpt shown in Figure 5.2, which tracks circulation for a comic book collection's first 10 months, shows *Hellboy* was one of the top titles. This library will want to explore *Hellboy*

Title	Vol.	Date Item Created	Total Checkouts	Total Renewals	Last Checked Out	DUE DATE
The Sandman / Neil Gaiman, writer	v.7	24-06-08	9	1	28-10-08 17:06	30-01-09
Watchmen / Alan Moore, writer Dave Gibbons, illustrator		01-04-08	8	1	02-12-08 14:24	- -
The Sandman / Neil Gaiman, writer	v.3	24-06-08	8	1	20-11-08 13:31	- -
The Sandman / Neil Gaiman, writer	v.1	23-06-08	7	5	21-09-08 16:10	27-01-09
Batman, the Dark Knight returns / Frank Miller with Klaus Janson and Lynn Varley		23-06-08	7	2	03-12-08 22:46	27-01-09
The Sandman / Neil Gaiman, writer	v.2	24-06-08	7	0	18-09-08 17:14	27-01-09
The Sandman / Neil Gaiman, writer	v.6	24-06-08	7	0	29-10-08 17:14	30-01-09
The Sandman / Neil Gaiman, writer	v.9	24-06-08	7	0	03-11-08 13:14	03-02-09
Harley Quinn. Preludes and knock-knock jokes / written by Karl Kesel, pencils by Terry Dodson with Craig Rousseau		24-06-08	6	1	12-11-08 17:08	25-01-09
Jinx : the definitive collection / by Brian Michael Bendis for David Engel		24-06-08	6	1	09-12-08 09:00	26-01-09
Hellboy / by Mike Mignola	v.3	23-06-08	6	1	26-11-08 13:25	05-02-09
The Sandman / Neil Gaiman, writer	v.5	24-06-08	6	0	30-10-08 16:07	- -
Tank Girl 2 / Alan Martin & Jamie Hewlett		24-06-08	5	0	12-11-08 17:08	26-01-09
All-star Superman / written by Grant Morrison, pencilled by Frank Quitely	v.1	24-06-08	5	0	12-01-09 12:47	05-02-09
The Sandman / Neil Gaiman, writer	v.4	24-06-08	5	4	07-10-08 00:46	- -
The Sandman / Neil Gaiman, writer	v.10	24-06-08	5	0	03-11-08 13:14	- -
Showcase presents Batman	v.1	24-06-08	4	6	14-09-08 12:32	26-01-09
Bone / by Jeff Smith		24-07-08	4	2	16-10-08 16:36	26-01-09
Inhumans / Paul Jenkins, writer, Jae Lee, artist		24-06-08	4	1	20-10-08 21:01	30-01-09
Frank Miller's Sin City. Vol. 1. The hard goodbye / Frank Miller		30-06-08	4	6	09-12-08 09:31	05-02-09
The amazing Spider-man [electronic resource] : the complete collection		13-03-08	4	0	19-12-08 13:08	- -
Hellboy / by Mike Mignola	v.1	23-06-08	4	5	01-10-08 20:48	- -
Buddha / Osamu Tezuka	v.1	24-06-08	4	2	11-12-08 17:19	- -
Batman chronicles	v.1	24-06-08	4	1	18-11-08 13:42	- -
Top 10 / Alan Moore, writer Gene Ha, finishing artist	v.1	24-06-08	3	6	12-11-08 15:14	25-01-09
Top 10 / Alan Moore, writer Gene Ha, finishing artist	v.2	24-06-08	3	2	18-09-08 14:46	26-01-09
House of M. Uncanny X-Men / writer, Chris Claremont, pencils, Alan Davis inks, Mark Farmer ... [et al]		24-06-08	3	4	08-10-08 12:26	26-01-09
The Essential Wolverine / featuring Chris Claremont & John Buscema, Archie Goodwin & John Byrne	v.1	24-06-08	3	5	18-09-08 19:17	26-01-09
Phoenix / by Osamu Tezuka [English translation by Dadakai Jared Cook, Shinji Sakamoto, and Frederik L. Schodt]	v.1	24-06-08	3	1	15-10-08 18:27	27-01-09
Dreams / David Mack		23-06-08	3	0	17-11-08 22:10	30-01-09
Buddha / Osamu Tezuka	v.8	24-06-08	3	1	15-09-08 13:45	02-02-09
Blade : undead again / writer, Marc Guggenheim, artist, Howard Chaykin		24-06-08	3	5	14-09-08 12:32	03-02-09
Birds of prey : old friends, new enemies / [Gail Simone, writer Ed Benes ... [et al.]		24-06-08	3	2	15-10-08 18:27	05-02-09
Frank Miller's Sin City. vol. 2, A dame to kill for / Frank Miller		30-06-08	3	2	02-10-08 16:08	05-02-09
Fruits basket / Natsuki Takaya [translators, Alethea Nibley and Athena Nibley]	v.2	30-06-08	3	1	07-12-08 13:51	05-02-09

Figure 5.2

Excerpt of a Circulation Report on the First 10 Months of a Graphic-Novel Collection spinoffs, other titles in this genre, titles by the same creators, or even search for *Hellboy* on commercial book sites such as Amazon.com in order to use recommendation features such as "Customers Who Bought This Item Also Bought . . . "

Titles that were least used should also be reviewed. These may have been good selections that somehow failed to connect with potential readers. For example, if a library finds that *Fruits Basket*, a teen-oriented manga, did not circulate, it should review the shelving location and promotional materials used.

Another interesting way to look at reports is to see how many times later volumes of series circulated when compared with the first volume. Suppose *Naruto*, v. 1, circulated many times, but volumes 2, 3, and 4 circulated only a few times? Especially if use of later volumes tapers to zero, the library may not want to continue this series. Clearly, readers are able to find *Naruto*, but perhaps their interest is not sustained through the entire series. A good thing to double check is the catalog record: if one finds *Naruto* in the online catalog, are all volumes found with equal ease? Some catalog systems may make long series appear to end after 10 volumes, as shown in Figure 5.3. If usage drops off after vol. 10, a poor display may be the cause.

On the other hand, if later volumes are circulating frequently, then buying more volumes of the series is an obvious choice, since it maintains interest and avoids a sudden end to an ongoing story.

Other ways to expand the collection are perhaps less obvious. For instance, if circulation reports show a particular writer's or artist's works have been checked out more often than others, then adding more volumes from that creator's body of works is advisable (see Chapter 3, under "Creators"). If a popular volume of a title is involved in a crossover (see Chapter 2, "Arcs/Crossovers"), then the library might want to buy the main collection of the crossover or other volumes that are involved in the crossover; likewise, if the main volume collecting the crossover is popular, adding other titles from that crossover would be an excellent choice.

Author	Kishimoto, Masashi
Title	Naruto / story and art by Masashi Kishimoto ; [English adaptation by Jo Duffy ; translation, Katy Bridges, Mari Morimoto]
Publisher	San Francisco, Calif. : VIZ Media, 2003
Local Note	Comic books, strips, etc

Location	Call number	Status
Carrier Lib-Browsing	PN6790.J33 K555 2003 v.1	AVAILABLE
Carrier Lib-Browsing	PN6790.J33 K555 2003 v.2	AVAILABLE
Carrier Lib-Browsing	PN6790.J33 K555 2003 v.3	AVAILABLE
Carrier Lib-Browsing	PN6790.J33 K555 2003 v.4	AVAILABLE
Carrier Lib-Browsing	PN6790.J33 K555 2003 v.5	AVAILABLE
Carrier Lib-Browsing	PN6790.J33 K555 2003 v.6	AVAILABLE
Carrier Lib-Browsing	PN6790.J33 K555 2003 v.7	AVAILABLE
Carrier Lib-Browsing	PN6790.J33 K555 2003 v.8	AVAILABLE
Carrier Lib-Browsing	PN6790.J33 K555 2003 v.9	AVAILABLE
Carrier Lib-Browsing	PN6790.J33 K555 2003 v.10	AVAILABLE

View additional copies or search for a specific volume/copy

Bookmark URL for this catalog record:
http://leo.jmu.edu:80/record=b2135114~S0

Figure 5.3
Screenshot Showing Initial Display of Holdings for Naruto. The library has volumes 1–28.

After reviewing usage of the existing collection, libraries will want to consider entirely new titles, as discussed in Chapter 7.

CONCLUSION

Creating a mainstream comic book collection does not need to be expensive, but it should be purposeful and tied directly to users' interests. Existing holdings in graphic novels can be supplemented by a selection of mainstream comic titles in various genres (see Chapter 4). If comic books are new, libraries should review relevant policies to be sure they address comic books' special needs. Funding for a new or expanded collection should be tied to the library's mission. Any popular-reading comics collection should be evaluated using circulation information to grow the collection to reflect readers' interests.

NOTES

1. However, even in this short time frame, many of these titles have gone out of print.
2. Karen Potash of OverDrive, e-mail message to author, April 27, 2010.
3. Other options include calling (888) COMIC-BOOK (266-4226) or using The Master List at http://www.the-master-list.com.
4. Details can be found at http://www.diamondbookshelf.com/public/default .asp?t=1&m=1&c=20&s=176&ai=7121.
5. Sharon Bodtorf of Wert Bookbinding, attachment to e-mail message to author, February 15, 2008.

REFERENCES

Archie Digital Comics. "Sign Up—Archie Digital." http://www.archiedigital.com/sign-up (accessed April 27, 2010).

Diamond Bookshelf. "Ordering Information." http://www.diamondbookshelf.com/public/ default.asp?t=1&m=1&c=20&s=176&ai=7121 (accessed April 22, 2010).

H. W. Wilson Company. "Graphic Novels Core Collection." http://www.hwwilson.com/ databases/graphicnovels_core.cfm (accessed April 26, 2010).

ICv2.com. "Top 10 Comics Business Events of 2009." January 5, 2010, http://www.icv2.com/ articles/news/16589.html (accessed April 22, 2010).

Ihnatko, Andy. "ComixOlogy's Marvel iPad App Shows Promise for Digital Comics." *Chicago Sun-Times*, March 31, 2010. http://www.suntimes.com/technology/ihnatko/2134294, marvel-ipad-comixology-ihnatko-033110.article (accessed April 22, 2010).

Marvel.com. "Marvel Ratings System." Marvel Subscriptions, http://subscriptions.marvel.com/ v3/pages/ratings.htm (accessed October 25, 2010).

6

Cataloging

Cataloging and shelving graphic novels are two different aspects of the same concern: access. Getting graphic novels into the hands of readers involves presenting the books' metadata in a way that will mean something to the core audience and other readers, advertising the collection through the catalog and its location in the library, and figuring out how the collection fits into the library's workflow and space. Even experienced catalogers may encounter novel conundrums, such as determining whether a graphic novel is a monograph or a serial; which information to use for the title; what to put in notes fields and subject headings; and determining main and added entries. This chapter will discuss each issue in turn and provide two examples. It will also discuss issues related to location of the collection.

MONOGRAPHS, SERIALS, OR BOTH?

What kind of material are graphic novels? On one hand, they could be cataloged as single-volume monographs. They are, after all, complete stories in one volume, generally with unique titles that differentiate themselves from other, similar volumes. However, in many cases, their original formats—comic books—are quite obviously serials; they are released in consecutive issues, with numerical and chronological designations that are meant to be continued indefinitely. When those comics are reprinted, the reprint line is expected to last as long as the original series.

Some graphic novels are quite obviously monographs. *Watchmen*, for example, was meant to be complete in one volume. Limited series are often reprinted in one volume and should usually be considered monographs. Other graphic novels might obviously be part of a serial in their original, comic book form but be a monograph when collected. For example, writer Steve Engelhart, along with artists Len Wein and Marshall Rogers, created a run of stories in *Detective Comics* #469–479 in the 70s. Although those stories began as part of the serial *Detective Comics*, they were reprinted as *Batman: Strange Apparitions*, which was complete in one volume. Although Batman's story and series went on, the graphic novel is meant to capture a time and the creators' viewpoint; there will be no future volumes of the series because those creators did not leave any more similar work to be reprinted, and other nearby issues will not likely be reprinted in a linked series.

On the other hand, some stories may be complete in one volume yet be seen as a series or multivolume work. Frank Miller's *Sin City* volumes are numbered consecutively, yet each tells a story that is independent of others in the series. However, they share a common setting and feature occasional appearances by characters from previous stories. For these reasons, the titles should be read in order and are therefore considered part of one overall story.

For most superhero graphic novels that reprint recent comic books, it is probably best to catalog them as multivolume works. Most of these titles rely on continuity, making it helpful for users to read the books in a certain order to get the most out of them. The stories and characters extend across multiple volumes, telling if not one story, at least a series of interrelated ones. Unlike serial prose titles like the Harry Potter or Nancy Drew series, the series title is a separate part of the title and is emphasized before the volume title (see Example 2 below). Most titles have volume numbers, which makes putting the volumes in order simple.[1]

Occasionally, the numbering on graphic-novel series is restarted to show the presence of a new creator or story direction. In this case, the new numbering should be given a new record, although this can lead to confusion; for instance, if v. 1 of the second series is followed on the shelves by v. 2 of the first, readers will be puzzled. Use the list of reprinted issues as a guide; this information can be found on the back cover or in the indicia, which is generally inside the front cover or on the t.p. verso.

Some catalogers might argue the serial nature of the works trump other concerns, especially with manga, which rarely have volume titles. Still, even though cataloging graphic novels as serials solves some problems, such as Cuttering and the complications of individual volume names, it is probably not the best option. While cataloging the books as serials simplifies the records, it makes them more opaque, leaving less information for readers. Readers may have trouble in some systems placing holds on materials (Serchay 2008). From a shelving point of view, most libraries physically separate their serials from the monograph collections, which can make them more difficult for readers to find and for librarians to promote.

Whichever choice you make, heed the cataloger's mantra and be consistent. This should go without saying, but sometimes inconsistencies creep in because information can be hidden or encoded in a way comic book publishers and readers do not see as hidden at all. For instance, catalogers may not perceive that certain volumes should be linked. In the second series of *Birds of Prey* reprints, for instance, the volume numbers were omitted, but the individual volumes in the series are as closely linked as any other major superhero title. This lack of numbering could lead to confusion no matter how the series is cataloged. It may take a little detective work to discover the connection between and the order of the volumes, but putting these hidden series into single records not only allows the catalog to be consistent but also organizes the titles into a more useful format. Series titles can be hyperlinked to launch new searches, and volume numbers can be added to reflect the intended reading order.

TITLE ACCESS

When it comes to the title proper, consistency may be more important than literal transcription. The title pages in collected editions are not always the best sources for gathering information. Artists and editors often creatively lay out the title pages in ways that might obscure information to catalogers (see examples below). Some may leave off the series title, leaving a contextless and useless volume title for the 245 (title statement) field. Some title pages can lack information entirely. DC's and Marvel's black-and-white reprint lines (Showcase Presents and Essentials, respectively) often have no creator information on their title page, crediting creators from each of the 20–30 individual reprinted issues on the t.p. verso and following pages. As mentioned above, the indicia can also hold vital information about the book's title.

However, catalogers should not be afraid to use the Internet to help decide what the title of the work is. Catalogers, with justification, can choose a wide variety of titles for a series, depending on the volume. Here are some titles for Marvel's *Essential Avengers* series drawn from WorldCat:

- *Essential Avengers*
- *Stan Lee presents The essential Avengers. (vol. 1)*
- *Essential Avengers 4: Avengers #69–97 & Incredible Hulk #140*
- *Essential Avengers 5*
- *Avengers. vol. 6, Avengers #120–140, Giant-size Avengers #1–4, Captain Marvel #33 & Fantastic Four #150*
- *Essential Avengers. vol. 7*

Although each title might be individually justified, only the titles that include *Essential Avengers* at the beginning are collectively justified. When these titles are solicited by Marvel, they are referred to as *Essential Avengers*; on Amazon, they are listed as *Essential Avengers*; on the Marvel Web site, they fall under the title *Essential Avengers*. On other, less official Internet forums, they are most often referred to as *Essential Avengers*. Using the other titles—omitting "Essential" or including the content information or "Stan Lee Presents"—confuses readers who are actually looking for the *Essential Avengers*. Having "Avengers" in the title might help, but there are many Avengers reprint titles: *Avengers, Essential Avengers, Avengers Visionaries, Mighty Avengers, New Avengers, Dark Avengers, Young Avengers*, and even *Pet Avengers*. Obviously, alternate titles are going to be very important with multivolume works.

Whichever is selected as the title proper, it is important to have access through the other possible titles as well. The graphic novel's subtitle should be given its own 246 (varying form of title) field for users who are looking for one particular volume. But be careful; too many variant titles can lead to confusion, especially if they are too vague, such as "Avengers," or too common, such as the publisher's name at the beginning of the title. Be sure to use 490 (series statement) fields to link books in the same reprint line, such as Marvel Essentials or DC Showcase. Although these lines have different content, they are part of the same superhero universe, and they present stories in a similar fashion.

NOTES FIELDS

Notes fields can also be used to convey information specific to graphic novels. If a series changes its name, the 500 (general note) field can be used to guide readers to where the story is continued (or is continued from). As the Cataloging Department at the University of Illinois (2005) notes, it can also be used to alert readers of whether a manga volume is reprinted in its original reading order (panels right to left, from the "back" of the book to the front) or whether it has been flopped to make it look more familiar to American readers ("Graphic Novels" 2005). Noting nonstandard sizes—especially the digest size common to manga—might help users find the smaller, more easily overlooked volumes. The size information is in the 300 field as well, but making a note of it will make the information stand out.

For libraries that collect graphic novels that appeal to a wide range of ages, another use for the 500 field is to display publishers' recommended age ranges for the book. This is a tricky consideration. Publishers' age ratings may not be accurate or may not align with those of your community. These ratings may also have a chilling effect on the circulation of a book, either by claiming a book is too mature for a younger audience or too immature for an adult or college student. If the graphic-novel collection is supposed to serve a younger audience, displaying an erroneous rating that proclaims the title is meant for adults may also confuse children and their parents (Goldsmith 2005).

Many catalog records of collected editions include a 505 (contents) note. For records describing multivolume works, they are indispensible. Listing the name of each volume allows users to confirm or discover that books they thought stood alone are actually part of a larger whole. Each volume name should additionally be given an alternate title field. The 505 field is also the most useful place in the record for noting the volume and issue numbers of the reprinted comics, giving the reader more information about where the collection falls in the character's and publisher's history. The year of the volume's first issue might be more useful, in this case, than the actual volume number for comic titles with several volumes.

If the record is for a stand-alone monograph, resist the impulse to give additional title entries to the titles of the individual stories included in the collection. These titles are rarely known by even the most diehard comics fan, and transcribing these titles would be akin to including the names of chapters of a novel: useful for completeness's sake but generally not worth the time. Among the 11 issue titles in *Daredevil Visionaries*: Frank Miller, v. 3, for instance, are the generic titles "Siege," "Resurrection," "Child's Play," "Roulette," and "Guts." Giving these volumes a 700 (added personal name) field would clog the catalog with unhelpful titles.

SUBJECT AND TITLE HEADINGS

Subject headings necessitate careful decisions. Library of Congress (LC) subject headings are often an awkward fit for fiction, which includes most popular graphic novels. Other subject headings, such as *Olderr's Fiction Subject Headings*, *ALA's Guidelines on Subject Access to Individual Works of Fiction, Drama, Etc.*, and *Unreal! Hennepin County Library Subject Headings for Fictional Characters and Places* may be helpful in this regard, especially the latter; many comics publishers use shared universes, so common fictional locales, objects, and characters will appear in graphic novels from different comics titles. For most libraries, however, these alternate sources will not be an ideal solution, as they introduce extra procedures and non-LC subject headings into the workflow (Gatley, Wallace, and Waye 2005). Institutions that wish to create robust graphic-novel research collections might find this adaptation useful, though.

LC subject headings are still the best option for most libraries, but which ones will help users find the collection? While the free-floating subdivision "Comic books, strips, etc." is useful for nonfiction graphic novels, it does not help users who are trying to find graphic novels as a whole, and it can scare away users who have a distaste for the comic book medium. Using "Graphic novels" or "Comic books" as a genre heading (field 655) can be helpful, even though these terms name the format rather than the genre. Adding a heading for specific genres of graphic novels, such as "superheroes" or "fantasy," gives an extra level of granularity, and users who are hoping to find manga could find this type of heading invaluable. However, if users do not expect to be able to search on these terms, then they may lack usefulness. At James Madison University, catalogers created a 740 entry for the name of the graphic-novels collection and added the entry to every record in the comic-book collection, thus linking all the volumes in the popular graphic-novels collection. This also makes it easy to generate reports for analyzing collection usage (see Chapter 5).

Uniform title fields (730) and subject headings for specific characters can also aid users in finding graphic novels featuring their favorite characters. Be careful, though, especially with uniform titles; although some titles may seem similar enough to fall under the same uniform title, readers might consider them very different. *Ultimate X-Men*, for instance, is similar to other X-Men titles, but readers who searched on the uniform title "X-Men (Comic strip)"[2] might not expect to find a volume of *Ultimate X-Men*. Although the two titles have similarities, and *Ultimate X-Men* was based on the X-Men concept, the characters and storylines can diverge greatly. They do not share a universe or continuity—in fact, Marvel Comics created *Ultimate X-Men* as part of an alternative to the continuity-heavy Marvel Universe.

Whatever decisions are made, public-services librarians should discuss the collection and related procedures with catalogers. Catalogers want to get the records right, and without feedback from and about users, the way they catalog the collection might not be right for users. Likewise, if public-services librarians are aware of cataloging procedures, they will be more effective in assisting users.

MAIN ENTRY/CUTTERING

The main entry for a work is the person or group chiefly responsible for a work, and although the main entry may not concern most comics fans, it can have major implications in the catalog record's appearance and Cutter numbers. AACR2 rule 21.24 says that when there is collaboration between the artist and writer, the first person named on the title page should be given the main entry and the second-named person should get an added entry (Joint Steering 1998). Putting aside the aforementioned lack of clear information on title pages in some graphic novels, this means most main entries will be writers, as most comics list the writer first. From the point of view of consistency, this is admirable. But given the collaborative nature of comics work, the artist may do as much or more creative work on the book, especially artists who also help the writer plot the story. If there is more than one writer but only one artist, the artist will be similarly slighted. In other situations, the artist may be of more interest than the writer, so keeping the artist's works together may be of more interest.[3] The easiest option, however, is to choose either the artist or writer to always be the main entry and to maintain consistency; catalogers will be left with fewer questions, and readers will be able to adapt more readily.

Usually, whoever gets the main entry will also form the basis of the Cutter number. However, this may not be the best choice for filing. As David S. Serchay (2008) points out, this can spread consecutive volumes of a series across the collection—for example, volumes 7, 8, and 9 of *Ultimate X-Men* would appear in separate locations since they were written by three different people.[4] Although many readers will follow writers and artists to whatever projects they work on, the superhero genre has survived by training readers to follow the series and characters. Perhaps more importantly, this style of Cuttering could divide a continuing story. Therefore, Cuttering by title makes more sense.

However, even this has complications. Series can change titles, which can put consecutive volumes well apart, and DC and Marvel have series of collected editions dedicated to reprinting material that inserts the line's name as the first word of the title (e.g., *Essential Fantastic Four* and *Showcase Presents Green Lantern*). Cuttering these under "Essential" or "Showcase" would group the titles with all the other Essential or Showcase volumes, which collect many different characters. Serchay (2008) suggests Cuttering by the character name might help. This seems the best way to direct readers to the stories that might interest them, but that may put a burden on shelvers as popular characters such as Batman and Spider-Man will collect a large mass of volumes that may be difficult to put in any consistent order.

Another question is how many creators should get added entries. While many graphic novels will have only a writer and an artist, multiple writers and artists can be present, especially for collections that reprint more than a half-dozen issues. How much of a contribution must a creator make to get an entry? In an Essential or Showcase volume, there may be a half-dozen or more writers or artists who have minimal contributions but no one who has contributed to more than a quarter of the issues in the book. This also raises the question of which types of creators should be credited—although writers and pencilers/artists are recognized as important, other jobs are not always. Inkers, colorists, letterers, and editors are rarely given as much credit as writers and pencilers, despite the considerable influence each job can have on the finished product. AACR2 rule 21.30A suggests giving entries to up to three people in each category (such as writers and illustrators); if four or more are listed, only one need be given an added entry (Joint Steering 1998). However, in the latter case, the rule also suggests choosing the first-named person the added entry; it is a better idea to get a rough idea of which creator contributed to the most issues and make that writer or artist the added entry.

CATALOGING EXAMPLES

Below, two typical examples of collected editions will be examined. Each will be cataloged in two different ways: as a monograph and as a monographic series. MARC coding will be shown at three places during each example, with the monograph record on the left and the monographic series record on the right.

Example #1: *Essential Spider-Woman, vol. 1*

The first step is to determine the book's title. Figures 6.1 and 6.2 show the cover and title page for *Essential Spider-Woman, vol. 1*, and the artistic way they are laid out obscures any obvious title. "To know her is to fear her" and "Stan Lee Presents" are mere taglines and certainly not part of the book's title; Stan Lee has presented thousands of Marvel Comics over the last four decades, and "To know her is to fear her"

Figure 6.1
The cover of *Essential Spider-Woman, vol. 1*; art by Joe Sinnott.
© 2005 Marvel Comics.

is a slogan, meant to help sell the book, that is present on the covers of many individual comics collected in the volume. The words at the bottom of the page list the contents of the volume. That leaves "Essential Spider-Woman" (or possibly "Spider-Woman Essential") as the title. A search of Amazon.com, Marvel.com, or any number of resources listed in Chapter 9 shows the former title is better known. But that's not the entire title; the cover and the spine list "vol. 1" as well, so that should be added to a monographic record. However, a check of those Web resources also reveals there is a second volume of *Essential Spider-Woman*; if the acquisition of *Essential Spider-Woman, vol. 2*, is planned or even possible, "vol. 1" should obviously be omitted, and the volume should be catalogued as a monographic series.

What other titles should be included in the record? Given the prominent placement of "Spider-Woman" on the title page and in the contents, a 246 field should be created for "Spider-Woman." However, the other two serials listed—*Marvel Two-in-One* and

Figure 6.2
The title page of *Essential Spider-Woman, vol. 1*. © 2005
Marvel Comics.

Marvel Spotlight—should be relegated to a note field listing the contents. The book is, however, part of two series: Marvel's Essential series, which reprints large chunks of older Marvel comics in black and white, and Essential Spider-Woman. The latter does not need a 490 (series title) field since it is the same title as the book itself, and the authority control has an entry for the former, which can be seen in Figure 6.5 in an 830 (uniform title) field. However, that leaves the question of precisely what should be placed in the 490 field. The title and credits pages and the cover are not helpful in this regard—the word "Essential" is the only part of the series listed on any of those sources.[5] The back cover features an advertisement for the "Marvel Essentials Library," which is the best series name provided in this volume.

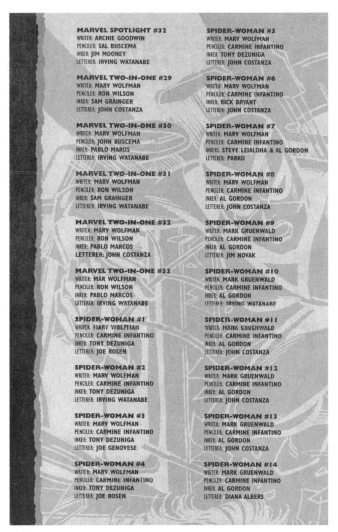

Figure 6.3
The first credits page for *Essential Spider-Woman, vol. 1.*
© 2005 Marvel Comics.

If the library's graphic-novel collection has a name or there is a name that ties together the various graphic-novel titles the library owns, place it in a 740 (uncontrolled related title) field, as shown below.

Next is the decision of who should be credited as the main entry and who should be included as an added entry. As seen in the two credit pages (Figures 6.3 and 6.4), writer Mark Gruenwald contributed to 12 issues, and Marv Wolfman wrote 13. Usually, writers have longer runs on titles than artists, but penciler Carmine Infantino drew 18 of the book's 31 issues. This makes him the logical choice for main entry for the monographic record. but a check of online resources shows he contributed very little to v. 2 ("Spider-Woman"), so he should remain an added entry for the monographic series (see Figure 6.6). Gruenwald and Wolfman also deserve added entries. Michael Fleisher, who wrote the

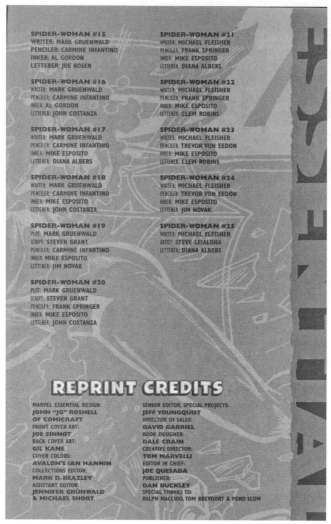

Figure 6.4
The second credits page for *Essential Spider-Woman, vol. 1.*
© 2005 Marvel Comics.

last five stories in the volume, is also an excellent choice for an added entry; another candidate is Ron Wilson, who penciled four issues.

Local practices can specify additional entries for creators who made small contributions to large volumes like this, but it quickly leads to a long list of entries for people with minimal contributions and is against the advice of AACR2 rule 21.30A. Patrons who are fans of John Buscema, for instance, may be interested to know he contributed to this volume, but because his contribution comes to about 20 out of more than 600 pages, it's likely that all but Buscema's most dedicated fans will consider the listing of little use. Writers and pencilers whose work amounts to fewer than four issues—about the length of the shortest comics collections—should probably be omitted, even if their efforts were among the three largest in their category for the volume.

Figure 6.5

Sample MARC Records without Subject or Name Headings for *Essential Spider-Woman, vol. 1*

Monograph record	Monographic series record
245 00 $a Essential Spider-Woman, $n vol. 1 / $c	245 00 $a Essential Spider-Woman / $c
246 1 $a Spider-Woman	246 1 $a Spider-Woman
260 $a New York : $b Marvel Comics, $c 2005.	260 $a New York : $b Marvel Comics, $c 2005-.
300 $a v. : $b chiefly ill. ; $c 26 cm.	300 $a v. : $b chiefly ill. ; $c 26 cm.
	490 1 $a Marvel essentials library
490 1 $a Marvel essentials library	500 $a "To know her is to fear her!"— Cover and T.p.
500 $a "To know her is to fear her!"— Cover and T.p.	500 $a At head of title: Stan Lee presents.
500 $a At head of title: Stan Lee presents.	500 $a Volume 1 originally published in single magazine form in Marvel spotlight #32, Marvel two-in-one #29-33, Spider-Woman #1-25, c1977-1979.
500 $a Originally published in single magazine form in Marvel spotlight #32, Marvel two-in-one #29-33, Spider-Woman #1-25, c1977-1979.	740 0 $a Graphic novel collection.
740 0 $a Graphic novel collection.	830 0 $a Essential (Marvel Comics Group).
830 0 $a Essential (Marvel Comics Group).	

Most of the rest of the people listed on this page should not get entries. Letterers and colorists[6] can safely be omitted no matter how great their contributions. The same goes for editors, including the comics' original editor (not credited in this example), reprint editors, or editors in chief. However, although inkers can usually be left out, an inker who is well known for writing or penciling may be given an additional entry.

There is one possible exception to the rule about minimal contributions mentioned above. Although writer Archie Goodwin and artist Sal Buscema contributed only one issue to the collection, they did create the character of Spider-Woman (Mangels 2004).[7] Just as certain creators, such as Bob Kane for Batman, are credited for their individual creations in comics and other media, it may make sense for a library to add an entry for these creators. However, given how little influence Buscema and Goodwin had on Spider-Woman—they worked on the character for only the first issue in this 31-issue collection, which reprints her appearances chronologically—it probably is not a good idea to add entries for them here.

One final note about personal entries: If a library that catalogs this book as a monographic series adds the second *Essential Spider-Woman* volume, it should be prepared to add more entries for creators to the record. In this case, that could include four names that are not already part of this record—another argument for being selective on whom to give additional entries to. An online check of the credits for v. 2's contents—*Spider-Woman*

Figure 6.6

Sample MARC Records without Subject Headings for *Essential Spider-Woman, vol. 1*

Monograph record	Monograph series record
100 1 $a Infantino, Carmine.	245 00 $a Essential Spider-Woman / $c [various writers and artists].
245 10 $a Essential Spider-Woman, $n vol. 1 / $c [various writers and artists].	246 1 $a Spider-Woman
246 1 $a Spider-Woman	260 $a New York : $b Marvel Comics, $c 2005-.
260 $a New York : $b Marvel Comics, $c 2005.	300 $a v. : $b chiefly ill. ; $c 26 cm.
300 $a v. : $b chiefly ill. ; $c 26 cm.	490 1 $a Marvel essentials library
490 1 $a Marvel essentials library	500 $a "To know her is to fear her!"—Cover and T.p.
500 $a "To know her is to fear her!"—Cover and T.p.	500 $a At head of title: Stan Lee presents.
500 $a At head of title: Stan Lee presents.	500 $a Volume 1 originally published in single magazine form in Marvel spotlight #32, Marvel two-in-one #29-33, Spider-Woman #1-25, c1977-1979.
500 $a Originally published in single magazine form in Marvel spotlight #32, Marvel two-in-one #29-33, Spider-Woman #1-25, c1977-1979.	700 1 $a Fleischer, Michael.
700 1 $a Fleischer, Michael.	700 1 $a Gruenwald, Mark.
700 1 $a Gruenwald, Mark.	700 1 $a Infantino, Carmine.
700 1 $a Wilson, Ron.	700 1 $a Wilson, Ron.
700 1 $a Wolfman, Marv.	700 1 $a Wolfman, Marv.
740 0 $a Graphic novel collection.	740 0 $a Graphic novel collection.
830 0 $a Essential (Marvel Comics Group).	830 0 $a Essential (Marvel Comics Group).

#26–50—shows no writer or penciler contributed to more than half the issues in the two *Essential Spider-Woman* volumes ("Spider-Woman").

Subject headings can be assigned at the cataloger's discretion; examples for *Essential Spider-Woman*, v. 1, can be seen in Figure 6.7. However, adding the generic subject "Comic books, strips, etc." is not necessary if there is some other obvious way to direct students to the libraries' collection of graphic novels, such as the collection name in a 740 field or a hyperlinked local genre note, such as a 655 field.

Example #2: *Birds of Prey: The Battle Within*

For *Birds of Prey: The Battle Within*, the choice of title is much simpler. Although the title is so small it almost seems hidden on the title page (not reproduced here), there

Figure 6.7

Sample Finished MARC Records for *Essential Spider-Woman, vol. 1*

Monograph record	Monograph series record
100 1 $a Infantino, Carmine.	245 00 $a Essential Spider-Woman / $c [various writers and artists].
245 00 $a Essential Spider-Woman, $n vol. 1 / $c [various writers and artists].	246 1 $a Spider-Woman
246 1 $a Spider-Woman	260 $a New York : $b Marvel Comics, $c 2005-.
260 $a New York : $b Marvel Comics, $c 2005.	300 $a v. : $b chiefly ill. ; $c 26 cm.
300 $a v. : $b chiefly ill. ; $c 26 cm.	490 1 $a Marvel essentials library
490 1 $a Marvel essentials library	500 $a "To know her is to fear her!"— Cover and T.p.
500 $a "To know her is to fear her!"— Cover and T.p.	500 $a At head of title: Stan Lee presents.
500 $a At head of title: Stan Lee presents.	500 $a Volume 1 originally published in single magazine form in Marvel spotlight #32, Marvel two-in-one #29-33, Spider-Woman #1-25, c1977-1979.
500 $a Originally published in single magazine form in Marvel spotlight #32, Marvel two-in-one #29-33, Spider-Woman #1-25, c1977-1979.	650 0 $a Heroines in literature $v Comic books, strips, etc.
650 0 $a Heroines in literature $v Comic books, strips, etc.	650 0 $a Heroes $v Comic books, strips, etc.
650 0 $a Heroes $v Comic books, strips, etc.	655 4 $a Superhero comic books, strips, etc.
655 4 $a Superhero comic books, strips, etc.	700 1 $a Fleischer, Michael.
700 1 $a Fleischer, Michael.	700 1 $a Gruenwald, Mark.
700 1 $a Gruenwald, Mark.	100 1 $a Infantino, Carmine.
700 1 $a Wilson, Ron.	700 1 $a Wilson, Ron.
700 1 $a Wolfman, Marv.	700 1 $a Wolfman, Marv.
740 0 $a Graphic novel collection.	740 0 $a Graphic novel collection.
830 0 $a Essential (Marvel Comics Group).	830 0 $a Essential (Marvel Comics Group).

is no difficulty figuring out what the title is once "Birds of Prey: The Battle Within" is found on the cover (Figure 6.8) or the t.p. verso (Figure 6.9). The only choice, really, is to decide whether to catalog this as a monograph or a monographic series.

Although the book does not give an indication of this, there are a series of trade paperbacks reprinting *Birds of Prey*. Catalogers need to be aware that just as the stories in graphic novels often take place in a wider fictional universe, the collections of these stories may be part of a wider series as well. The most obvious source for this information, the

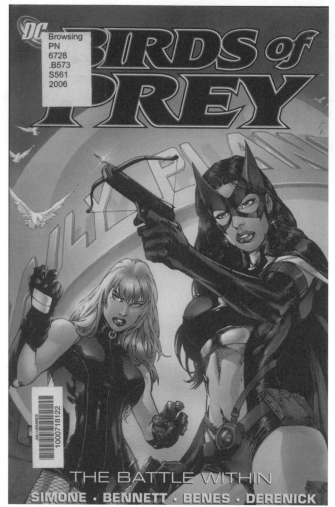

Figure 6.8
The cover of *Birds of Prey: The Battle Within*; art by Ed
Benes. *Birds of Prey: The Battle Within* © 2006 DC Comics.
All Rights Reserved.

DC graphic novels page (http://www.dccomics.com/dcu/graphic_novels), lists 12 volumes
with *Birds of Prey* at the beginning of their titles, although no numbering or order (other
than alphabetical) is given. "Mike's Amazing World of DC Comics," an impressive fan
site maintained by Mike Voiles, lists the same 12 volumes, giving them volume numbers
based on chronological order (Voiles, "Guide"). *The Battle Within* is listed as v. 6. However, the book's listing on Amazon.com says the book is v. 4 (Amazon.com). Both of these
sources can have their potential weaknesses—the former is maintained by a single person,
and the latter's information concerns are more commercial than bibliographic—so which
is better in this case?

    The discrepancy lies in the comics reprinted and the absence of numbering by the
publisher. Voiles begins his numbering with the oldest trade paperback with the name

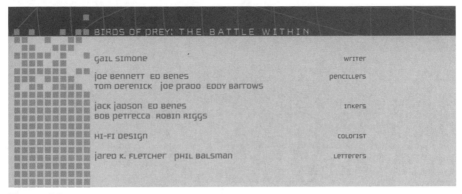

Figure 6.9
The t.p. verso of *Birds of Prey: The Battle Within*. *Birds of Prey: The Battle Within* ©
2006 DC Comics. All Rights Reserved.

Birds of Prey: 1999's *Birds of Prey*, which reprints various one-shots and limited series written by Chuck Dixon that shows the Birds of Prey team being formed. The next volume, *Birds of Prey: Old Friends, New Enemies*, is also written by Dixon and reprints the first six issues of the *Birds of Prey* title. Amazon gives no numbers to these volumes and lists *Birds of Prey: Of Like Minds*, which reprints #56–61, as v. 1. *Of Like Minds* is the beginning of writer Gail Simone's tenure on the title, and it begins a run of almost 70 consecutive issues of *Birds of Prey* reprinted by DC. Since issues #7–55 have not been reprinted in a volume titled *Birds of Prey*, Voiles calls *Of Like Minds* v. 3.

Amazon's numbering is preferable in this case, for several reasons. One is that renumbering a reprint series when a new writer or penciler begins working on a title is common. Another is that *Birds of Prey* #7–55 might be reprinted at some point in the future, and Voiles's numbering leaves no space for them, while Amazon's allows volumes to be added to the first series. Amazon's higher visibility as a source of information is also a basis for using its numbering system, although it is the weakest reason of the three.

Additional titles are a bit easier than with *Essential Spider-Woman*. Since the series title would be the same as the 245 $a title, there's no need to add a series entry. The subtitle (or volume title, for monographic serials) can be given an additional entry: a 246 field for monographs, a 740 field for monographic serials (see Figure 6.10).

Main and additional entries for creators are also simpler with *Birds of Prey* than for the large, thematically varied *Essential Spider-Woman*. There is only one writer credited: Gail Simone. As she is the only creator who fulfilled her role unaided throughout the book, she should be the main entry. Interestingly, she also was the main writer throughout most of the Amazon-numbered series, writing 7 of the 10 volumes,[8] so she is also a logical choice for the main entry of a monographic series.

For the pencilers, it is a bit more difficult. Joe Bennett is the first-listed penciler, but how much did he contribute? Did the other pencilers make a large contribution? The title page and t.p. verso are silent on the individual contributions of the artists; the credits that would usually be on the title pages of the individual comics issues have been removed from the reprinted collection. They are listed on the covers to

Figure 6.10

Sample MARC Records without Subject or Name Headings for *Birds of Prey: The Battle Within*

Monograph record	Monograph series record
245 10 $a Birds of Prey, $n [vol. 4] : $c The battle within / $c	245 00 $a Birds of Prey / $c
246 1 $a Battle within	260 $a New York : $b DC Comics, $c c2006.
260 $a New York : $b DC Comics, $c c2006.	300 $a 234 p. : $b chiefly col. ill. ; $c 26 cm.
300 $a 234 p. : $b chiefly col. ill. ; $c 26 cm.	500 $a Vol. 4 "originally published in single magazine form in Birds of Prey #69-75"—T.p. verso.
500 $a "Originally published in single magazine form in Birds of Prey #69-75"—T.p. verso.	740 02 $a Battle within.

the individual issues, but the credits do not differentiate between pencilers and inkers. To find out which penciler contributed what, the cataloger will have to seek outside information. DC's site has no further explanation, but Voiles has an issue-by-issue breakdown on his page on the book (Voiles, "Birds"). Bennett indeed did do the most work, penciling 5 of the 10 issues. Ed Benes and Thomas Derenick

Figure 6.11

Sample MARC Records without Subject Headings for *Birds of Prey: The Battle Within*

Monograph record	Monograph series record
100 1 $a Simone, Gail.	100 1 $a Simone, Gail.
245 10 $a Birds of Prey, $n [vol. 4] : $c The battle within / $c [Gail Simone, writer; Joe Bennett [et al.], pencilers].	245 00 $a Birds of Prey / $c [various writers and artists].
246 1 $a Battle within	260 $a New York : $b DC Comics, $c c2006.
260 $a New York : $b DC Comics, $c c2006.	300 $a 234 p. : $b chiefly col. ill. ; $c 26 cm.
300 $a 234 p. : $b chiefly col. ill. ; $c 26 cm.	500 $a Vol. 4 "originally published in single magazine form in Birds of Prey #69-75"—T.p. verso.
500 $a "Originally published in single magazine form in Birds of Prey #69-75"—T.p. verso.	700 1 $a Bennett, Joe, $d 1968-
700 1 $a Bennett, Joe, $d 1968-	700 1 $a Benes, Ed.
740 0 $a Graphic novel collection.	740 02 $a Battle within.
	740 0 $a Graphic novel collection.

each contributed two issues as well, with Benes inking Joe Prado's single issue. Benes also inked his own work, something the other pencilers did not do, and a look at the credits on Voiles's site for previous *Birds of Prey* volumes show Benes was the regular series artist before this volume. Catalogers could follow the AACR2 rule and list Bennett as the sole penciler for the monograph, but a monographic serial record should include Benes because of his long contribution to the title (see Figure 6.11).

Again, remember to add titles and format entries to keep the collection and medium together.

The subject headings are similar to the ones in the first example, with a few additions based on the differences between the two books (see Figure 6.12).

Figure 6.12

Sample Finished MARC Records for *Birds of Prey: The Battle Within*

Monograph record	Monograph series record
100 1 $a Simone, Gail.	100 1 $a Simone, Gail.
245 10 $a Birds of Prey, $n [vol. 4] : $c The battle within / $c [Gail Simone, writer; Joe Bennett [et al.], pencilers].	245 00 $a Birds of Prey / $c [various writers and artists].
246 1 $a Battle within	260 $a New York : $b DC Comics, $c c2006.
260 $a New York : $b DC Comics, $c c2006.	300 $a 234 p. : $b chiefly col. ill. ; $c 26 cm.
300 $a 234 p. : $b chiefly col. ill. ; $c 26 cm.	500 $a Vol. 4 "originally published in single magazine form in Birds of Prey #69-75"—T.p. verso.
500 $a "Originally published in single magazine form in Birds of Prey #69-75"—T.p. verso.	650 0 $a Computer hackers $v Comic books, strips, etc.
650 0 $a Computer hackers $v Comic books, strips, etc.	650 0 $a Heroines in literature $v Comic books, strips, etc.
650 0 $a Heroines in literature $v Comic books, strips, etc.	650 0 $a Heroes $v Comic books, strips, etc.
650 0 $a Heroes $v Comic books, strips, etc.	650 0 $a Women with disabilities $v Comic books, strips, etc.
650 0 $a Women with disabilities $v Comic books, strips, etc.	655 4 $a Superhero comic books, strips, etc.
655 4 $a Superhero comic books, strips, etc.	700 1 $a Bennett, Joe, $d 1968-
700 1 $a Bennett, Joe, $d 1968-	700 1 $a Benes, Ed.
740 0 $a Graphic novel collection.	740 02 $a Battle within.
	740 0 $a Graphic novel collection.

COLLECTION LOCATION

The main priority for shelving should be to facilitate access; for a collection designed to appeal to popular tastes, like a graphic-novel collection, increasing circulation is an additional remit.

For libraries that shelve fiction in specially designated fiction areas, broken down by genres, the solution is obvious, if not easily achieved: carve out space within the fiction area and designate it a graphic-novel area. Finding the space might be more easily said than done, but it is the most direct solution, allowing for high visibility and easier promotion.

There are difficulties with this idea beyond finding the space, of course. Some graphic novels are not fiction; these can be given their own section within the graphic-novel collection, interfiled with the rest of the collection, or filed within the stacks. A larger concern is age appropriateness. Some sort of designation should be given if the collection contains materials of different maturity levels: a prefix to the call number or a different shelving section, for example. Given the difficulty of shoehorning a single new collection into the stacks, finding room for two might be impossible, so the latter might not be practical.

The Vancouver Public Library has a slight variant on the idea: its graphic novels are interfiled with the appropriate fiction genres. As a result, the library has experienced a dramatic increase in circulation (Gatley, Wallace, and Waye 2005). This scheme makes sense in many ways; most graphic novels *are* fiction, it allows fans of writers who create both graphic novels and fiction to find their content in one place, and it places the material in a more browsing-friendly area, one with a high amount of traffic. However, it requires browsers to know which genre superhero and borderline stories fall into, and it assumes users browse by the name of the writer rather than artist or (most likely) the characters involved.

Shelving by call numbers within the stacks may have an advantage in that the appropriate shelves should be easy to find for most users. The disadvantages outweigh that small advantage, however. It is difficult to promote a collection tucked away in the stacks. The Dewey Decimal Classification (DDC) puts graphic novels at 741.5, with extensions based on a creator's country. This is not a useful place for graphic novels, as it groups the medium with books on drawing (between metalwork and decorative arts, neither of which seem to have a high similarity with graphic novels). This classification can become crowded, with books about the medium of comics, comic strips, and graphic novels all being lumped together in one undifferentiated spot (Goldsmith 2005). Although the DDC has considered further subdivision of graphic novels, it has not done so yet (Beall 2006); developing those subdivisions as a local practice would be time consuming, but it might be worth the effort. The Library of Congress numbers, PN6700–6790, are slightly more conducive to shelf browsing, as the PN is a section devoted to literature.

Interfiling is also an option, but when graphic novels are spread throughout the library's holdings, there is no "graphic-novel collection" any more. Interfiling can be useful for libraries that collect graphic novels on a wide variety of topics, and the DDC does suggest persuasive and nonfiction graphic novels be classified with the subjects they cover. It is, however, not a way to build interest in a particular collection.

CONCLUSION

Graphic novels and collected editions have nuances that make their cataloging more difficult than the slight difference in format would seem to indicate. Titles and creators are obscured by graphic concerns; they are collaborative works that can have a dozen or more people involved; they are a hybrid form of monograph and serial. The decision of where to put the volumes adds an extra complication.

This chapter has presented options for both cataloging and shelving. It is important to choose what best fits your library. Solutions this chapter dismissed may end up being the best for your situation, because they meet your need for granularity or simplicity or hit a middle ground between them. Solutions this chapter easily endorsed may be impractical or not robust enough. These decisions must be made with the input of all the parties involved, each considering workflow and the access of the patrons. It does not help either party to implement procedures by fiat.

NOTES

1. However, some series omit volume numbers. Detective work is necessary in these cases to supply the correct numbers; Example 2 in this chapter and see Chapter 9, under "Lists of Graphic Novels and Their Contents."

2. The X-Men are not part of a comic strip, despite the title heading.

3. Some libraries—especially Dewey libraries—might decide to classify graphic novels as fiction. The necessity of grouping graphic novels by only one facet of creativity, either writing or illustrating, is a large downside to this idea.

4. The volumes were written by Mark Millar, Brian Michael Bendis, and Brian K. Vaughn, respectively.

5. The "Marvel Comics" logo on the upper left of the cover is more likely branding rather than title information.

6. Colorists are not credited in *Essential Spider-Woman, vol. 1*, because it is a black-and-white reprint. The colorists' work does not appear in the volume. See Figure 6.9 for credits with colorists.

7. Inker Jim Mooney might also be considered one of Spider-Woman's creators; arguments about who created which characters are rarely clear-cut affairs.

8. This can be seen by clicking on the links to the books from Voiles's page at http://dcindexes.com/tpbs/dblist.php?group=dcu.

REFERENCES

Amazon.com. "Birds of Prey Vol. 4: The Battle Within." http://www.amazon.com/Birds-Prey-Vol-Battle-Within/dp/1401210961/ref=sr_1_1?ie=UTF8&s=books&qid=1272599836&sr=8-1 (accessed April 29, 2010).

Beall, Julianne. "741.5 or Graphic Novels in the DDC." April 7, 2006, http://www.powershow.com/view/365f-NGRmO/741_5_or_graphic_novels_in_the_DDC (accessed April 30, 2010).

Gatley, Randy, Christine Wallace, and Donna Way. "Boom: Graphic Novel Explosion @ Your Library." Vancouver: University of British Columbia, School of Library, Archival, and Information Studies, 2005. http://www.slais.ubc.ca/courses/libr517/04-05-wt2/projects/booom/print.html (accessed April 26, 2010).

Goldsmith, Francisca. "Graphic Novels Now: Building, Managing, and Marketing a Dynamic Collection." Chicago: American Library Association, 2005.

"Graphic Novels." Urbana-Champaign: University of Illinois University Library, 2005. http://www.library.illinois.edu/cam/specialtype/graphic.html (accessed March 17, 2010).

Joint Steering Committee for Revision of AACR. "Anglo-American Cataloging Rules." 2nd ed. London: Library Assocation; Chicago: American Library Association, 1998.

Mangels, Andy. "Spider-Woman." In *The Superhero Book: The Ultimate Encyclopedia of Comic-Book Icons and Hollywood Heroes*, edited by Gina Misoroglu with David A. Roach, 464–66. Detroit, MI: Visible Ink, 2004.

Serchay, David S. *The Librarian's Guide to Graphic Novels for Children and Tweens*. New York: Neal-Schuman, 2008.

"Spider-Woman." Unofficial Handbook of Marvel Creators, edited by Markus Müller, http://www.maelmill-insi.de/UHBMCC/spwoman2.htm#S5734 (accessed April 29, 2010).

Voiles, Mike. "Birds of Prey: The Battle Within." Mike's Amazing World of DC Comics, http://dcindexes.com/tpbs/dblist.php?group=dcu&comicid=37114 (accessed April 29, 2010).

Voiles, Mike. "The Guide to DC Graphic Novels and Collected Editions." Mike's Amazing World of DC Comics, http://dcindexes.com/tpbs/dblist.php?group=dcu (accessed April 29, 2010).

7

An Effective Collection: Guidelines for Promotion

Comic book collections have an enormous advantage when it comes to promotion: their exciting visual imagery automatically attracts patrons. Mainstream comics certainly have an advantage over literary graphic novels when it comes to promotion. Although, as this book explains, there is more to mainstream comics than superhero stories, characters like Spider-Man and Iron Man have star power from their appearances in major motion pictures. Mainstream comics survive by being popular and attracting new readers, so their publishers have already worked hard to make the titles and covers appealing to readers.

This chapter will first discuss public relations considerations, including identifying audiences and creating messages. Next, it will suggest ways to create a promotional environment for the collection. Finally, it will present ideas for communicating about the collection.

PUBLIC RELATIONS, PROMOTION, AND ADVERTISING

According to Lisa Wolfe, author of *Library Public Relations, Promotions, and Communications* (2005), public relations and promotion are different concepts. Public relations is "the business of trying to convince the public to have understanding for and goodwill toward a person, firm, or institution," whereas promotion is "trying to further the growth or development of something." A comic book collection will benefit from both. Public relations is important for comic books because the public has preconceived notions about them, based on whatever personal experiences they have had with comics in the past. Some may think of comics as children's fare; others may think only of disproportionate women in spandex jumpsuits. A good PR plan will develop messages that will help shape patrons' view of the collection. Promotion is important for connecting with existing comic book readers and encouraging new readers to sample the collection. Advertising, a specific aspect of promotion, is "calling something to the attention of the public" and is also important for libraries adding comic books for the first time because readers may not expect the library to have comic books (Wolfe 2005, 18).

Libraries may already have organizational public relations, promotional efforts, or marketing campaigns. Larger libraries may even have a staff person specifically designated to support these efforts. If so, the comics collection can use these resources. However, the person who knows the most about the new collection will still need to provide information about the collection and encourage the library to promote it as part of larger efforts.

If the library does not have an existing PR plan or promotional efforts, the comics collection would make excellent fodder for a project-based public relations plan. Always consider how the comics collection might connect with the library strategic plan or a current initiative of library administration, which is perhaps the most important internal audience. They ultimately control whether the collection is funded and where it is located. They may even have to deal with patrons or the press about objections to the collection.

DEVELOPING MESSAGES ABOUT THE COLLECTION

Part of public relations is developing a set of messages that can be used for various promotional efforts and communications. The following list of questions is proposed by Wolfe when developing a public relations/communication plan:

- What do you want to tell people? What is the message?
- Who do you want to tell? Is there more than one potential audience?
- When do you want to communicate your message? Public libraries might want to use the comic book collection as part of a summer reading program. Academic libraries might want to target students early in the semester, when students may have more spare time for pleasure reading.
- Why do you want to tell people about the collection? Do you want them to do anything? (Wolfe 2005, 44)

Many libraries would like to be all things to all people, but when crafting a project-based public relations plan, try to think of various audiences that might be attracted to different titles or genres and develop separate messages for each. For comic books, this might include new or existing comic book readers, children, or adults. Libraries will also always have an internal audience: library staff and administration. Circulation staff, for example, should know enough about the collection to say, "We plan to add new comic book titles each month," when a patron checks out a graphic novel. Administrators should have ready answers about how the collection fits into the library's mission. One of the messages an academic library might want to develop for both faculty and library administration might be "Comic books are used heavily in some areas of scholarly research." Librarians would want to be ready with links to related conferences, journals, and scholarly monographs. A public library might want to emphasize to parents how comic books can encourage reluctant readers to spend time with a book. Libraries that are making a new venture with a comic book collection might want to tell everybody, "Yes, we actually have comic books!" A well-rounded suite of messages and supporting information can be used and reused in multiple types of promotional materials and public relations efforts. The next part of this chapter will discuss creating a promotional environment for a comic book collection.

PHYSICAL LOCATION AND DISPLAY

Libraries developing a new comic book collection will obviously need to consider where to locate the items. Their physical location and display can greatly affect the collection's use (see Chapter 6, under "Collection Location"). Promotional displays about the collection elsewhere in the library can also increase circulation. Creating a promotional environment also means giving some thought to the virtual community that has the potential to form around the collection.

Comics are visual materials, and the comics collection needs to be located in a high-traffic area where people can see it. The display should be attractive, with a variety of covers facing out. Comfortable seating in the area is a plus, so people can read a few pages and determine which titles they want to check out. If possible, locate the collection in an area where staff can see it, too. As with any browsing collection, regular attention will keep the area tidy and organized.

Brochures or fliers about the collection should be available in the same area. A standard brochure could feature the following information:

- The size and scope of the collection
- How to search in the library catalog for comic books and/or graphic novels
- Policies related to the collection (checkout periods, how to renew)
- How to recommend a comic book title for acquisition or give comic books to the library
- Contact information for feedback about the collection

A supplementary brochure for new comic book readers might have:

- An explanation of why the library has a comic book collection
- Comic book title recommendations for new comics readers
- A few recommendations for books *about* comics, such as *Understanding Comics* by Scott McCloud

Academic libraries might wish to offer an additional brochure focusing on scholarly publishing about comics, including academic journals that have published articles about comic books, comic book characters, or related topics; academic conferences relating to comic books; and research databases that include coverage of comic book–related topics. Ask academics who use the collection for research to let the library know about their work. Invite them to make a presentation in the library on their research topic.

Cosette Kies urges libraries not to overlook the traditional book list as an inexpensive way to "publicize unusual subjects" (2003, 112–13). With comics, they can be used to draw readers' attention to different facets of the collection, such as specific genres, characters, or themes. The content from these brochures should also be included on the library's Web site. Figure 7.1 shows some examples of informational materials.

PROMOTIONAL DISPLAYS INSIDE AND OUTSIDE THE LIBRARY

Most libraries have bulletin boards and display cases that provide opportunities to showcase the comics collection inside the library building. Academic and school libraries have numerous additional opportunities outside the library building, including

JMU LIBRARIES COMIC BOOKS COLLECTION

What is included in the new comic books collection?
- mainstream titles such as *Spider-Man, Superman, X-Men, Iron Man*
    - some on DVD in Media Resources
    - some in print
- non-superhero titles such as *Usagi Yojimbo, The Sandman, Fables, Buddha*
- graphic novels such as *Watchmen* and *Batman: The Dark Knight Returns*

Can I check out the comic books?
Yes!! We will analyze checkout statistics to inform future decisions about buying comic books.

How can I search for comic books at JMU Libraries?
Search in LEO Library Catalog on <u>Comic Books Collection</u> for a list!

I am sort of interested, but don't want to read about men in tights. What do you recommend?
- *Fables* deals with various characters from fairy tales and folklore.
- *Usagi Yojimbo* is a samurai story set in medieval Japan. Although the characters look like animals, it's not for young children.
- *Alias* and *Queen and Country* feature a private investigator in the US and a UK spy respectively.
- *Fruits Basket* is one of the top Japanese 'manga' titles, and follows the life of a high-school student investigating a zodiac curse!

Are these books for children?
Do not assume that "comic books" means "kids." Some of the titles in this collection have adult content such as violence, drugs, and occasional nudity. As with any book, movie, or TV show, it is important for parents to decide what is age-appropriate.

Why does JMU Libraries have comic books?
This collection was funded as an experimental collection development project. In addition to being fun to read, comic books and characters have become part of mainstream popular culture and could easily be used as primary sources for research into gender, sociology, literature, and more!

Figure 7.1
An Example of a Brochure Describing a Comic Book Collection

school hallways, dining facilities/lunchrooms, and for academic libraries, residence halls. Another place to put a promotional display is on the screensaver of the library's public terminals. If the library has a standard screensaver, perhaps a comic book collection screensaver could be used to promote specific events or during a specific week of the year.

Because of their visual nature and popularity, comic books offer several opportunities for more permanent art to be displayed near the collection or in highly visible areas of the library. Be sure to locate purchased materials in a high-traffic area and/or use secure methods in order to avoid theft. Examples of affordable and compelling graphics include the following:

- The American Library Association offers numerous posters and other promotional materials. Search on "Graphic Novels and Comics" at http://www.alastore.ala.org.
- Surface View offers high-quality canvas and satin prints of Marvel comic book covers and panels ranging from £70–£250 (http://surfaceview.co.uk/two).
- Rizzoli's Expanding Universe Wall Chart ($45) displays a 12-foot Marvel Comics family tree (http://www.rizzoliusa.com/catalog/display.pperl?isbn=9780789399649).

Your local comic book shop may also have extra promotional posters they are willing to contribute, especially if you are able to buy some titles from them for the collection or give them credit near the poster for the donation.

BUILDING A COMMUNITY AROUND COMIC BOOKS

As soon as readers discover the new comic book collection, they may wish to be notified of new additions to the collection and related events. One idea is to create a Facebook page for the library comics collection. This will reach only people who have a Facebook account, but it is a great way to create viral publicity, especially in today's school and academic environments.

Libraries may also wish to create a mailing list sign-up sheet, Web form, or some other method of collecting contact information. The advantage of having a mailing list as opposed to offering an RSS feed is that you will have a better estimate of how many people are in your community. It may be beneficial to store this information in a spreadsheet or database that also allows addresses to be included. Figure 7.2 provides tips for writing e-mails to current or potential collection users.

A community group can easily turn into a base of support for the collection. If you need evidence of the collection's use to justify new purchases, ask people on the list to send an e-mail or a letter to your library's decision makers. You can also ask this

---

Sending e-mails to the library's local community can be a great way to market the comic book collection. In addition to announcing a new collection or new additions, e-mails can be used as part of other marketing efforts. If the library plans to have an event, speaker, or contest or is conducting a poll or survey, using e-mail will help get the word out.

Some tips for effective marketing e-mails are:

- Be sure the subject line is targeted toward your audience and contains the most interesting keywords possible. For example, "Free Comic Book Day at Smith Library, January 10th" will likely get more readers than "Smith Library to Host January Event"

- With comic books, do not hesitate to use top-shelf character names and book titles. *Good*: "Smith Library has a new mainstream comic book collection."

  Better: "Smith Library's new comic book collection features popular characters such as Spider-Man and Superman."

- The e-mail should be no more than a few sentences. Include a URL for more information.

- Always include the library's comic book collection home page URL and contact information.

Figure 7.2
Tips for Sending E-mails to Your Local Community

group for input on potential acquisitions or new trends and formats. Finally, like other niche collections, the comic book collection has the potential to attract in-kind gifts or offers of help. Individuals may wish to donate part or all of a personal comic book collection. They may know someone in the comic book industry who might be willing to speak at an event. They may have good advice about discounts at local comic book shops.

EVENTS TO PROMOTE THE COLLECTION

The launch of a new (or newly envisioned) comic book collection provides the perfect opportunity for a themed event in the library. Public, academic, and school libraries can all take advantage of a kickoff event. Libraries with younger readers may want to have "Spider-Man" or another character actually visit the library for the event. Events might feature comic book–themed food like bat-shaped cookies for Batman; small giveaways, preferably with information about the collection attached; or door prizes. Contests in reading, writing, or art are another way to involve patrons and promote the collection at the same time.

Free Comic Book Day, which is usually held the first Saturday in May, is one of the best opportunities to promote a library comic book collection and comic books in general (http://www.freecomicbookday.com). Libraries and educators can acquire selected titles from the organization and give them away to patrons (educators@freecomicbookday .com). Public libraries have frequently used this day to host a comic-related speaker or event. To see a wide variety of library events related to Free Comic Book Day, simply Google "free comic book day library."

Movie nights are an excellent opportunity to promote both print comic books and related videos and games (see Chapter 8). For example, just before the 2010 release of *Iron Man 2*, the Jefferson Township Public Library in New Jersey had a pizza and movie night featuring the first *Iron Man* movie. Similarly, Huntington Beach Public Library posted a Facebook announcement related to the movie, complete with links to the library catalog: "And while you wait for opening weekend, might we suggest checking out some *Iron Man graphic novels*, the *first movie*, or even *Sherlock Holmes* for a Robert Downey, Jr. fix?" (http://www.facebook.com/note.php?note_id=385929347629). For more on comic book movies, see Chapter 8, under "Films." A similar avenue of promotion involves games nights; for more details, see Chapter 8, under "Games Days/Nights."

Libraries with comic book collections will find visually compelling materials to round out exhibits and provide special book lists for themed events. For example, a library might have events promoting women writers during Women's History Month, and a selection of comic books by women writers could make an interesting addition. For inspiration, the Friends of Lulu awards provide good examples of new female talent and past women comics creators as well as women-friendly work in comics. Awards are voted on by members each summer (http://friendsoflulu.wordpress.com/lulu-awards).

Universities and high schools may have student clubs whose interests include comic books, and should facilities permit, the club could be invited to have meetings in the library. Many student organizations are willing to do fund-raisers such as bake sales to support their favorite causes—perhaps the library's new comics collection could be their next cause, and the money raised could go to purchase new acquisitions with the group's input. (See Figure 7.3 for another opportunity to work with college students on promoting the collection.)

Some courses at colleges and universities frequently include a requirement to find a "real-life" client in need of marketing materials or a marketing campaign. Marketing classes, for example, might require students to develop a mini-campaign (McGeachin and Ramirez 2005). Graphic design classes may be charged with developing visual materials such as brochures. Academic libraries at schools offering these majors can identify potential classes through the course catalog and contact professors about this opportunity.

Students are usually looking for fun projects. A comic book collection offers visually compelling materials and may already be of personal interest to some students. The library's campus location is an additional bonus, as students will not need to travel off campus to visit with their "clients." Students may develop promotional materials, coordinate an event, work on a Web site, or even suggest new media to promote the collection.

Figure 7.3
Working with a Marketing Class to Promote the Collection

At any event, try to offer an evaluation form, even if it asks only two or three key questions, so that this information can be included with future collection requests.

Developing a promotional environment for comic books will position a library to create and send effective communications about the collection. This will be discussed in the next section.

COMMUNICATIONS ABOUT THE COLLECTION

Libraries have many means of communication with their patrons, and the comic book collection can take advantage of both usual and new methods. After setting the collection up for success, promotional communication about the comics collection will get the word out to the various audiences served by the collection. Lisa Wolfe offers a three-question list to use when developing communications:

1. What do you want the audience to remember?
2. What action do you want them to take?
3. How will this action require them to change thoughts or behavior? (2005, 32)

Whether creating a Web page, newsletter article, or press release, the library should answer these three questions each time it prepares to send a communication.

PROMOTING THE COLLECTION ON THE LIBRARY WEB SITE

The library Web site is one of the easiest places to promote the comic book collection. At a minimum, have a home page for the collection with all the information provided in the supplemental materials such as brochures and promotional displays. Include contact information for users who want to make recommendations or have questions.

The comics page is also a great place to connect readers with related library materials: journals, reference books, and books about comic books. Provide links that launch searches into the catalog on subject headings and authors related to comic books; Chapter 6 discusses how to catalog comic books for effective search and retrieval in the catalog. Comic book Web pages on the library site can provide easy entry into the catalog.

```
Metadata found in the web page http://www.lib.jmu.edu/resources/comics/

<head>
<title>Comic Books and Graphic Novels at JMU Libraries</title>

<meta name="keywords" content="comic books, graphic novels, x-
men, wolverine, marvel, dc comics, captain america, iron man,
hulk, comics, comic collection" />

<meta name="description" content="JMU's comic books and graphic
novel collection contains mainstream comic book titles such as
Iron Man, Spider-Man, and Captain America, as well as
independent titles such as Buddha and Usagi Yojimbo.  All comic
books and graphic novels can be checked out. " />
</head>
```

Search engine results for "jmu comic books" in Google
(Note: the second page listed does not have a meta description tag, which is why the search
engine has provided a description of its own by grabbing arbitrary text)

Comic Books and Graphic Novels at JMU Libraries
JMU's comic books and graphic novel collection contains mainstream
comic book titles such as Iron Man, Spider-Man, and Captain America, ...
www.lib.jmu.edu/resources/comics/ - Cached

Collecting Graphic Novels and Comic Books
Batgirl Comic In Fall 2008, JMU Libraries began to purchase a selection of
mainstream comic books and graphic novels, starting with about 170 graphic novel ...
www.lib.jmu.edu/edge/Spring2009(2)/article4.aspx - Cached

Show more results from www.lib.jmu.edu

Figure 7.4
Example of HTML Metadata for a Library Web Page about Comic Books

Make sure the Web pages about comic books have good metadata so users can find them using Google and the library Web site search engine. Be sure any subpages also have their own metadata. With good metadata, your Web pages can appear at the top of Google results lists for searches that include some local information, such as the name of your library, university, or town. Figure 7.4 shows an example of metadata and how it can affect search engine results displays. Searching on "jmu comic books" in Google produces the James Madison University library's comic book home page as the first result—as it should.

Depending on your local community, there may be local groups or organizations that might wish to link to your comic book home page. If you know of any, consider sending them an e-mail and asking them to link to the library's comic book Web site.

USING LIBRARY NEWSLETTERS AND OTHER PUBLICATIONS

Library newsletters are an obvious place to promote a new collection, ongoing additions to the collection, and related events. If the library is part of a larger organization, its publications might also be an option. Student newspapers may be willing to send a reporter and write an article. Alumni newsletters at colleges and universities are always looking for stories to attract different segments of their audience. Public libraries are already likely aware of local newspapers or publications that might be interested in the collection. Local coffee shops and bookstores often have magazine and newspaper racks with local publications, if inspiration is needed.

A similar idea to the library newsletter is creating postcards specifically about the collection. On a college campus, these might be distributed across campus for little or no expense or be offered on a rack in the library (Cosgrove 2005). Again, the attractive visual nature of comic books will make it easy to find compelling graphical images. Comic book publishers can authorize the use of licensed images; both DC Comics (http://www.dccomics.com/dccomics/about/dcc_randp.pdf) and Marvel Comics (http://marvel.com) have dedicated permissions departments that provide a quick turnaround for requests.

USING PRESS RELEASES

If other publications might potentially be interested in the collection, it is important to manage the message through press releases. Good public relations about comics is important because they can be so easily stereotyped and misunderstood. Head off potentially negative or inaccurate presentations of the collection by taking proactive steps. Even if the publication sends a reporter to gather information, it is all too easy to confuse facts and figures. Numbers, URLs, and names should be clearly spelled out in the press release to avoid misinformation. Lisa Wolfe provides templates and suggestion for writing press releases (2005, 122–28). Finally, be sure to have a colleague and someone in the library administration review the press release.

When writing the press release text and working with reporters, consider carefully the potential for "spin" on any story about the collection. Reporters may opt for quick and easy headlines like "Biff! Pow! Bang!" which may perpetuate the stereotype of comic books as campy superhero stories rather than promote a carefully selected collection composed of a wide range of genres (see Chapter 4). In addition to being sure your statements match up to the desired message, ask the reporter what his or her interest in the story is to see if they are investigating a particular angle. Also, ask the publication to let you know when a promised article is likely to appear. With students, be sure they are aware of copyright restrictions on images that they are hoping to include.

USING SURVEYS AND POLLS TO PROMOTE
AND BUILD THE COLLECTION

Not only can you use a survey to help select titles for an initial collection, but a survey effort can also have a promotional effect. For example, a graphic novel–readers' survey at the Octogone Library in the LaSalle borough of Montreal began, "Did you know that your library has one of the most extensive collections of manga, comic books, and graphic novels (*bandes dessinees*) on the Island of Montreal? It's true, and we're always trying to touch it up for you" (Charbonneau 2005, 40).

Polls are another quick way to promote the collection. For example, you could include a poll (or a link to a poll) on your library home page for two weeks asking visitors to vote on which new comic book series should be added to the library's collection, with a list of several candidates. Not only will the library get input on which series titles would be most popular, the comics collection gets screen space on the library home page, and the poll provides a convenient excuse to send out an e-mail invitation to your local community.

NEW MEDIA FOR PROMOTION

Web 2.0 media offer additional opportunities for promotion. Be sure to run any ideas past the library's main PR person or the library administrators, who might be aware of related efforts or institutional guidelines about Web 2.0 use. Ideas for using Web 2.0 include the following:

- As mentioned earlier, set up a Facebook page devoted to the comics collection. Use it to advertise new additions, feature polls or surveys about the collection, and link to relevant Web sites or events.
- Create a Twitter account for the collection. Since Facebook can now be set up to update Twitter, the library can have two Web 2.0 channels but have to remember to update only one.
- Create a short YouTube video showing the size and location of the collection. Be sure to post a link to the video from the collection's Facebook page. *YouTube: An Insider's Guide to Climbing the Charts*, by Alan Lastufka and Michael W. Dean, provides full details on how to make and market compelling short videos (2008).

Meredith Farkas's *Social Software in Libraries* (2007) offers an excellent overall introduction to Web 2.0 technologies.

SHARING WITH OTHER PROFESSIONALS

If recent conference presentations, poster sessions, and exhibits are any indication, other library professionals are interested in comics collections in libraries.[1] Consider preparing a poster session or presentation about the new comics collection or some specific aspect such as promotion techniques, selection policies, or evaluation. In addition to giving and receiving professional advice, such efforts will be of interest to the library administration. Share information about the program with the library dean, director, or school principal. Let them know how "hot" comics are at professional conferences, in exhibits, or in other presentations.

SPECIFIC PROMOTION TECHNIQUES FOR SCHOOL LIBRARIANS

School libraries have several additional opportunities for promoting the comics collection beyond those already discussed in this chapter. When the collection is launched, fliers about the comic book collection or related events can be placed in teachers' mailboxes. If possible, school librarians could attend a staff meeting with teachers and make a brief announcement about the launch of the collection and about new developments. Pass out a colorful handout with facts and figures about the collection.

School libraries might also consider holding a "family night" or open house with refreshments, displays, handouts, and a follow-up e-mail after the event (Yoke 2003, 44). McGown says families "will be the biggest supporters in your school community" if they are given the opportunity (1997, 5). By involving families, the library may receive offers to volunteer or contribute in-kind gifts. Offering a newsletter to families is a way to continue developing the library's relationship with this community. School libraries often have an advantage in having a volunteer office or PTA/PTO. There may be volunteers with design expertise, PR, or marketing experience. When working on PR, marketing, and promotion of the comics collection, school library media specialists should consider sending information to PR staff at the school-district level in case they want to use it in larger efforts such as districtwide newsletters (Wolfe 2005, 13).

MARKETING THE COMIC BOOK COLLECTION TO WOMEN

Although women are making significant inroads into the comic book industry, the majority of popular titles are written, drawn, and read by males. But an increasing number of girls are reading comic books, with 39.5 percent of girls aged 6 to 8 and 44 percent of girls aged 9 to 11 reading comic books (Packaged Facts 2008). Figure 7.5 provides a list of comic books that feature women or were authored by women. Many of the suggestions in this chapter can be applied to marketing for both men and women. However, it is important to remember who is being targeted.

- Women who grew up reading teen comic books as girls may not be aware of adult-level comic books that would interest them.
- Women who are entirely new to comic books may assume they are all about superheroes in spandex, with wildly unrealistic body types.
- Mothers may be on the lookout for titles that will interest their daughters and sons.

The comic books below demonstrate the variety of comic book genres written by or featuring women. For additional suggestions, refer to Sequential Tart (http://www.sequentialtart.com) and Friends of Lulu (http://friendsoflulu.wordpress.com).

Air, created by writer G. Willow Wilson and artist M. K. Perker, combines a spy-adventure tale with a love story. The main character is Blythe, a onetime flight attendant who now has the ability to travel in alternate dimensions.

Birds of Prey, written by Gail Simone and others and drawn by a variety of artists, features three women as a superhero team.

ElfQuest, created by Wendy Pini and Richard Pini in the late 1970s and now reprinted in full-color hardcover editions, follows a tribe of elves on a primitive planet. It is aimed at young adults.

Girls with Slingshots, created by Danielle Corsetto, was started as a Web comic in 2004 and features the adventures of the cynical Hazel, the spirited Jamie, and a cactus named Pedro. Collected editions are available at http://www.daniellecorsetto.com/gwsstore_books.html.

Persepolis, written and drawn by Marjane Satrapi, is an autobiographical graphic novel depicting her childhood up to her early adult years in Iran during and after the Islamic revolution.

Rin-ne, written and illustrated by top manga author Rumiko Takahashi, is a Japanese manga series licensed in the United States by Viz Media. The series follows Sakura Mamiya, a girl who gained the power to see ghosts after an incident as a child. Takahashi is also the writer of *InuYasha* and *Ranma ½,* two other extremely popular manga and anime.

Wonder Woman, which began in 1942 and has been written by Jodi Picoult (2007) and Gail Simone (2007 to 2010); Simone was the 2009 Friends of Lulu Hall of Fame Inductee.

Figure 7.5
Women-Written Comic Books and Comic Books Featuring Strong Women Characters

Communications to market the collection toward women might look different than those designed for male readers. In her book *Marketing to Women* (2006), Martha Barletta identifies specific themes that affect how women make purchasing decisions; themes relevant to a comic book collection are summarized here. First, Barletta suggests women are more likely than men to think in terms of people (46). For a comic book collection, this means featuring descriptions of who the characters are as people, what drives them, and why they act the way they do. Another important theme to target is teamwork. Compared to men, Barletta says, "Women test equally high on internal competitiveness or the drive to achieve her personal best, but the drive to conquer someone else is not nearly as strong" (53). Luckily, comic books abound with teams—however, they are not always emphasized. Another way to improve marketing communications to women is to include more details. Barletta states that while men like things to be simplified, for women, "Details not only add richness and depth but are necessary to an understanding of the situation" (69). She suggests giving women lots of specifics rather than making a long story short (77–78). This might mean brochures with more complete descriptions of characters and stories. Finally, Barletta notes that women care a great deal about challenge and achievement (88), which is often overlooked in marketing to women, but they do not necessarily enjoy "boastful, bragging, and swaggering" behavior (89). Comic book heroes can be portrayed both ways.

A good example of these differences can be found in the blog Fantastic Fangirls (http://fantasticfangirls.org). A post invited its staff to answer the question, "What comic book character would you like to give a holiday present to, and what would you give him or her?" Fangirl Caroline answered, "I'd get the New Avengers a kitchen table." Here's part of her reasoning:

> The cast of Brian Michael Bendis's New Avengers have been hiding out/living together in Steve Rogers' old house in New York City. This time has corresponded with, in my opinion, a creative Renaissance for the book, and also, within the context of the story, an important time for the Avengers as a group. It's been about Clint Barton finding his place as a leader (regardless of the costume he wears), Bucky Barnes re-discovering his ability to be part of a team of heroes and to function in the modern world (same comment about costume), Carol Danvers figuring out where she really belongs, Bobbi Morse and Jessica Drew being alive and their real selves again, Peter Parker remembering to trust his team, Luke Cage and Jessica Jones figuring out how their marriage fits with their super-identities, and Wolverine never, ever doing the dishes." (Pruett 2009)

Unlike the myriad, male-authored blog posts about the New Avengers scattered across the Internet, which often focus on specific events and whether the blog author likes how the story is shaping up, this blog takes a different look at a standard superhero comic title, and this post highlights all of Barletta's themes above.

When you plan events and services for women, consider incorporating opportunities to create connections among individuals. Marketing events and services targeting women may include:

- A comic book discussion group
- A blog where women are encouraged to recommend or review a favorite comic book or answer a comic-themed question each month
- A "Pampered Chef"–style party where the products being sold are the library's new comic books
- Opportunities to volunteer at a fundraiser for comic books

In an effort to avoid stereotypes and generalizations, it would be easy to skip over this section. But if you pay attention to commercial advertising efforts, there really is a difference between women and men when it comes to marketing. Do not assume that all the above suggestions will apply to all women or that men will not come to interactive events: just consider offering multiple messages for multiple audiences.

CONCLUSION

Developing good public relations, promotions, and advertising for a graphic-novel collection can be fun and easy. However, attention must be paid to developing strategic messages for specific audiences. The exciting visual imagery of comic book covers makes them ideal candidates for a public-use area and related displays and events. Promoting the collection on the library Web site, in library newsletters, and to local publications can help spread the word, as can surveys and polls. Reaching diverse readers with information about the collection will increase use and drive continued development of the collection.

NOTE

1. At the 2010 ALA Annual Conference, the American Library Association featured at least five separate events directly related to comic books (http://www.nxtbook.com/nxtbooks/hall-erickson/ala_2010conference/#/0); the Association of College and Research Libraries included two poster sessions related to comic books at the 2009 National Conference (http://www.eshow2000.com/acrl/2009/conference_program.cfm); and the Public Library Association featured the daylong preconference "Librarians Get Graphic," with presenters from libraries and the comics industry, at the PLA 2010 National Conference (http://www.placonference.org/pdf/pla_2010_prelim_pgm.pdf).

REFERENCES

American Library Association. "ALA Store." http://www.alastore.ala.org (accessed October 26, 2010).

Barletta, Martha. *Marketing to Women: How to Understand, Reach, and Increase Your Share of the World's Largest Market Segment.* 2nd ed. Chicago: Dearborn Trade, 2006.

Charbonneau, Olivier. "Adult Graphic Novels Readers: A Survey in a Montreal Library." *Young Adult Library Services* 3, no. 4 (2005): 39–42.

Cosgrove, John A. "Drop Them a Postcard: Another Way to Reach Your Patrons." *College and Undergraduate Libraries* 12, no. 1–2 (January 2006): 93–100.

Kies, Cosette. *Marketing and Public Relations for Libraries.* Scarecrow Library Administration Series, 10. Lanham, MD: Scarecrow Press, 2003.

Lastufka, Alan, and Michael W. Dean. *YouTube: An Insider's Guide to Climbing the Charts.* Sebastopol, CA: O'Reilly Media, 2008.

McGeachin, Robert B., and Diana Ramirez. "Collaborating with Students to Develop an Advertising Campaign." In *Real-Life Marketing and Promotion Strategies from College Libraries*, edited by Barbara Whitney Petruzzelli, 139–52. Binghamton, NY: Haworth Press, 2005.

McGown, S. "Survival Alphabet Soup." *Library Talk* 10, no. 5 (1997): 5–6.

Packaged Facts. *The Kids and Tweens Market in the U.S.* 9th ed. Rockville, MD: Packaged Facts, 2008.

Pruett, Caroline. "Q&A #52 What Comic Book Character Would You Like to Give a Holiday Present to, and What Would You Give Him or Her?" December 15, 2009. http://fantasticfangirls .org/?p=1634 (accessed April 26, 2010).

Rizzoli New York. "Marvel: The Expanding Universe Wall Chart." Rizzoli International Publications, http://www.rizzoliusa.com/catalog/display.pperl?isbn=9780789399649 (accessed October 26, 2010).

Surface View. "Surface View Two." http://surfaceview.co.uk/two (accessed October 26, 2010).

Yoke, B. "Open Doors to Collaboration with an Open House." *Library Media Connection* 22, no. 1 (2003): 44–45.

Wolfe, Lisa A. *Library Public Relations, Promotions, and Communications: A How-to-Do-It Manual.* 2nd ed., How-to-Do-It Manuals for Libraries, 126. New York: Neal-Schuman, 2005.

RECOMMENDED READINGS

Farkas, Meredith. *Social Software in Libraries: Building Collaboration, Communication, and Community Online.* Medford, NJ: Information Today, 2007.

Miller, Steve. *Developing and Promoting Graphic Novel Collections.* New York: Neal-Schuman, 2005.

Walters, Suzanne. *Library Marketing that Works!* New York: Neal-Schuman, 2004.

8

Comics in Other Parts of the Library

Graphic-novel collections are visually distinct from the rest of the collection; the covers and spines will likely be more colorful and dynamic than their neighbors. But the collections are thematically similar to at least two other categories of library materials: audiovisuals and games.

Graphic novels, films and TV, and games are not part of the traditional view of library collections. Films and television shows worked their way into the library as part of audiovisual collections, suffering through their times as the newest collection—the collection that library staff and administration were not truly sure should be part of the library. But those days are past, and movies and films are fully ensconced in the library. Graphic-novel collections will cease to be on the fringes of library collections one day, especially since so many comic book stories show up in TV and film. Games are even newer and have yet to gain the acceptance that even graphic novels have. But adding comic-related films, TV shows, and games can help create a well-rounded collection.

FILMS

Superheroes have been seen as box-office gold for the last decade, despite several flops and missteps. DC characters have been featured in movies as far back as the 40s, when Batman and Superman appeared in separate movie serials. The *Batman* movie (1966), based on the TV series starring Adam West, was goofy and over the top, spurring no cinematic imitators. The superhero genre laid fallow in film until 1978's *Superman*, starring Christopher Reeve, became a success and spawned three sequels of successively lesser quality plus a mostly forgotten *Supergirl* movie. *Batman* (1989), starring Michael Keaton and directed by Tim Burton, appeared after the Superman franchise ran out of steam; *Batman* inspired three sequels itself before it too wore out its welcome.

During the late 80s and early 90s, Marvel attempted to get into movies, but films based on its characters, including Captain America, the Punisher, and the Fantastic

Four, tended to be direct-to-video flops or worse.[1] But it was not until a movie based on an obscure vampire hunter—*Blade*—was released in 1998 that Marvel had a hit on its hands. Since then, the company's movie franchises have been consistently financially if not critically successful; even the panned 2003 *Hulk* grossed $245 million worldwide (Box Office Mojo). Since 2000, Marvel characters have been the stars of almost two dozen movies. More are on the way: Marvel formed its own movie company to produce films based on its characters, and in 2009, Disney bought Marvel, uniting the company's characters with a large entertainment corporation.

Marvel's success marked a new era for films based on comic books. DC returned Batman to the big screen in 2005 (*Batman Begins*) and Superman in 2006 (*Superman Returns*). Actor Heath Ledger won an Oscar for his role as the Joker in the 2008 sequel to *Batman Begins*, *The Dark Knight*. In 2009, the movie adaptation of one of the greatest comics stories, *Watchmen*, was released. Even lesser-known characters were able to climb onto the silver screen; *Hellboy* (2004) and *Hellboy II: The Golden Army* (2008) were based on Mike Mignola's comics for Dark Horse, and action movies based on writer Alan Moore's non-superhero characters, such as *From Hell* (2001), *V for Vendetta* (2005), and *The League of Extraordinary Gentlemen* (2003), were also produced. Superhero movies that were not based on existing properties became more common as well; *Unbreakable* (2000), *The Incredibles* (2004), *Sky High* (2005), *My Super Ex-Girlfriend* (2006), *Hancock* (2008), and *Megamind* (2010) all used the superhero concept.[2] See Table 8.1 for a more thorough (but not exhaustive) list of superhero movies based on comics.

Even for those who acknowledge the variety of the medium of comics, there is a tendency to think of comic book movies as over-the-top, big-budget summer blockbusters. However, there is a wide range of movies that are not action-oriented or special-effects laden. Those interested in quieter fare can choose from movies such as *American Splendor* (2003), which details comics creator Harvey Pekar's life and career; *Ghost World* (2001), a coming-of-age story about two teenage girls; and *Persepolis* (2007), author Marjane Satrapi's story of growing up during the Iranian Revolution.

Movies have done a surprisingly good job of capturing the different comic genres, given that using comics as a source material did not become popular until after superheroes had squashed most of the other genres. A list of films made from sources other than superhero comics can be found in Table 8.2; Figure 8.1 recommends titles for a core collection of comic book movies.

TELEVISION

Superheroes have had a less shining path in live-action television than on the silver screen. Television episodes have much lower budgets than movies, causing programs to skimp or rely on ingenuity for the special effects that are crucial to the genre. Even today, when network television commonly uses computer graphics, superheroes have a hard time succeeding in this medium. There are some standouts, however; see Table 8.2 for a list of recommendations for a core collection of comics characters on television.

Surprisingly, although Marvel has had more successful movies over the past decade, DC has been much more successful on television—and not just in the last decade, but since *Adventures of Superman* began its six-season run in 1952. In the mid-60s, *Batman* was briefly a sensation, and in the 70s, *Wonder Woman* ran for three seasons. In the 80s, *Flash* lasted for only one year, but *Lois and Clark: The New Adventures of Superman*

Table 8.1
Superhero Movies Based on Comics

Marvel	DC
Blade (1998)	*Batman* (1966)
Blade II (2002)	*Batman* (1989)
Blade: Trinity (2004)	*Batman and Robin* (1997)
Daredevil (2003)	*Batman Begins* (2005)
Elektra (2005)	*Batman Forever* (1995)
Fantastic Four (2005)	*Batman Returns* (1992)
Fantastic Four: Rise of the Silver Surfer (2008)	*Catwoman* (2004)
	The Dark Knight (2008)
The First Avenger: Captain America (2011)	*Green Lantern* (2011)
	Steel (1997)
Ghost Rider (2007)	*Supergirl* (1984)
Howard the Duck (1986)	*Superman* (1978)
Hulk (2003)	*Superman II* (1981)
Incredible Hulk (2008)	*Superman III* (1983)
Iron Man (2008)	*Superman IV: The Quest for Peace* (1987)
Iron Man II (2010)	*Superman Returns* (2006)
Punisher (1989)	*Watchmen* (2009)
Punisher (2004)	
Punisher: War Zone (2008)	**Other**
Spider-Man (2001)	*The Green Hornet* (2011)
Spider-Man 2 (2004)	*Kick-Ass* (2010)
Spider-Man 3 (2007)	*Mystery Men* (1999)
Thor (2011)	*Spawn* (1997)
Wolverine (2009)	*The Spirit* (2008)
X-Men (2000)	
X2 (2003)	
X-Men: First Class (2011)	
X-Men: The Last Stand (2006)	

ran from 1993 to 1997. *Smallville*, which recounts the adventures of a young Clark Kent, is the longest lived of the lot: it began in 2001, and the 2010–2011 season marks its tenth on television. Marvel, on the other hand, has had only one live-action series on network television: *The Incredible Hulk*, which ran for a respectable five seasons (1977–1982). Table 8.3 lists some live-action superhero series based on comics.

Four of the most prominent TV series based on non–comic book superheroes are *The Greatest American Hero*, *Heroes*, *No Ordinary Family*, and *The Cape*. *The Greatest American Hero*, which ran from 1981 to 1983, is better known for its theme song and as a pop culture reference than for anything about the series, which featured a teacher who was given a superpowered suit by aliens but could not get the hang of any of the suit's abilities. *Heroes*, which began its four-season run in 2006, centered around the

Table 8.2
Comic Book Movies in Other Genres

Horror

30 Days of Night (2007)

The Crow (1994)

Swamp Thing (1982)

Tales from the Crypt (1972)

Tales from the Crypt: Demon Knight (1993)

Tales from the Crypt: Bordello of Blood (1994)

Science Fiction

Barb Wire (1996)

The Guyver (1991)

Judge Dredd (1995)

The League of Extraordinary Gentlemen (2003)

Men in Black (1997)

Men in Black II (2002)

Rocketeer (1991)

Tank Girl (1995)

Teenage Mutant Ninja Turtles (1990)

*Teenage Mutant Ninja Turtles II:
The Secret of the Ooze* (1991)

Teenage Mutant Ninja Turtles III (1993)

V for Vendetta (2006)

Crime

A History of Violence (2005)

The Losers (2010)

Red (2010)

Road to Perdition (2002)

Sin City (2005)

Wanted (2008)

Humor

The Mask (1994)

Manga/Manhwa

Akira (1988)

Dragonball Evolution (2009)

Ghost in the Shell (1995)

Nausicaä of the Valley of the Wind (1984)

Oldboy (2003)

Priest (2011)

Alternative/Biographical

American Splendor (2003)

Art School Confidential (2006)

Ghost World (2001)

Persepolis (2007)

Scott Pilgrim vs. the World (2010)

Fantasy

Avatar: The Last Airbender (2010)

Bulletproof Monk (2003)

Constantine (2005)

From Hell (2001)

Hellboy (2004)

Hellboy II: The Golden Army (2008)

Red Sonja (1985)

Western

Cowboys and Aliens (2011)

Jonah Hex (2010)

Children's comics

*The Adventures of Tintin: Secret of
the Unicorn* (2011)

Josie and the Pussycats (2001)

Richie Rich (1994)

Other

300 (2007)

Monkeybone (2001)

Akira (1988): One of the classics of anime, *Akira* is a futuristic story of Neo-Tokyo, which is wracked by biker gangs and political unrest. The movie is fast paced and extremely well animated and displays the futuristic imagery anime is known for, although some may object to its violence and occasionally disturbing scenes.

Batman (1989): The first mass-market attempt to reclaim Batman from his goofy 60s image, *Batman* combined director Tim Burton's moody and dark Gotham City and Danny Elfman's memorable score to create a movie no one would dare think of as "campy." Outstanding performances by Michael Keaton (as Batman / Bruce Wayne) and Jack Nicholson (as the Joker) helped make *Batman* a success.

The Crow (1994): Starring Brandon Lee, the son of Bruce Lee who died during filming, *The Crow* is a dark, moody tale of supernatural revenge that in some ways resembles *Batman* (1989) sans the braying, brightly painted clown; Roger Ebert called *The Crow* "a stunning work of visual style," although critics noted the movie's slight plot (Ebert 1994).

The Dark Knight (2008): The comic-book movie with the largest box office take ever, *The Dark Knight* built upon the 2005 Batman relaunch (*Batman Begins*) by bringing back Christopher Nolan (director), Christian Bale (Batman / Bruce Wayne), and Michael Caine (Alfred). But it was Heath Ledger's disturbing portrayal of the Joker that stole the show; Ledger won a posthumous Oscar for the performance.

Hellboy (2004): Adapting writer/artist Mike Mignola's demonic everyman for the big screen, director Guillermo del Toro managed to preserve the spooky drama, action, and humor of the original. The cast is strong for what, at the time, was a little-known character, featuring Ron Perlman (Hellboy), Selma Blair (Liz Sherman), and John Hurt (Trevor Bruttenholm).

Iron Man (2008): *Iron Man* eschewed the dark dramatics of *The Dark Knight* and other superhero movies for a tongue-in-cheek action movie, and it worked. Witty performances by Robert Downey Jr. (Iron Man/Tony Stark) and Gwyneth Paltrow (Pepper Potts) created a fun superheroic alternative to the more successful *Dark Knight*.

Persepolis (2007): The black-and-white animated French adaptation of Marjane Satrapi's memoir about growing up during and after the Islamic Revolution in Iran was highly praised by critics. Although foreign subtitled animated films will not appeal to all patrons, Satrapi's story is movingly and stylishly told. The film won the Jury Prize at the 2007 Cannes Film Festival and was nominated for the Academy Award for the Best Animated Feature.

Road to Perdition (2002): Although most viewers did not know it, *Road to Perdition* was based on a trio of crime comics by Max Allen Collins, each with a different artist. The movie had perhaps the most distinguished cast ever in a comic book movie (Tom Hanks, Paul Newman), was nominated for six Academy Awards (including Best Supporting Oscar for Newman), and won the Academy Award for Cinematography.

Spider-Man (2001): Although preceded by *Blade* and *X-Men*, *Spider-Man* was the movie that proved the success of Marvel movies was real. Director Sam Raimi made a movie that was true to the character's comic book stories without slavishly following the original tales, and Tobey Maguire (Spider-Man/Peter Parker), Kirsten Dunst (Mary Jane Watson), and Willem Dafoe (Norman Osborn/Green Goblin) did an excellent job with the material.

Superman (1978): The modern era of superhero movies began with director Richard Donner's *Superman*. Christopher Reeve (Clark Kent/Superman) seemed born for the role of the clean-cut icon, and the box-office returns and special effects paved the way for the many comic book movies that followed.

X2 (2003): Improving on the enjoyable original X-Men movie, Bryan Singer's sequel belongs among the best Marvel movies. Although it has been criticized for focusing too much on one character (Wolverine), it does an excellent job dealing with the themes of alienation and prejudice that are central to the X-Men comics.

Figure 8.1
Eleven Comic Book Movies for a Core Collection

Table 8.3
Live-Action TV Shows Based on Comic Books

DC	Marvel
Adventures of Superman (1952–1958)	*Blade: The Series* (2006)
Batman (1966–1968)	*Incredible Hulk* (1978–1982)
Birds of Prey (2002–2003)	*Mutant X* (2001–2004)
The Flash (1990–1991)	**Other**
Human Target (2010–)	*The Tick* (2001–2002)
Lois & Clark: The New Adventures of Superman (1993–1997)	*The Walking Dead* (2010–)
Smallville (2001–2011)	
Wonder Woman(1975–1979)	

lives of a small group of people who discovered they had powers after a solar eclipse. In the 2010–2011 season, two new series about original superheroes made their debuts: *No Ordinary Family*, a drama about a typical American family that gained superpowers after a trip to the Amazon, and *The Cape*, which featured the adventures of a police officer who gains special abilities after being framed for a crime he did not commit and being left for dead.

Although superheroes are barely a blip on the network primetime radar, they are a mainstay of animated television. Originally a Saturday morning diversion, superhero cartoons have made their way to cable networks, particularly the Cartoon Network and Disney XD. Although animation is better able to handle the special effects needed to make a workable superhero show, older series frequently look dated, with art that appears rough or animation with reduced rate of frames per second. An exception is a set of 17 color, animated shorts based on Superman made by Fleischer Studios and Famous Studios from 1941 to 1943, which stand out in design and animation quality.

Of the many superhero cartoons, a few distinguish themselves. *Super Friends* featured the major DC heroes and ran, under several similar names, for 13 seasons between 1973 and 1986. Although the seasons were of variable quality, the series featured some excellent voice work and set popular expectations of DC heroes for a generation. *Batman: The Animated Series*, which aired from 1992 to 1995, also had exceptional voice talent, and its sophisticated stories and aesthetic—a dark, art-deco Gotham City from some unspecified past—garnered it high praise. *Superman: The Animated Series* (1996–2000) featured a similar art style but translated it into Superman's bright, cheerful Metropolis. *Justice League* (2001–2004) and *Justice League Unlimited* (2004–2006) featured similar concepts and characters as *Super Friends* but updated the style and improved the story quality.

Marvel's animated offerings did not begin so auspiciously; in 1966, *Marvel Super Heroes* aired weekdays, featuring a new hero each day. The animation could charitably be called "limited"—the art was photocopied from comics, with mouths and limbs being the only things animated on the screen. *X-Men* (1992–1997) introduced characters from what was the most popular comics series at the time to television. *Spider-Man: The Animated Series* (1994–1998) was a welcome update of Spider-Man from a pair of earlier, forgettable (except for the theme songs) series. *X-Men: Evolution* (2000–2003) successfully recast the X-Men and their enemies as high school students, replacing the team's usually deadly animosities with high-school rivalries.

For those unfamiliar with manga, anime makes an excellent introduction to the stories, although the story arcs may differ significantly. Also, most of what comes to America is action-oriented, so the diversity of manga does not always come through by looking at English-language anime. *Inu Yasha* and *Tenchi Muyo!* both feature romance plots woven around science fiction/fantasy stories and are popular with both boys and girls. *Sailor Moon* is remarkable for not only starring a female protagonist but also making her the leader of a mostly female heroic team that battles to save Earth. *Case Closed* and *Lupin III* are both crime series; Lupin is an elite criminal who pulls off implausible heists with his crew in each episode, while *Case Closed* stars Detective Conan, a detective who continues to fight crime after he is transformed into a small boy. *Naruto* follows a young orphan living in a ninja village as he tries to gain respect and power on his quest to become the village's leader. *Dragon Ball* has a similar coming-of-age plot, although its protagonist searches for the eponymous mystic objects of power. *One Piece* is also a quest story; in the series, a group of pirates are in search of the title treasure. *Yu-Gi-Oh!* and *Zatch Bell!* both center around duels—*Yu-Gi-Oh!* in a fictional card game called "Duel Masters" and *Zatch Bell!* in a millennial demon tournament. *Ranma ½* is the story of a young boy trained in the martial arts who changes gender when splashed with cold water.

When adding anime to a library's collection, it is important to know how the American versions may differ from the original Japanese episodes. Some versions are subtitled for the English-language market, but most are dubbed, especially those series that have appeared on American TV. Also, some series have been edited for content; those that have not may be more violent or explicit than those who are familiar with the series from television might be expecting. Some books on anime can be found in Appendix C, under "Manga and Anime"; Web sites that review anime can be found in Chapter 9, under "Reviews."

A list of animated series based on comic books can be found in Table 8.4. Titles recommended for a core collection of TV series based on comic books can be found in Figure 8.2.

USING THE AUDIOVISUAL COLLECTION

There are many ways in which the graphic novel and audiovisual collections can support and enhance each other. The easiest way is through joint promotions. Materials created for one collection can mention the other, and signs and materials that promote one collection can be placed with the other. Audiences who are interested in one collection might reasonably be considered good targets for promotional materials about the other. Libraries can also have a comic book movie night, in which a general audience is invited to watch a movie that has some connection to comics (see Chapter 7, under "Events to Promote the Collection").

Depending on the library's strategies for building the graphic-novel and audiovisual collections, the acquisition of new titles for both collections can be coordinated. If the graphic-novel collection has a focus—such as particular characters, companies, or genres—the audiovisual collection can add new titles that mirror that focus. The graphic-novel collection can add titles related to movies or TV series that are already present in the audiovisual collection. If a graphic novel that has been added to the collection is a major inspiration for a movie, then that movie should be considered for the

Table 8.4
Animated TV Shows Based on Comic Books

DC	Marvel
The Batman	*Avengers: Earth's Mightiest Heroes*
Batman Beyond	*Avengers: United They Stand*
Batman: The Animated Series	*Fantastic Four* (four different series)
Batman: The Brave and the Bold Justice League	*Incredible Hulk* (two different series)
Justice League Unlimited	*Iron Man*
Krypto the Superdog	*Iron Man: Armored Adventures*
Legion of Superheroes	*Spectacular Spider-Man*
Super Friends	*Spider-Man and His Amazing Friends*
Superman: The Animated Series	*Spider-Man* (three different series)
Teen Titans	*The Super Hero Squad Show*
	Wolverine and the X-Men
Manga	*X-Men*
Bleach	*X-Men: Evolution*
Case Closed	
Dragon Ball Z	**Other**
Ghost in the Shell: Stand Alone Complex	*Sam & Max: Freelance Police*
InuYasha	*Teenage Mutant Ninja Turtles*
Lupin III	*The Tick*
Naruto	
One Piece	
Ranma ½	
Sailor Moon	
Tenchi-Muyo	
Yu-Gi-Oh!	
Zatch Bell!	

audiovisual collection. Because of their popular and colorful nature, the audiovisual collection may benefit from having comic-related titles in promotional materials for the library at large.

TRADITIONAL GAMES

Many different types of traditional games might tie in to a graphic-novel collection. The simplest is a superhero-themed version of a traditional board or card game, such as a Marvel or Superman version of Monopoly, Uno, or Stratego.[3] These games are much like playing chess with a novelty set of pieces: the rules are the same, even if the pieces look different. Many newly created board games based on DC and Marvel superheroes are also available, but these games usually get only middling ratings from games sites like BoardGameGeek.com. These games frequently fail to capture the feel of

Batman: The Animated Series (1992–1995): A stylish, high-quality animated series that may be the greatest TV superhero series ever. Not only did it adapt *Batman* stories faithfully and compellingly, but it also had an effect on the comics, with two supporting characters from the show being written into the comic book universe.

Incredible Hulk (1977–1982): Along with fellow 70s superhero show *Wonder Woman*, *Incredible Hulk* was one of the few live-action shows to capture the feel of the comic book stories on which it was based without looking silly or campy at the time. Today, both it and *Wonder Woman* have a high amount of nostalgia value for older patrons and might represent a good opportunity to introduce those patrons to the graphic novel collection.

Justice League/Justice League Unlimited (2001–2006): Continuing the superhero universe created in *Batman: The Animated Series* and *Superman: The Animated Series*, *JL/JLU* combined the team concept of the 70s favorite *Super Friends* with more modern and rich storytelling to create one of the strongest superhero cartoons ever.

Naruto/Naruto Shippuden (2002–present): Based on the very popular manga series, these anime series follows teen ninja Naruto Uzumaki as he grows in power. Although there is some violence, the original series (*Naruto*) should be accessible to both teens and adults.

Sailor Moon (1992–1997): One of the early anime series to break into American television, *Sailor Moon* stands out for featuring a predominantly female cast. Although other series, such as *Tenchi Muyo!* and *InuYasha*, had females in strong supporting roles, *Sailor Moon* showed females could take the heroic lead.

The Tick (1994–1996): A hilarious sendup of comic book tropes, *The Tick* mixed barely competent superheroes with ridiculous supervillains possessing on-the-nose names to create the funniest comic book TV show.

Figure 8.2
Six Comic Book TV Shows for Library Collections

graphic novels; slapping the name of a hero or company onto the box does not instill excitement or fun in the game. Three types of games that do a better job of tapping into those feelings—and thus linking it to the library's comic book collection—are role-playing games, video games, and miniatures games.

ROLE-PLAYING GAMES

In role-playing games (RPGs), players "assume roles . . . and cooperatively seek to overcome obstacles and resolve conflicts placed before them by the game master" (Snow 2007). Each player is given or creates a list of statistics describing her character's physical and mental attributes; the players then decide the actions of their individual characters. The players and game master develop a story together, with the narrative structure laid out by the game master altered, enhanced, and confirmed by the choices of the players. Success or failure is often dictated by rolls of dice, ranging from the standard six-sided dice to less familiar polyhedral dice. These games allow players to tell their own stories. They can try to recreate their favorite storylines or characters, or they can try to tell new stories, the kind they would like to read about but have not been able to find. Allowing these games into the library cements the link between those stories and the library.

Dungeons & Dragons, a fantasy game, is the first and most famous RPG, but there have been many superhero RPGs since. The two most popular superhero RPGs are

Champions and Mutants & Masterminds. Champions is the older game, having been first published by Hero Games almost 30 years ago. Therefore, the game may be familiar to more players, possibly causing less confusion and less time lost while explaining the rules. The rules are also very flexible, making it easier to fit new players' ideas into the game. However, Champions is very math intensive, and it requires a large number of six-sided dice to play. Mutants & Masterminds is much newer, first published in 2002 by Green Ronin Press. The game is based on the d20 system that was developed for the third edition of Dungeons & Dragons; this means that although the game itself may be less familiar to gamers, the underlying mechanics are very familiar to many. Unfortunately, the Mutants & Masterminds version of the system is a highly modified form of the d20 system, thus mitigating that familiarity.

If either game is used for a library event—or if another superhero RPG is chosen—it is important to make sure the mechanics of the system are as transparent as possible. Giving players characters that have already been created[4] is one way to ease the strain, especially if annotations are made that allow players to put the character's statistics into context. The game master should also be prepared to handle as much of the game mechanics as possible to relieve the players from the burden of learning the rules quickly. This can put a strain on even an experienced game master, so finding someone with experience to run or help with the game is recommended. Academic and school libraries may be able to partner with student organizations for help; public libraries may be able to find local gaming groups or game masters at their local game or comics shop.

VIDEO GAMES

Video games are extremely popular, with more than $19.7 billion in sales in 2009 (Associated Press 2010). This type of game also has strong ties to comic books (see Table 8.5), and libraries can use those links and the games' popularity to draw attention to their collection.

There are several different styles of video games. Some of the most common are:

- Fighting games, in which two or more players control characters who spar in a bout
- Shooters, which are focused on projectile combat; they can be either first person, in which the action is seen over the character's shoulder, or third person, which allows the character to be seen
- Action-adventure games, which concentrate on exploration, gathering items, solving puzzles, and fighting
- Role-playing games, which allow players to control one or more characters who increase in power, abilities, and prestige as the game goes along
- Strategy games, which are based around planning and tactics—these are the video games most closely related to board games
- Music games, in which players tap buttons in certain sequences in order to simulate playing music.

The best choice of a game for a library event depends on a number of factors. For most game nights, games that encourage a regular rotation of players are probably the best choices. Fighting games allow for frequent substitution of players and make for easy tournaments, although some library users might be uneasy about the violent

Table 8.5
Video Games Based on Comic Books

Marvel

Fantastic Four on Game Boy Advance, Nintendo GameCube, PlayStation 2, and Xbox

Fantastic Four: Rise of the Silver Surfer on Nintendo DS, PlayStation 2, PlayStation 3, Wii, and Xbox 360

The First Avenger: Captain America on PlayStation 3 and Xbox 360

Ghost Rider on Game Boy Advance, PlayStation 2, and PSP

Hulk on Nintendo GameCube, PC, PlayStation 2, and Xbox

Incredible Hulk: Ultimate Destruction on Nintendo GameCube, PlayStation 2, and Xbox

Iron Man on Nintendo DS, PlayStation2, PlayStation3, PSP, Wii, and Xbox 360

Iron Man 2 on Nintendo DS, PC, PlayStation 3, PSP, Wii, and Xbox 360

Marvel vs. Capcom 2: New Age of Heroes on PlayStation 2, PlayStation 3, Xbox, and Xbox 360

Marvel Nemesis: Rise of the Imperfects on Game Boy Advance, Nintendo GameCube, PlayStation 2, PSP, and Xbox

Marvel Super Hero Squad: Infinity Gauntlet on Nintendo DS, PlayStation 3, Wii, and Xbox 360

Marvel: Ultimate Alliance on Game Boy Advance, PC, PlayStation 2, PlayStation 3, PSP, Wii, Xbox, and Xbox 360

Marvel: Ultimate Alliance 2 on Nintendo DS, PlayStation 2, PlayStation 3, PSP, Wii, and Xbox 360

Punisher on PC, PlayStation 2, and Xbox

Spider-Man 2 on Game Boy Advance, N-Gage, Nintendo DS, Nintendo GameCube, PC, PlayStation 2, PSP, and Xbox

Spider-Man 3 on Nintendo DS, PlayStation 2, PlayStation 3, PSP, Wii, and Xbox 360

Spider-Man: Friend or Foe on Nintendo DS, PlayStation 2, PSP, Wii, and Xbox 360

Spider-Man: Shattered Dimensions on Nintendo DS, PC, PlayStation 3, Wii, and Xbox 360

Spider-Man: The Movie on Game Boy Advance, Nintendo GameCube, PlayStation 2, and Xbox

Spider-Man: Web of Shadows on PlayStation 2, PlayStation 3, PSP, Wii, and Xbox 360

Ultimate Spider-Man on Nintendo GameCube, PlayStation 2, PC, and Xbox

X-Men: The Official Game on Nintendo GameCube, PlayStation 2, PC, Xbox, and Xbox 360

X-Men Legends on N-Gage, Nintendo GameCube, PlayStation 2, and Xbox

X-Men Legends II: Rise of Apocalypse on N-Gage, Nintendo GameCube, PC, PlayStation 2, PSP, and Xbox

X-Men Origins: Wolverine on Nintendo DS, PC, PlayStation 2, PlayStation 3, PSP, Wii, and Xbox 360

DC

Batman Begins on Game Boy Advance, Nintendo GameCube, PlayStation 2, and Xbox

Batman Vengeance on Game Boy Advance, Nintendo GameCube, PC, PlayStation 2, and Xbox

Batman: Arkham Asylum on PC, PlayStation 3, and Xbox 360

Batman: Dark Tomorrow on Nintendo GameCube and Xbox

Batman: Rise of Sin Tzu on Game Boy Advance, Nintendo GameCube, PC, PlayStation 2, and Xbox

(*continued*)

Table 8.5 (continued)

Batman: The Brave and the Bold on Nintendo DS and Wii
Catwoman on Game Boy Advance, Nintendo GameCube, PC, PlayStation 2, and Xbox
DC Universe on PC and PlayStation 3
Justice League Heroes on Nintendo DS, PlayStation 2, PSP, and Xbox
Lego Batman on Nintendo DS, PC, PlayStation 2, PlayStation 3, Wii, and Xbox 360
Mortal Kombat vs. DC Universe on PlayStation 3 and Xbox 360
Superman Returns on Nintendo DS, PlayStation 2, Xbox, and Xbox 360
Superman: Shadow of Apokolips on Nintendo GameCube and PlayStation 2
Superman: The Man of Steel on Xbox
Teen Titans on Nintendo GameCube, PlayStation 2, and Xbox
Watchmen: The End Is Nigh on PC, PlayStation 3, and Xbox 360

Manga
Astro Boy on PlayStation 2
Digimon Rumble Arena 2 on Nintendo GameCube, PlayStation 2, and Xbox
Digimon World Data Squad on PlayStation 2
Dragon Ball Z: Budokai on Nintendo GameCube, PlayStation 2, and Xbox
Dragon Ball Z: Budokai Tenkaichi on PlayStation 2
Dragon Ball Z: Burst Limit on PlayStation 3 and Xbox 360
Dragon Ball Z: Raging Blast 2 on PlayStation 3 and Xbox 360
Dynasty Warriors: Gundam on PlayStation 3 and Xbox 360
Fullmetal Alchemist and the Broken Angel on PlayStation 2
Ghost in the Shell: Stand Alone Complex on PlayStation 2 and PSP
InuYasha: Feudal Combat on PlayStation 2
InuYasha: The Secret of the Cursed Mask on PlayStation 2
JoJo's Bizarre Adventure on Dreamcast, PlayStation, and PlayStation 2
Lupin III: Treasure of the Sorcerer King on PlayStation 2
Mobile Suit Gundam: Journey to Jaburo on PlayStation 2
Mobile Suit Gundam: Zeonic Front on PlayStation 2
Naruto: Clash of Ninja on Nintendo GameCube
Naruto: Clash of Ninja Revolution on Wii
Naruto: Ultimate Ninja on PlayStation 2
Naruto: Ultimate Ninja Storm on PlayStation 3 and Xbox 360
Naruto: Uzumaki Chronicles on PlayStation 2
One Piece Grand Battle on Nintendo GameCube and PlayStation 2
One Piece: Unlimited Adventure on Wii
Shaman King: Power of Spirit on PlayStation 2
Super Dragon Ball Z on PlayStation 2
Wangan Midnight Maximum Tune 3 DX on PlayStation 3

Table 8.5 (continued)

Yu-Gi-Oh! 5D's: Wheelie Breakers on Wii

Yu-Gi-Oh! The Duelists of the Roses on PlayStation 2

Zatch Bell! Mamodo Battles on Nintendo GameCube and PlayStation 2

Zatch Bell! Mamodo Fury on Nintendo GameCube and PlayStation 2

Other

Asterix & Obelix: Kick Buttix on PlayStation 2

Comic Jumper: The Adventures of Captain Smiley on Xbox 360

The Darkness on PlayStation 3 and Xbox 360

Hellboy: The Science of Evil on PlayStation 3, PSP, and Xbox 360

Judge Dredd: Dredd vs. Death on Nintendo GameCube, PC, PlayStation 2, and Xbox

Spawn: Armageddon on Nintendo GameCube, PlayStation 2, and Xbox

Teenage Mutant Ninja Turtles on Nintendo GameCube, PC, PlayStation 2, and Xbox

TMNT Chronicles on PC, PlayStation 3, PSP, Wii, and Xbox 360

Turok: Evolution on Game Boy Advance, Nintendo GameCube, PC, PlayStation 2, and Xbox

Turok on PC, PlayStation 3, and Xbox 360

XIII on Mac, Nintendo GameCube, PC, PlayStation 2, and Xbox

content of these games. Strategy games are less explicitly violent and can offer chances to switch players, but they can be harder to find with superhero themes. It is important to pay attention to the age rating of these games and to match the age level of the expected attendees. Game reviews can help ensure no one is unpleasantly surprised by the game's quality or content. Also, since games are available on many different video-game systems, make sure the game is available on a platform available to your library.

Table 8.5 provides a list of video games based on different kinds of comic books. This list is not exhaustive, and new platforms for old games and new titles are being added all the time.

MINIATURES GAMES

Miniatures games are an older type of game than either video or role-playing games, as games based upon miniature representations of fighting forces have been around since the beginning of the twentieth century—in fact, author H. G. Wells invented a miniature game, called "Little Wars," in 1913. Most miniature games since then have revolved around wars, be they modern, historical, or science fictional. Today, there are three games based on superhero miniatures, each suited for library events.

The most popular one is Heroclix, a collectible game[5] based on the "clicking" mechanic of WizKids' MechWarrior (science fiction) and Mage Knight (fantasy) games. Heroclix miniatures are sold in "packs," which contain five randomly selected figures; the figures vary in power and rarity. In Heroclix, figures have certain powers and characteristics that change when they are "damaged" by another figure's attack; the success or failure of the attack is determined by rolling two six-sided dice. The damage is represented by turning (or "clicking") the figure's base, revealing a new set of powers and characteristics. Each figure has a point value, and players assemble teams whose point values add up to a certain predetermined limit. Games continue until all but one player's characters are knocked out or a time limit is reached. The game was first released in 2002, and in the years following, more than 3,000 different figures have been produced, giving the game a great deal of adaptability. Although the game was discontinued for a year (2008–2009), Heroclix has returned with releases throughout 2010 and beyond.

Marvel Attacktix is, like Heroclix, a collectible miniatures game. Released by Hasbro in 2006 and compatible with the previously released Star Wars and Transformers figures, Marvel Attacktix is a simpler game than the other two. No dice are required, no map or terrain tiles are needed, and the mechanics are more rudimentary than either of the other two miniature games, with movement being the only numerical consideration. There is a great deal of reliance on hand-eye coordination, with players firing small plastic missiles at the other player's figures; knocking a figure over removes it from the game. Games can be very quick, depending on the shooting skill of the players.

Heroscape is a game system that has produced miniatures from several different genres and time periods, including cowboys, Vikings, Romans, wizards, and dinosaurs. Unlike Heroclix or Attacktix, Heroscape is not a collectible game; although the game has several expansion sets, buyers always know what game pieces come in the boxes they buy. Like Heroclix, however, players choose the miniatures on their team. Each miniature has a card with statistics; damage, which is determined by special dice, is counted with markers rather than clicking. Hasbro released a Marvel-themed set in 2007, including 10 figures and terrain on which to play the game.

GAMES DAYS/NIGHTS

To promote the library and its collections, some libraries have sponsored games events (Helmrich and Neiburger 2005; Reed 2008; Sutton and Womack 2006; Vance 2009). These events invite users into the library to play games, usually a video, card, or traditional board game. But there is no reason why a library cannot use a games event to promote its comic book collection or vice versa. If the library does not have anyone on staff who is familiar with these games, outside help may be recruited. Again, libraries associated with high schools or universities may be able to get help for gaming nights—either with organizing or promoting—through gaming or hobby clubs associated with the school. Public libraries may wish to consult local gaming or comic book stores for advice on which games might best match up with the collection or users or even joint promotions.

National Gaming Day, which is held on a Saturday in the middle of November, is an excellent opportunity to use these kinds of games to emphasize the collection. Part of the Campaign for America's Libraries, National Gaming Day is an ALA-organized event that encourages libraries to use games to reach out to their communities. The event, which "focuses on the social and recreational side of gaming" (ALA 2009), uses both board and video games to promote libraries. In 2008, 2009, and 2010, libraries served as part of a nationwide video-game tournament, and Hasbro, the event's main sponsor, distributed free games to registered libraries. However, each library can decide to organize game events of their own choosing, and all three of the above discussed types of games would be excellent choices for the event. For more details, see http://ngd.ala.org.

CONCLUSION

The characters, titles, and style of comic books have spread into other areas of pop culture, giving librarians a rare opportunity. With a little extra thought, the opportunities to get graphic novels to work with the rest of the library's collections—and to get the rest of the collections to work with the graphic-novel collection—are many. Films, television, and games give libraries a chance not only to promote the graphic novel collection but also to build enthusiasm for many nontraditional areas of the library.

NOTES

1. The *Fantastic Four* (1994) movie was never released, although this was intentional; the movie was made to extend the movie rights to the property for the producers.

2. Such movies did exist before the twenty-first century, with *Darkman* (1990)—directed by *Spider-Man*'s Sam Raimi and starring Liam Neeson—being the most prominent.

3. Most of the Monopoly variants, such as Marvel Comics, Batman, Batman and Robin, Fantastic Four, Spider-Man, and X-Men Monopoly, were released by USAopoly but are out of print and may be expensive or hard to find. Stratego: Marvel Heroes, also based on a Hasbro product, may similarly be difficult to find. Specialized versions of Uno, such as Batman, Batman Begins, Fantastic Four, Incredible Hulk, Spider-Man, Superman, and X-Men Uno, were produced by Sababa Games, while Mattel concentrated on movie and TV versions of heroes: Superman Returns, The Batman, Spider-Man, Batman Begins, and Dark Knight Uno.

4. Players in RPGs are usually allowed to create their own characters, giving them a sense of connection with and investment in the game. However, time constraints and the aforementioned unfamiliarity with the system make leaving that to players an unwise option.

5. The first collectible game was Magic: The Gathering, a fantasy-themed card game that was released in 1993. Magic sold 15 randomly selected cards per pack, with certain cards being rarer or more powerful than others. Players assembled their cards into decks, hoping to find a combination of cards that worked well together. The combination of collecting and customizable game play quickly made its publisher—Wizards of the Coast—a force in the games market.

REFERENCES

American Library Association. "Celebrate National Gaming Day @ Your Library!" November 10, 2009. http://www.ala.org/ala/newspresscenter/news/pressreleases2009/november2009/ngd09_pio.cfm (accessed March 17, 2010).

Assosciated Press. "Hardware Boosts December Video Game Sales." MSNBC.com, January 15, 2010. http://www.msnbc.msn.com/id/34868317 (accessed April 26, 2010).

Box Office Mojo. "Hulk." http://www.boxofficemojo.com/movies/?id=hulk.htm (accessed
    March 17, 2010).
Ebert, Roger. "The Crow." *Chicago Sun-Times*, May 13, 1994. http://rogerebert.suntimes.com/
    apps/pbcs.dll/article?AID=/19940513/REVIEWS/405130302/102302/1023 (accessed
    April 17, 2010).
Helmrich, Erin, and Eli Neiburger. "Video Games as a Service: Hosting Tournaments at Your
    Library." *Voice of Youth Advocates* 27, no. 6 (2005): 450–53.
Reed, Jason. "Young Adults, Video Games, and Libraries." *Bookmobile and Outreach Services* 11,
    no. 1 (2008): 63–78.
Snow, Cason. "Dragons in the Stacks: An Introduction to Role-Playing Games and their Value to
    Libraries." *Collection Building* 27, no. 2 (2008): 63–70.
Sutton, Lynn, and H. David "Giz" Womack. "Got Game? Hosting Game Night in an Academic
    Library." *College and Research Libraries News* 67, no. 3 (March 2006): 173–76.
Vance, Dorothy. "Playing Games for Fun and Learning @ Your Library." *Mississippi Libraries*
    73, no. 1 (2009): 11–13.

9

Web Resources

The world of graphic novels may seem bewildering to newcomers. Fortunately, there are a host of Web sites to help those who are interested in the medium.

Several types of Web sites can be a boon to libraries with comics collections. Publishers' Web sites are authoritative but are geared more toward sales to individual readers than toward libraries' needs. Comics news sites offer the latest updates about popular comic book creators and tie-ins. Other sites provide information about sales figures and the popularity of new titles. Reviews of comics may be helpful for making acquisitions decisions, although reviews of the collected editions may be harder to come by. Lists of collected editions and their contents are another useful tool for librarians, as are recommendations. Sites on comics for younger readers can also help librarians decide what to acquire. Finally, sites dedicated to women in the comics world can help libraries market their collections toward women and develop more diverse collections.

Because so many graphic novels are released each year and characters and popular creators change from year to year, book resources can become out of date or incomplete within a few years. For that reason, this chapter omits books in favor of Web sites. However, some books will retain some or all of their usefulness, regardless of age; for a bibliography of those books, please see Appendix C.

PUBLISHERS

Comics publishers' own Web sites (see Figure 9.1) vary in helpfulness for those looking to buy collected editions. DC's Web site (http://www.dccomics.com) is the most useful of the major publishers. On their "Graphic Novels" pages, they list all of the trade paperbacks and hardcovers they have published. The only disadvantage is that the lists are separated by imprint; the mainstream superhero books, for instance, are on a different list than their Vertigo titles or their "DC Kids" books, which may feature superheroes but are written and drawn for young audiences.[1] The site also offers DC's "30 Essential Graphic Novels" (http://www.dccomics.com/sites/essential30), although

DC: http://www.dccomics.com

Marvel: http://marvel.com

Dark Horse: http://www.darkhorse.com

Image: http://www.imagecomics.com

IDW: http://www.idwpublishing.com

Figure 9.1
Publishers' WebSites in Brief

it seems heavy on books that feature Batman, are published under the Vertigo imprint, or are written by Alan Moore.

Marvel Comics (http://marvel.com) doesn't have a separate graphic novels or collected editions page. Instead, the company's "Comics" page (http://marvel.com/comic_books) allows users to see the company's offerings by clicking on the "Browse Comic Books" button. The comics and collected editions can be viewed by character, series, creator, event, or on-sale date. Each category can be filtered by the other categories (except "event"), age rating, and format (comic, digest, hardcover, or trade paperback). Multiple filter categories can be selected, but some filters allow only one choice (hardcover or trade paperback can be chosen as a format, but not both, for instance). The date filter can be limited to a selected month or a range of months. However, both the browsing and search functions of the Web site are somewhat unreliable, and using Google site search might be a more dependable way to search Marvel's past offerings.

Dark Horse Comics (http://www.darkhorse.com) similarly filters its products by their release date, although it does have a "Books" section, which promotes new and upcoming releases and has links to book previews. The "Upcoming" and "New Releases" section can be filtered by title, creator, or genre, and the directory can be changed to an alphabetical list. Dark Horse also has a "Best Sellers" link under its "Books" section, although there are no criteria or dates listed for the 10-item list. Both comics and books are also sorted into "Zones," which groups the publisher's products into a limited number of genres and title characters. The site also has a "Libraries" area (http://libraries.darkhorse.com), which provides links to recent and upcoming releases ("Current / Upcoming" tab), its books by suggested age ("Backlist" tab), links to reviews of its books ("Reviews" tab), and a core title list ("Bestsellers" tab).

Image Comics's site (http://www.imagecomics.com) lists this week's and upcoming comics and collections, but there is no separate page for trade paperbacks or hardbacks. The back catalog can be found using the "Coming Soon" tab on the schedule page (http://www.imagecomics.com/schedule.php), allowing navigation by month of release. There is no search function on the site. For more information, the "Links" page directs users to the individual studios' pages. IDW (http://www.idwpublishing.com) has a catalog page (http://www.idwpublishing.com/catalog), listing releases by series title. The site has a Google-powered search box as well.

COMICS NEWS

There are several comic book news sites (see Figure 9.2). Comic Book Resources (http://comicbookresources.com) and Newsarama (http://www.newsarama.com) are the

---

The Beat: http://www.comicsbeat.com

Comic Book Resources: http://comicbookresources.com

Comics Alliance: http://www.comicsalliance.com

Newsarama: http://www.newsarama.com

Publisher's Weekly*'s Comics News*: http://www.publishersweekly.com/pw/by-topic/
book-news/comics/index.html

Figure 9.2
Comics News in Brief

leading sites; CBR won the Eisner Award[2] for "Best Comics-Related Publication/
Journalism" in 2009, while Newsarama won the award in 2008. Both sites feature interviews, previews and solicitations, and articles on comics and the people who make them.
CBR features columns by Marvel editor in chief Joe Quesada ("Cup o' Joe") and prominent comics retailer Brian Hibbs ("Tilting at Windmills"); it was the former home of
"Lying in the Gutters," a popular comics rumor column by Rich Johnston. Newsarama
has a slightly wider scope; although it primarily covers comics, it also devotes coverage
to "genre entertainment" in media such as film, TV, and video games (Newsarama).
Primarily, these sites can update librarians on popular creators' latest projects and inform
them about tie-ins to comics, which may be useful for promotion (see Chapter 7).

Publisher's Weekly's Comics News page (http://www.publishersweekly.com/pw/
by-topic/book-news/comics/index.html) is a bit more useful for librarians interested in
comic books, though it is primarily focused on smaller comics publishers. The site has
news and interviews focused on the comics industry, but the news is primarily focused on
publishers and collections. Reviews of collections and comics are also included as
well as a monthly graphic-novel best-seller list. *Publisher's Weekly* also offers subscriptions to its "Comics Week" electronic newsletter (http://www.publishersweekly
.com/pw/email-subscriptions/index.html).

"The Beat," which was formerly a part of *Publisher's Weekly*, is a blog covering "comics culture" (http://www.comicsbeat.com). This gives the blog considerable leeway for
diversions, but it also covers mainstream comics and smaller publishers in admirable
depth. The site also has an extensive list of links to other sites related to comics. An interesting feature of "The Beat" is three monthly columns that look at the sales of comics
from DC, Marvel, and other publishers (categorized as "Indie"). Although none of these
lists include collected editions, these three columns look through the sales of comics
titles, compiled through data gained from ICv2.com,[3] and compare the most recent
month's sales to previous months. The columnists also try to explain—or puzzle out—
the reasons for a title's increase or decline (usually decline) in sales. This can let librarians know which titles are likely to remain popular in preparation to buying the collected
editions. These sales figures include sales to the direct market only and don't include
sales through other channels, such as subscriptions, bookstores, and newsstands.

Comics Alliance (http://www.comicsalliance.com) is a slightly different comics
news site. Like other sites in this category, it features news of major and minor comic
book companies and interviews with creators, but Comics Alliance distinguishes itself
by featuring more humor and original creative content than most news sites. Like most
of the leading sites that feature comics as a culture rather than a publishing medium, it

drifts into coverage of TV, movies, and video games that are somewhat tenuously connected to comics. It is part of AOL's "Asylum" network of sites.

SALES

Other sites can tell librarians which collected editions are the most popular. ICv2.com is perhaps the best known and most quoted of those sites. The site, which covers many areas of pop culture, collects sales data from the direct market. This allows them to assemble a monthly "Top 300 Graphic Novels" list, complete with estimated sales to comic book stores; the archives can be found at http://www.icv2.com/articles/home/ 1850.html. (A "Top 300 Comic Book" list can also be found at this archive, but although they provide the figures for the columnists at "The Beat," ICv2.com's sales columns do not have the same depth of analysis as "The Beat" does; see the preceding section.) These lists do not always consider bookstores or non-comics Internet retailers.

Other sites, however, can help fill in that gap in knowledge. Amazon.com has a graphic novels and comics bestseller list, which is updated hourly (http://www .amazon.com/gp/bestsellers/books/4366). The rapid updating can makes it difficult to notice long-term trends, although each entry does list the number of weeks each book has been in Amazon's top 100 graphic novels. Another flaw for librarians who are buying for a graphic novel collection is that the list often contains collections of comic strips—a different genre, although similar in some ways—and non–comic books by comics creators such as Neil Gaiman.

In 2009, the *New York Times* started publishing "Graphic Books" bestseller lists, compiling the top-10-selling hardcover, paperback, and manga books in bookstores nationwide (http://artsbeat.blogs.nytimes.com/tag/graphic-books-best-seller-lists). The lists are updated weekly and tell how long each book has been on the list. Since many collections' sales are evergreen, this means some titles (mainly paperbacks) will stay on the list for a long time, despite having been available for years before the *Times* started the lists. Still, it is probably the best snapshot of what is currently most popular outside the direct market.

Figure 9.3 summarizes the sites for sales figures and their URLs. For a list of resources on where to buy the graphic novels, see Chapter 5, under "Where to Buy Comic Books."

REVIEWS

Finding reviews of comics is easy; finding reviews of collected editions is more difficult. Still, as trade paperbacks and hardback editions become more popular, reviews of these books are becoming more prevalent. Although not an exhaustive list,

---

Amazon.com: http://www.amazon.com/gp/bestsellers/books/4366

The Beat: http://www.comicsbeat.com/category/sales-charts

ICv2.com: http://www.icv2.com/articles/home/1850.html

New York Times *Graphic Books Bestseller List:* http://artsbeat.blogs.nytimes.com/tag/ graphic-books-best-seller-lists

---

Figure 9.3
Comics Sales in Brief

the following sites have a large archive of graphic-novel reviews and have been updated recently:

- Collected Comics Library, which features reviews mainly in podcast form (http://www.collected comicslibrary.com)
- Collected Editions (http://collectededitions.blogspot.com)
- Comics Bulletins' Line of Fire Reviews (http://www.comicsbulletin.com/reviews/tpb.htm)
- Diamond Bookshelf (http://www.diamondbookshelf.com), a part of the Diamond Comic Distributors site, which combines original reviews with selected graphic-novel reviews from *Publisher's Weekly*, *Library Journal*, and *School Library Journal*
- Graphic Novel Reporter, although it has few superhero comic reviews (http://www .graphicnovelreporter.com)
- Grovel, although its superhero reviews cover mainly DC, including its Vertigo and America's Best Comics imprints (http://www.grovel.org.uk; formerly Graphic Novel Reviews)
- Masked Bookwyrm (http://www.pulpanddagger.com/maskedbookwyrm)
- No Flying, No Tights, which has short reviews, aimed mainly at teens, of books from a wide variety of genres (http://www.noflyingnotights.com)
- Trade Talks, which focuses on superhero titles, especially from Marvel (http://tradetalks .blogspot.com)[4]
- The Weekly Crisis, under its "Trade Waiting" label (http://www.weeklycrisis.com/search/label/ Trade Waiting)

User-contributed book reviews can also be found at Amazon.com, although these reviews are of uncertain quality and sometimes lack critical insight.

Occasionally, to get an idea of the quality of a book, librarians can look at reviews of individual issues from a collection. *The Comics Journal* (http://www.tcj.com), which started as a print magazine but has migrated to an online presence with semiannual print publication, is one of the foremost sources of comics journalism and has a great deal of reviews and comics news. However, it is famously dismissive of superhero comics. Comics Worth Reading (http://comicsworthreading.com) provides a range of reviews of both superhero and other genres, single issues and collections. Comic Book Galaxy (http://www.comicbookgalaxy.com/reviews.html) and Comics Daily (http://www .alternatecover.com) provide reviews of both single-issue comics and collections. The superhero stories reviewed by Read About Comics (http://www.readaboutcomics .com) are generally in single-issue form, and there are many reviews of books from smaller publishers. Both Newsarama and Comic Book Resources have reviews that concentrate on superhero stories. Long-time Internet comics commentators Marc-Oliver Frisch (http://comiksdebris.blogspot.com) and Paul O'Brien (http://www .housetoastonish.com) do weekly reviews, with the occasional review of a set of single-issue comics that might end up as a collected edition. The Kid's Comic Book Reviews (http://kidscomicbooks.blogspot.com) looks at comics from a unique point of view— the reviews are written by an nine-year-old, with minimal help from his father.

Reviews of manga and anime are not often found on the same site as reviews of American comics. Fortunately, plenty of sites can help fill that gap. Here is a sample:

- Anime News Network, which not only has reviews of anime and rankings of the most popular anime but is also an excellent source for news on anime and new releases (http://www .animenewsnetwork.com)

- Comic Book Bin (http://www.comicbookbin.com/manga.html)
- Gilles's Service to Fans Page has anime and manga recommendations and resources; anime and manga guides for parents, librarians, and teachers by librarian Gilles Poitras; and supplements and companions to Poitras's books on anime and manga (http://www.koyagi.com)
- Manga for Parents and Kids has a few reviews but more importantly has a guide and a glossary to manga (http://www.manga4kids.com)
- Manga Recon at Pop Culture Shock (http://www.popcultureshock.com/manga/index.php/category/reviews/manga-reviews)
- Manga Reviews (http://mangareviews.wordpress.com)
- Manga Worth Reading (part of Comics Worth Reading), with reviews by Joanna Draper Carlson, a long-time Internet commenter on comics (http://comicsworthreading.com/category/manga)
- Mangalife.com (http://www.mangalife.com/reviewsarchive.htm)
- Mania.com, which is part of a larger entertainment site, has a large collection of anime and manga reviews (http://www.mania.com/reviews_by_title.php)

There are also sites for those looking for a more scholarly examination of comics. The Comix-Scholars Discussion List (http://www.english.ufl.edu/comics/scholars) allows academic researchers, critics, and teachers to communicate about comics. Comicsresearch.org (http://comicsresearch.org) provides bibliographies with tables of contents for books about comic books and strips.

A few of the many outstanding review sites and their URLs are listed in Figure 9.4.

LISTS OF COLLECTED EDITIONS AND THEIR CONTENTS

An excellent resource for librarians looking for worthwhile graphic novels is the Trade Paperback List (http://tplist.millarworld.net/index.html). Although the site has not been updated since 2008, it does have an archive of "Books of the Week" picks, highlighting standout graphic novels. Books are listed by series title and include a short description, including the issues that were reprinted in the volume. This can be helpful if a library decides to collect all the stories in a title; regular collections might skip an issue or three because of a crossover while maintaining consecutive numbering on the reprint

---

Collected Comics Library: http://www.collectedcomicslibrary.com

Collected Editions: http://collectededitions.blogspot.com

Comic Book Galaxy: http://www.comicbookgalaxy.com/reviews.html

Comics Bulletins' Line of Fire Reviews: http://www.comicsbulletin.com/reviews/tpb.htm

Comics Worth Reading: http://comicsworthreading.com

Gilles' Service to Fans Page: http://www.koyagi.com

Manga for Parents and Kids: http://www.manga4kids.com

Mania.com: http://www.mania.com/reviews_by_title.php

The Kid's Comic Book Reviews: http://kidscomicbooks.blogspot.com

Figure 9.4
Reviews in Brief

volumes, but if those skipped issues were reprinted during the time the site was updating, the Trade Paperback List tells users where. The site can also help librarians trying to discover if they have all the volumes of a series that unhelpfully omits volume numbers on its reprints (such as DC's *Birds of Prey*; see Chapter 6, Example #2). The site's maintainers claim it will be updated again as soon as it is converted into a database-driven format.

Other sites can also help librarians discover information about trade paperback contents and series. DC's "Graphic Novels" pages, as mentioned above, are a great resource in this regard; on the off chance DC's site does not provide enough help, the "TPB Guide" at Mike's Amazing World of DC Comics (http://dcindexes.com/tpbs) can help fit in the gap. The Unofficial Handbook of Marvel Creators (http://www .maelmill-insi.de/UHBMCC/datafr.htm) can fill in the same sorts of information for Marvel comics, although its frame-based design is a bit trickier to navigate than the other two. For references on comics from all publishers, the Grand Comics Data Base (http://www.comics.org) is an excellent resource. Wikipedia and Amazon.com may also be helpful, but they are less reliable than the other Web sites for contents and series information.

Every month, each comic book company releases a list of what they will publish in three months' time. These advance solicitations are generally released during the third week of every month;[5] the information can be found on various news sites, and they generally contain the same, copied information from Diamond Comic Distributors' *Previews*. The listings usually contain the book's price, page count, and creators and include a short paragraph describing the book's contents. The solicitations also mention when the books will be released to the direct market (books may be released at the same time or later to other markets). Solicitations can be found at most major comic book news sites on the Web, such as Newsarama or Comic Book Resources (http://www .comicbookresources.com/?page=archive&type=kw&key=solicitations). Although entries on Amazon.com and other sites may list books scheduled to come out after the most recent set of solicitations, these entries are tentative at best and cannot be relied upon.

One of the best all-around sites for librarians looking for information on DC and Marvel trade paperbacks and hardcover collections is the Collected Editions Discussion Forums (http://marvelmasterworksfansite.yuku.com/directory). These forums can help librarians keep track of solicitations, possible future releases beyond solicitations, and current collections. There are frequent quick reviews, and the members are always willing to give an opinion on collections, if asked. Keep in mind, though, that the users here do tend to be more interested in collections of older material. Of particular interest are the Marvel Masterworks Message Board (http://marvelmasterworksfansite.yuku.com/ forums/1), which deals with all Marvel reprint collections, and the DC Archives Message Board (http://marvelmasterworksfansite.yuku.com/forums/6), which covers all DC TPBs and hardcover collections.

A brief summary of the sites discussed in this section can be found in Figure 9.5.

AGE-APPROPRIATE MATERIAL

Finding comics that match the age groups of users is an important concern, and fortunately, many Web resources can help. The Graphic Novels in Libraries mailing list (http:// groups.yahoo.com/group/GNLIB-L) is geared toward public and school librarians.

Comic Book Resources solicitations: http://www.comicbookresources.com/?page
=archive&type=kw&key=solicitations

DC Archives Message Board: http://marvelmasterworksfansite.yuku.com/forums/6

Marvel Masterworks Message Board: http://marvelmasterworksfansite.yuku.com/forums/1

Mike's Amazing World of DC Comics: http://dcindexes.com/tpbs

The Unofficial Handbook of Marvel Creators: http://www.maelmill-insi.de/UHBMCC/
datafr.htm

Trade Paperback List: http://tplist.millarworld.net/index.html

Figure 9.5
Collected Editions and Their Contents in Brief

The list shares reviews, resources, and notices about new titles. *School Library Journal*
places its graphic-novel review columns (http://www.schoollibraryjournal.com/csp/cms/
sites/SLJ/Reviews/GraphicNovels/index.csp) on its Web site; the reviews are divided into
"Grade and Elementary School" and "High School" sections, with each paragraph-long
review receiving a more specific age range from the reviewer. Katherine "Kat" Kan writes
the "Graphically Speaking" column (http://www.voya.com/tags/graphic-novels) for the
bimonthly journal *Voice of Youth Advocates*. Kan has been producing her short, roundup
reviews since 1995. ALA's Young Adult Library Services Association (YALSA) publishes
a list of graphic novels recommended for young adults every year (archive at http://www
.ala.org/ala/mgrps/divs/yalsa/booklistsawards/greatgraphicnovelsforteens/gn.cfm). As
mentioned in the "Reviews" section, comic book reviews with young people in mind include
Manga for Parents and Kids (http://www.manga4kids.com) and The Kid's Comic Book
Reviews (http://kidscomicbooks.blogspot.com). Also, the not-for-profit organization Kids
Love Comics! (http://kidslovecomics.com) provides lists of recommended titles in further-
ance of their mission to "reintroduce kids' comics to mainstream America" (Kids Love).

Among publishers, Marvel (http://marvel.com/comic_books) has age ratings for all
of its publications online, and Dark Horse has recommended ages for all of its graphic
novels at http://libraries.darkhorse.com. Manga publishers Udon (http://www
.mangaforkids.com) and Viz (http://www.vizkids.com) have sites for their children's
lines as well.

Figure 9.6 summarizes the most notable of these sites.

Graphic Novels in Libraries mailing list: http://groups.yahoo.com/group/GNLIB-L

"Graphically Speaking" at VOYA: http://www.voya.com/tags/graphic-novels

Kids Love Comics!: http://kidslovecomics.com

School Library Journal *graphic novel reviews*: http://www.schoollibraryjournal.com/csp/
cms/sites/SLJ/Reviews/GraphicNovels/index.csp

YALSA Great Graphic Novels for Teens Archive: http://www.ala.org/ala/mgrps/divs/yalsa/
booklistsawards/greatgraphicnovelsforteens/gn.cfm

Figure 9.6
Age-Appropriate Material in Brief

Fantastic Fangirls: http://fantasticfangirls.org

Friends of Lulu: http://friendsoflulu.wordpress.com

Occasional Superheroine: http://occasionalsuperheroine.blogspot.com

Sequential Tart: http://www.sequentialtart.com

When Fangirls Attack: http://womenincomics.blogspot.com

Written World: http://ragnell.blogspot.com

Figure 9.7
Women in Comics in Brief

WOMEN IN COMICS

The representation of women in superhero comics is often controversial, and several sites exist to examine female comic characters and to support and publicize female creators. (These are presented in brief in Figure 9.7.) The organization Friends of Lulu (http://friendsoflulu.wordpress.com) is perhaps chief among these; the group exists to "increase female readership of comics, to promote the work of women in comics, to offer networking opportunities and general support to women in comics, and to facilitate communication among women and men who share the organization's purpose" (Friends of Lulu "FAQ"). The group also annually gives out the Lulu Awards to "bring attention to the best, most women-friendly and reader-friendly work in comics and to recognize the work of women comics creators of the past" at the San Diego Comic-Con (Friends of Lulu "Lulu").

Other Web sites can help librarians decide what material might appeal to (or deter) female readers. The sites include Sequential Tart (http://www.sequentialtart.com), a site written by a group of women and dedicated to highlighting women's influence on the comics industry; Occasional Superheroine (http://occasionalsuperheroine.blogspot.com), a blog by a female writer and former comic book editor that covers the comic book industry and other topics; When Fangirls Attack (http://womenincomics.blogspot.com), a multi-author blog that focuses on gender in comics and comics fandom; Fantastic Fangirls (http://fantasticfangirls.org), in which four female fans discuss comics in solo posts and in roundtable discussions; and Written World (http://ragnell.blogspot.com), in which a female comics fan comments upon superhero comics (mainly DC).

CONCLUSION

Although these Web sites are extremely helpful, they are just some of the hundreds of Internet sites on comics. Hidden gems lie undiscovered, and the fluid nature of the Internet means some resources listed in this chapter may become unavailable or stop updating and new sites will spring up. Web sites that offered information for free can change to a subscription model or pay-per-view model, as the *New York Times* is planning (Wauters 2010), or previously metered content can become free to all. Part of these sites' usefulness is to provide links to those new sites that will aid librarians in finding the best graphic novels available.

NOTES

1. These books are usually not part of mainstream DC continuity.

2. Handed out every year at the San Diego Comic-Con and named after influential comics creator Will Eisner (see Chapter 3), the Eisners consider themselves the "Oscars of comics" (San Diego Comic Con).

3. ICv2 stands for "Internal Correspondence, v. 2." *Internal Correspondence* was a publication for retailers by Capital City Distribution before Diamond acquired Capital City in 1996.

4. For the sake of full disclosure, this site is operated by Bryan D. Fagan, one of the coauthors of this book, and all of the reviews on the site are contributed by him.

5. Or possibly the fourth week, if the month has five Wednesdays.

REFERENCES

Friends of Lulu. "FAQ." http://friendsoflulu.wordpress.com/about (accessed March 17, 2010).

Friends of Lulu. "Lulu Awards." http://friendsoflulu.wordpress.com/lulu-awards (accessed March 17, 2010).

Kids Love Comics! "About Kids Love Comics!" http://kidslovecomics.com/klc_about.html (accessed April 28, 2010).

Newsarama, "About Us," http://newsarama.com/about_us (cited April 1, 2010).

San Diego Comic-Con. "Eisner Awards FAQ." http://www.comic-con.org/cci/cci_eisnersfaq .shtml (accessed April 14, 2010).

Wauters, Robin. "The *New York Times* Announces Paid Content Plans for 2011." Tech Crunch, January 20, 2010. http://www.techcrunch.com/2010/01/20/new-york-times-metered -model-2011 (accessed March 17, 2010).

Glossary

Anime: Japanese animation, sometimes inspired by (or inspiring) manga.

Arc: A group of linked comic book issues connected by plot, theme, or recurring characters.

Big Two: Marvel and DC, the two largest publishers of American comic books.

Bronze Age: The third age of comics, stretching from about 1970 to 1985–1986. Comic book stories tried to increase their relevance and inclusiveness, and fantasy comics became prominent for a while.

Collected edition: Comic book issues collected in a book form, either as a hardback, trade paperback, or digest; sometimes used interchangeably with "graphic novel."

Colorist: The person who adds color to finished, inked art.

Comic book: A magazine-type publication telling stories with words and illustrations. The term can also refer to the storytelling conventions or other properties of these magazines.

Continuity: The internally consistent logic of a story, or more relevantly to comics, of a publisher's output. Continuity demands that relevant changes and revelations of previous stories be observed or mentioned in future stories; however, some stories are explicitly or implicitly set outside of established continuity.

Creator-owned: Comic book work in which the writer and/or artists own a significant portion of the copyrights, royalties, and licensing.

Crossover: Arcs spread over two or more comic book titles.

Direct market: The sale of nonreturnable comic books by distributors to specialty comics shops.

Golden Age: The first age of comic books, lasting from the late 1930s to the late 1940s. The era marks the rise of superheroes and their first decline; during this period the conventions of the superhero genre were first set.

Graphic novel: A comic book story published in book form. Unlike a collected edition, a graphic novel does not have to have been published as a single-issue comic book form first.

Inker: An artist who takes the penciled drawings of the penciler and uses inks to make them darker. Also called a "finisher" or "embellisher."

Issue: A single publication of a comic book title, usually numbered in sequential order. Also called a "floppy" or "pamphlet."

Letterer: The person who adds text, such as dialogue, sound effects, credits, and story titles, to the art of a comic book.

Limited series: A comic book title that has its length set before the first issue is published. Usually, limited series (or "miniseries") are 1–12 issues long.

Manga: Comic books published in Japan or comics that conform to the stylistic forms of Japanese comics.

Miniseries: *See* Limited series.

Modern Age: The fourth and most recent era of comics, lasting from about 1985–1986 to the present. The Modern Age has seen more violence and mature content than previous eras, and the importance of continuity has diminished, as seen in the increase in reboots and revamps. There has also been a growing diversity of publishers and genres.

Penciler: The artist who takes the writer's script and turns it into images, which is generally done in pencil.

Plotter: The writer who creates the plot of a comic book.

Reboot: A term for throwing out past stories for a title, character, or concept and telling new stories based around the original idea. Examples of non-comics reboots include the 2004–2009 *Battlestar Galactica* television show and 2009 *Star Trek* film.

Retcon: Short for "retroactive continuity," the addition of new details into the continuity of a character or title.

Revamp: A term for throwing out some parts of the continuity of a title, character, or concept but keeping the rest and telling new stories based on the altered continuity.

Scripter: The writer who gives the penciler a script describing what to draw for a comic book. These scripts can be detailed or loose plots (*see* Plotter).

Shōnen: Boys' manga, which concentrates on action.

Shōjo: Girls' manga, which focuses on relationships and romance.

Silver Age: The second era of comic books, stretching from 1956 to about 1970. The era saw a rebirth of superheroes, the rise of Marvel Comics, a new vitality in art styles, and heroes with real-life problems.

Title: A comic book series consisting of consecutively numbered issues with the same name.

Trade paperback: A particular type of collected edition, printed at about the same size as the original comic books, with a flexible cardstock cover. Among readers, sometimes "trade paperback" is colloquially used for all collected editions or even all graphic novels.

Universe: A fictional world shared by characters. For instance, most of DC's superheroes inhabit the "DC Universe," which means the characters can meet, and continuity is shared between titles in that universe.

Volume: An iteration of a comic book title, which generally begins with issue #1. Volumes can begin or end at the publisher's whim. Two comic books published at different times with the same name are different volumes of the title.

Work for hire: Work in which a writer or artist owns little or none of the copyrights or royalties.

Writer: The person responsible for creating an idea for a story that artists can illustrate. Writers are generally responsible for the plot, the script, and the dialogue in a comic.

Appendix A

Initial Graphic Title List and Inclusion Criteria

Title	ISBN	Price (2008)	Publisher	Why included on list
Alias, v. 1	0785111417	$19.99	Marvel	Female lead role in private detective genre
Alias, v. 2: Come Home	0785111239	$13.99	Marvel	Female lead role in private detective genre
All-Winners 1	0785118845	$50.00	Marvel	Golden Age Marvel titles
Arana, v. 1: Heart of the Spider	0785115064	$7.99	Marvel	Hispanic female super hero
Avengers Comic Collection DVD-ROM		$39.99	Marvel	Full run of Avengers comics up to 2005
Batgirl: Year One	140120080X	$19.99	DC	Female lead role in the DC Universe (original Batgirl)
Batman Chronicles, v. 1	1401204457	$14.99	DC	Foundation piece—reprints character's appearances from the 30s and 40s
Batman Chronicles, v. 2	1401207901	$14.99	DC	Foundation piece—reprints character's appearances from the 30s and 40s

(continued)

(continued)

Title	ISBN	Price (2008)	Publisher	Why included on list
Batman Chronicles, v. 3	1401213472	$14.99	DC	Foundation piece—reprints character's appearances from the 30s and 40s
Batman Chronicles, v. 4	1401214622	$14.99	DC	Foundation piece—reprints character's appearances from the 30s and 40s
Batman: The Dark Knight Returns	1563893428	$14.99	DC	Often called the greatest Batman story ever told, written by Frank Miller
Birds of Prey, v. 2: Old Friends, New Enemies	1563899396	$17.95	DC	DC all-female team-up book
Birds of Prey: Of Like Minds	140120192X	$14.99	DC	DC all-female team-up book
Black Panther by Jack Kirby, v. 1	0785116877	$19.99	Marvel	1970s black lead role in a Marvel comic book
Black Widow, v. 1	0785107843	$15.95	Marvel	Modern female lead (spy genre)
Blade: Undead Again	0785123644	$14.99	Marvel	Modern black lead role
Bone: One Volume Edition	188896314X	$39.95	Cartoon Books	Beautiful epic fantasy; well reviewed
Buddha Vols. 1–8		$119.60	Vertical	Bestselling manga series by Osamu Tezuka
Captain America and the Falcon, v. 1: Two Americas	0785114246	$9.99	Marvel	Modern title with black costar (2000s)
Captain America and The Falcon: Secret Empire	0785118365	$19.99	Marvel	1970s title with black costar
Captain America Comic Collection DVD-ROM		$39.99	Marvel	Full run of Captain America to 2007
Catwoman, v. 1: Dark End of the Street	1563899086	$14.99	DC	Modern DC female lead role.
DC Comics Rarities Archives, v. 1	9781401200077	$52.95	DC	Golden Age sampler (hardback)

Title	ISBN	Price (2008)	Publisher	Why included on list
Elektra, v. 1: Introspect	0785109730	$16.99	Marvel	Modern female lead role
Emma Frost, v. 1: Higher Learning	0785114130	$7.99	Marvel	Modern female lead role
Essential Daredevil I	0785109498	$16.99	Marvel	Core comic character (1960s–1970s)
Essential Daredevil II	0785114629	$16.99	Marvel	Core comic character (1960s–1970s)
Essential Daredevil III	0785117245	$16.99	Marvel	Core comic character (1960s–1970s)
Essential Daredevil IV	0785127623	$16.99	Marvel	Core comic character (1960s–1970s)
Essential Defenders I	0785115471	$16.99	Marvel	Core comic characters (1970s)
Essential Defenders II	0785121501	$16.99	Marvel	Core comic characters (1970s)
Essential Defenders III	0785126961	$16.99	Marvel	Core comic characters (1970s)
Essential Luke Cage I	0785116850	$16.99	Marvel	The first African American lead role in a superhero comic
Essential Luke Cage, Power Man II	0785121471	$16.99	Marvel	Continuing the first black lead role in a superhero comic
Essential Ms. Marvel I	0785124993	$16.99	Marvel	Early female lead role; feminist (1970s)
Essential Official Handbook of the Marvel Universe I	0785119337	$16.99	Marvel	Reference title
Essential Official Handbook of the Marvel Universe, Deluxe Edition I	0785119345	$16.99	Marvel	Reference title
Essential Official Handbook of the Marvel Universe, Deluxe Edition II	0785119353	$16.99	Marvel	Reference title
Essential Official Handbook of the Marvel Universe, Deluxe Edition III	0785119361	$16.99	Marvel	Reference title

(*continued*)

(continued)

Title	ISBN	Price (2008)	Publisher	Why included on list
Essential Peter Parker, the Spectacular Spider-Man I	0785116826	$16.99	Marvel	Flagship superhero of the Marvel universe in the 1970s–1980s
Essential Peter Parker, the Spectacular Spider-Man II	0785120424	$16.99	Marvel	Flagship superhero of the Marvel universe in the 1970s–1980s
Essential Peter Parker, the Spectacular Spider-Man III	0785125019	$16.99	Marvel	Flagship superhero of the Marvel universe in the 1970s–1980s
Essential Savage She-Hulk I	0785123350	$16.99	Marvel	Early female lead role (lawyer); created by Stan Lee (1970s)
Essential Spider-Woman I	0785117938	$16.99	Marvel	Early female lead role (1970s)
Essential Spider-Woman II	0785117938	$16.99	Marvel	Early female lead role (1970s)
Essential Thor I	0785107614	$16.99	Marvel	Norse god adapted to superhero mythos
Essential Tomb of Dracula I	078510920X	$16.99	Marvel	Premier Marvel horror comic
Essential Wolverine I	0785102574	$16.99	Marvel	With Spider-Man, the most popular Marvel character
Essential Wolverine II	0785105506	$16.99	Marvel	With Spider-Man, the most popular Marvel character
Fables (all volumes)		$137.91	DC/Vertigo	Graphic novels based on classic folk and fairy tales
Fall 2007 Naruto Box Set, Volumes 1–27	1421518600	$119.67	VIZ	Manga, among the most highly ranked graphic novel on the 2006 overall bestseller list; more popular with boys
Firestar	0785122001	$7.99	Marvel	Original four-issue miniseries (1980s) with female lead role
Fruits Basket, Volumes 1–18 ($9.95 ea.) Box set is available for 1–4.	1598168622	$179.10	TokyoPop	Manga, among the most highly ranked graphic novel on the 2006 overall bestseller list; more popular with girls

Title	ISBN	Price (2008)	Publisher	Why included on list
Ghost Rider Comic Collection DVD-ROM		$27.99	Marvel	Full run of the series
Golden Age Marvel Comics 1	0785116095	$50.00	Marvel	Golden Age Marvel titles
Harley Quinn: Preludes and Knock-Knock Jokes	1401216285	$24.99	DC	Female lead role in the DC Universe
Hellboy, v. 1: Seed of Destruction	1593070942	$17.95	Dark Horse	Popular/supernatural new hero
Hellboy, v. 2: Wake the Devil	1593070950	$17.95	Dark Horse	Popular/supernatural new hero
Hellboy, v. 3: The Chained Coffin and Others	1593070918	$17.95	Dark Horse	Popular/supernatural new hero
House of M: Uncanny X-Men	9780785116639	$13.99	Marvel	Follows X-Men DVD; part of House of M crossover.
Incredible Hulk Comic Collection DVD-ROM		$39.99	Marvel	Full run of the series through 2006
Inhumans	0785107533	$24.95	Marvel	Great writing
Invincible Iron ManComic Collection DVD-ROM		$39.99	Marvel	Full run of the series through 2006
Jinx: The Definitive Collection	1582401799	$24.95	Image	Independent comic; female bounty hunter
Kabuki, v. 1: Circle of Blood	1887279806	$19.95	Image	Independent title; Japanese female lead role
Kabuki, v. 2: Dreams	1582402779	$12.95	Image	Independent title; Japanese female lead role
League of Extraordinary Gentlemen, v. 1	1563898586	$14.99	DC/ABC	Victorian characters gather to make super team; written by Alan Moore
Love & Rockets, v. 1: Music for Mechanics	093019313X	$18.95	Fanta-graphics	Written by Hispanic author team; independent; features strong female characters

(continued)

(continued)

Title	ISBN	Price (2008)	Publisher	Why included on list
Man of Steel poster		$14.00	ALA Graphics	$17'' \times 38''$ poster to market the collection
Marvel: Women of Marvel I	9780785122197	$24.99	Marvel	Anthology of various Marvel women characters from all time periods
Marvel: Women of Marvel II	9780785127086	$24.99	Marvel	Anthology of various Marvel women characters from all time periods
Mary Jane, v. 1: Circle of Friends	078511467X	$5.99	Marvel	Female perspective/ protagonist aimed at younger readers
Mary Jane, v. 2: Homecoming	0785117792	$6.99	Marvel	Female perspective/ protagonist aimed at younger readers
MW by Osamu Tekuza	1932234837	$24.95	Vertical	Bestselling manga by Osamu Tezuka
Phoenix Vols. 1–12 ($ 15.95 ea.)	1569318689	$191.40	VIZ	Manga; the life work of the "father of manga," Osamu Tezuka, translated into English
Promethea, Book 1	1563896672	$14.99	DC/ABC	Alan Moore writes woman's magical awakening
Promethea, Book 2	1563899574	$14.99	DC/ABC	Alan Moore writes woman's magical awakening
Queen & Country, v. 2: Operation: Morningstar	192999835X	$8.95	Oni	British secret agent title, female lead role
Runaways, v. 1: Pride and Joy	0785113797	$7.99	Marvel	Modern, well-written, diverse superhero team; family issues
Runaways, v. 2: Teenage Wasteland	0785114157	$7.99	Marvel	Modern, well-written, diverse superhero team; family issues
Runaways, v. 3: Good Die Young	0785116842	$7.99	Marvel	Modern, well-written, diverse superhero team; family issues

Title	ISBN	Price (2008)	Publisher	Why included on list
Sandman, v. 1–10		$149.90	DC/Vertigo	Neil Gaiman's magnum opus. One of the most important modern comic series
She-Hulk, v. 1: Single Green Female	0785114432	$14.99	Marvel	Modern interpretation of She-Hulk; humorous slant
She-Hulk, v. 2: Superhuman Law	0785115706	$14.99	Marvel	Modern interpretation of She-Hulk; humorous slant
Showcase Presents Batgirl, v. 1	1401213677	$16.99	DC	Lead female role in DC comic (1970s)
Showcase Presents Batman, v. 1	1401210864	$16.99	DC	Batman's stories from the beginning of the Silver Age
Showcase Presents Batman, v. 2	1401213626	$16.99	DC	Batman's stories from the beginning of the Silver Age
Showcase Presents Flash, v. 1	1401213278	$16.99	DC	Iconic DC superhero
Showcase Presents Green Lantern, v. 1	1401207596	$9.99	DC	Iconic DC superhero
Showcase Presents Green Lantern, v. 2	1401212646	$16.99	DC	Iconic DC superhero
Showcase Presents Jonah Hex, v. 1	140120760X	$16.99	DC	Western/supernatural genre comic
Showcase Presents Justice League of America, v. 1	1401207618	$16.99	DC	Premier DC superhero team
Showcase Presents Justice League of America, v. 2	1401212034	$16.99	DC	Premier DC superhero team
Showcase Presents Justice League of America, v. 3	978140121718-1	$16.99	DC	Premier DC superhero team
Showcase Presents Sgt. Rock, v. 1	978140121713-6	$16.99	DC	War comic; few are reprinted today

(continued)

(continued)

Title	ISBN	Price (2008)	Publisher	Why included on list
Showcase Presents Supergirl, v. 1	1401217176	$16.99	DC	Female lead
Showcase Presents Superman, v. 1	1401207588	$16.99	DC	Iconic superhero
Showcase Presents Superman, v. 2	1401210414	$16.99	DC	Iconic superhero
Showcase Presents Superman, v. 3	1401212719	$16.99	DC	Iconic superhero
Showcase Presents Teen Titans, v. 1	140120788X	$16.99	DC	DC superteam made of young adults
Showcase Presents Wonder Woman, v. 1	1401213731	$16.99	DC	DC's iconic female lead character; best-known female comics character
Silver Surfer and Fantastic Four Comic Collection DVD-ROM		$34.99	Marvel	Full run of both series to 2004
Sin City, v. 1 and 2		$34.00	Dark Horse	Modern noir tales; adults only
Spider-Girl, v. 1: Legacy	0785114416	$7.99	Marvel	Modern comic with female in lead role; appropriate for younger readers
Spider-Girl, v. 2: Like Father, Like Daughter	0785116575	$7.99	Marvel	Modern comic with female in lead role; appropriate for younger readers
Spider-Girl, v. 3: Avenging Allies	0785116583	$7.99	Marvel	Modern comic with female in lead role; appropriate for younger readers
Spider-Man Comic Collection DVD-ROM		$39.99	Marvel	Full run of *Amazing Spider-Man* to 2006 (does not contain *Peter Parker, the Spectacular Spider-Man*)
Strangers in Paradise, v. 1	1892597268	$17.95		Independent title; friendship/love between two female leads

Title	ISBN	Price (2008)	Publisher	Why included on list
Supergirl: Power	1401209157	$14.99	DC	Modern female lead role
Superman Chronicles, v. 1	9781401207649	$14.99	DC	Foundation piece— reprints character's appearances from the 30s and 40s
Superman Chronicles, v. 2	9781401212155	$14.99	DC	Foundation piece— reprints character's appearances from the 30s and 40s.
Superman Chronicles, v. 3	140121374X	$14.99	DC	Foundation piece— reprints character's appearances from the 30s and 40s
Tales of Super-natural Law	9780963395498	$16.95	Exhibit A Press	Comic written by a lawyer describing legal practices using supernatural examples
Tank Girl 2	184023492X	$16.95	Titan Books	Female lead in postapocalyptic landscape
Top Ten, Book 1	1563896680	$17.99	DC/ABC	Modern police story based on superher-oes; written by Alan Moore
Top Ten, Book 2	1563899663	$14.99	DC/ABC	Modern police story based on superheroes; written by Alan Moore
Ultimate X-Men Comic Collec-tion CD-ROM		$12.99	Marvel	Full run of the series to 2006
Usagi Yojimbo, v. 1-10		$159.50	Fanta-graphics and Dark Horse	Based on Japanese samurai and myth set in sixteenth century (1980s–present)
V for Vendetta	9780930289522	$19.99	DC	British dystopia written by Alan Moore
Watchmen	9780930289232	$19.99	DC	Considered one of the greatest comic stories ever told; written by Alan Moore
Wonder Woman Archives, v. 1-3		$150.00	DC	Golden Age Wonder Woman

(*continued*)

(continued)

Title	ISBN	Price (2008)	Publisher	Why included on list
Wonder Woman, v. 1: Gods & Mortals	1401201970	$19.99	DC	DC's iconic female lead character; best-known female comics character
Wonder Woman, v. 2: Challenge of the Gods	1401203248	$19.95	DC	DC's iconic female lead character; best-known female comics character
X-Men Comic Collection DVD-ROM		$39.99	Marvel	Full run of the series
X-treme readers poster		$14.00	ALA Graphics	22″ × 28″ poster to market the collection

SECOND YEAR ADDITIONS

Title	ISBN	Price (2009)	Publisher	Why included on list
Alias, v. 3: The Underneath	0785111654	$16.99	Marvel	Continues series starring female private detective
Alias, v. 4: The Secret Origins of Jessica Jones	0785111670	$17.99	Marvel	Continues series starring female private detective
Batman Chronicles, v. 5	9781401216825	$14.99	DC	Continues series; has circulated four times
Batman Chronicles, v. 6	9781401219611	$14.99	DC	Continues series; has circulated four times
Batman Chronicles, v. 7	9781401221348	$14.99	DC	Continues series; has circulated four times
Birds of Prey, v. 2: Sensei & Student	1401204341	$17.99	DC	Has circulated; continues series
Birds of Prey, v. 3: Between Dark and Dawn	1401209408	$14.99	DC	Has circulated; continues series
Birds of Prey, v. 4: The Battle Within	1401210961	$17.99	DC	Has circulated; continues series
Birds of Prey, v. 5: Perfect Pitch	1401211917	$17.99	DC	Has circulated; continues series
Birds of Prey, v. 6: Blood and Circuits	1401213715	$17.99	DC	Has circulated; continues series
Birds of Prey, v. 7: Dead of Winter	9781401216412	$17.99	DC	Has circulated; continues series
Birds of Prey, v. 8: Metropolis or Dust	9781401219628	$17.99	DC	Has circulated; continues series
Birds of Prey, v. 9: Club Kids	9781401221751	$17.99	DC	Has circulated; continues series
Catwoman, v. 2: Crooked Little Town	1401200087	$14.95	DC	Has circulated; continues series
Catwoman, v. 3: Relentless	1401202187	$19.95	DC	Has circulated; continues series
Catwoman, v. 4: Wild Ride	1401204368	$14.99	DC	Has circulated; continues series

(*continued*)

Title	ISBN	Price (2009)	Publisher	Why included on list
Civil War: Amazing Spider-Man	0785122370	$17.99	Marvel	Would continue DVD-ROM series
Civil War: Fantastic Four	0785122273	$17.99	Marvel	Would continue DVD-ROM series
Civil War: Road to Civil War	0785119744	$14.99	Marvel	Part of "Civil War" series
Elektra, v. 2: Everything Old Is New Again	0785111085	$16.99	Marvel	Martial-arts story with female hero
Elektra, v. 3: Relentless	0785112227	$14.99	Marvel	Martial-arts story with female hero
Elektra, v. 4: Frenzy	0785113983	$14.99	Marvel	Martial-arts story with female hero
Emma Frost, v. 2: Mind Games	0785114130	$7.99	Marvel	Continues series; high circulation
Emma Frost, v. 3: Bloom	0785114734	$7.99	Marvel	Continues series; high circulation
Essential Defenders IV	9780785130611	$16.99	Marvel	Continues series; has circulated
Essential Thor II	9780785133810	$16.99	Marvel	Continues series; has circulated
Essential Thor III	9780785121497	$16.99	Marvel	Continues series; has circulated
Essential Tomb of Dracula II	9780785114611	$16.99	Marvel	Continues series; has circulated
Essential Tomb of Dracula III	9780785115588	$16.99	Marvel	Continues series; has circulated
Essential Wolverine III	9780785105954	$16.99	Marvel	Continues series; has circulated; movie scheduled to come out
Essential Wolverine IV	9780785120599	$16.99	Marvel	Continues series; has circulated; movie scheduled to come out
Essential Wolverine V	9780785130772	$16.99	Marvel	Continues series; has circulated; movie scheduled to come out
Fables, v. 10: The Good Prince	9781401216863	$17.99	DC	Continues series; has circulated

Title	ISBN	Price (2009)	Publisher	Why included on list
Fables, v. 11: War and Pieces	9781401219130	$17.99	DC	Continues series; has circulated
Fantastic Four, v. 6: Rising Storm	0785115986	$13.99	Marvel	Continues DVD-ROM series
Fantastic Four: Beginning of the End	9780785125549	$12.99	Marvel	Continues DVD-ROM series
Fantastic Four: J. Michael Straczynski, v. 1	9780785120292	$14.99	Marvel	Famous author
Fantastic Four: The Life Fantastic	0785122753	$16.99	Marvel	Famous author
Fantastic Four: The New Fantastic Four	9780785124832	$15.99	Marvel	Would Continues DVD-ROM series
Fantastic Four: World's Greatest	9780785132257	$24.99	Marvel	Would Continues DVD-ROM series
Hellboy, v. 4: The Right Hand of Doom	1593070934	$17.95	Dark Horse	Top-circulating item; continues series
Hellboy, v. 5: Conqueror Worm	1593070926	$17.95	Dark Horse	Top-circulating item; continues series
Hellboy, v. 6: Strange Places	1593074751	$17.95	Dark Horse	Top-circulating item; continues series
Hellboy, v. 7: The Troll Witch and Others	1593078609	$17.95	Dark Horse	Top-circulating item; continues series
Hellboy, v. 8: Darkness Calls	9781593078966	$19.95	Dark Horse	Top-circulating item; continues series
Hellboy: Oddest Jobs	9781593079444	$14.95	Dark Horse	Top-circulating item; continues series
Hulk, v. 1: Red Hulk	9780785128816	$24.99	Marvel	Would Continues DVD-ROM series
Hulk: Incredible Herc	9780785129912	$14.99	Marvel	Continues DVD-ROM series
Hulk: Planet Hulk	0785122451	$39.99	Marvel	Continues DVD-ROM series
Iron Man, v. 3: Civil War	9780785123149	$11.99	Marvel	Would Continues DVD-ROM series

(*continued*)

(continued)

Title	ISBN	Price (2009)	Publisher	Why included on list
Iron Man, v. 4: Director of SHIELD	9780785122999	$14.99	Marvel	Would Continues DVD-ROM series
Iron Man, v. 5: Haunted	9780785125570	$26.99	Marvel	Would Continues DVD-ROM series
Kabuki, v. 3: Masks of the Noh	158240108X	$12.95	Image	Independent title; Japanese female lead role
Kabuki, v. 4: Skin Deep	1582400008	$12.95	Image	Independent title; Japanese female lead role
Kabuki, v. 5: Metamorphosis	1582402035	$24.95	Image	Independent title; Japanese female lead role
Kabuki, v. 6: Scarab	1582402582	$19.95	Image	Independent title; Japanese female lead role
League of Extraordinary Gentlemen, v. 2	1401201180	$14.99	DC	Continues series; has circulated three times
League of Extraordinary Gentlemen: Black Dossier	9781401203078	$19.99	DC	Continues series; has circulated three times
Love & Rockets, v. 4: Tears from Heaven	093019344X	$18.95	Fanta-graphics	Written by Hispanic author team; independent title; features strong female characters
Love & Rockets, v. 5: House of Raging Women	0930193695	$18.95	Fanta-graphics	Written by Hispanic author team; independent title; features strong female characters
Love & Rockets, v. 6: Duck Feet	0930193814	$18.95	Fanta-graphics	Written by Hispanic author team; independent title; features strong female characters
Love & Rockets, v. 8: Blood of Palomar	1560970057	$18.95	Fanta-graphics	Written by Hispanic author team; independent title; features strong female characters
Love & Rockets: New Stories #1	9781560979517	$14.99	Fanta-graphics	Written by Hispanic author team; independent title; features strong female characters

Title	ISBN	Price (2009)	Publisher	Why included on list
New Avengers, v. 3: Secrets and Lies	9780785117063	$14.99	Marvel	Would Continues DVD-ROM series
New Avengers, v. 4: Collective	9780785119876	$14.99	Marvel	Would Continues DVD-ROM series
New Avengers, v. 5: Civil War	0785122427	$14.99	Marvel	Would Continues DVD-ROM series
New Avengers, v. 6: Revolution	0785124683	$14.99	Marvel	Would Continues DVD-ROM series
New Avengers, v. 7: The Trust	9780785125037	$19.99	Marvel	Would Continues DVD-ROM series
New Avengers, v. 8: Secret Invasion, Book 1 (hardcover)	9780785129462	$19.99	Marvel	Would Continues DVD-ROM series
New Avengers, v. 9: Secret Invasion, Book 2 (hardcover)	9780785129486	$19.99	Marvel	Would Continues DVD-ROM series
Promethea, Book 3	9781401200947	$14.99	DC	Has circulated; famous author; continues series
Promethea, Book 4	9781401200312	$14.99	DC	Has circulated; famous author; continues series
Promethea, Book 5	9781401206208	$14.99	DC	Has circulated; famous author; continues series
Queen & Country: The Definitive Edition, v. 1	9781932664874	$19.95	Oni	Has circulated
Queen & Country: The Definitive Edition, v. 2	9781932664898	$19.95	Oni	Has circulated
Queen & Country: The Definitive Edition, v. 3	9781932664966	$19.95	Oni	Has circulated
Runaways, v. 7: Live Fast	0785122672	$7.99	Marvel	Would Continues series
Runaways, v. 8: Dead End Kids	9780785123897	$15.99	Marvel	Would Continues series
She-Hulk, v. 3: Time Trials	0785117954	$14.99	Marvel	Continues series; has circulated

(*continued*)

(continued)

Title	ISBN	Price (2009)	Publisher	Why included on list
She-Hulk, v. 4: Laws of Attraction	0785122184	$19.99	Marvel	Continues series; has circulated
She-Hulk, v. 5: Planet Without a Hulk	0785123997	$14.99	Marvel	Continues series; has circulated
She-Hulk, v. 6: Jaded	9780785125631	$14.99	Marvel	Continues series; has circulated
Showcase Presents Batman III	9781401217198	$16.99	DC	Continues series; has circulated
Showcase Presents Green Lantern III	9781401217921	$16.99	DC	Continues series; has circulated
Showcase Presents Justice League of America IV	9781401221843	$16.99	DC	Continues series; has circulated
Showcase Presents Sgt. Rock II	9781401219840	$16.99	DC	Continues series; has circulated
Showcase Presents Supergirl II	9781401219802	$16.99	DC	Continues series; has circulated
Showcase Presents Superman IV	9781401218478	$16.99	DC	Continues series; has circulated
Showcase Presents Teen Titans II	9781401212520	$16.99	DC	Continues series
Showcase Presents the Flash II	9781401218058	$16.99	DC	Continues series; has circulated
Showcase Presents Wonder Woman II	9781401219482	$16.99	DC	Continues series
Silver Surfer: In Thy Name	9780785127499	$10.99	Marvel	Continues DVD-ROM series
Silver Surfer: Requiem	9780785117964	$14.99	Marvel	Continues DVD-ROM series
Sin City, v. 3: The Big Fat Kill	9781593072957	$17.00	Dark Horse	High circulation volume (3–4)
Sin City, v. 4: That Yellow Bastard	9781593072964	$19.00	Dark Horse	High circulation volume (3–4)

Title	ISBN	Price (2009)	Publisher	Why included on list
Sin City, v. 5: Family Values	9781593072971	$12.00	Dark Horse	High circulation volume (3–4)
Sin City, v. 6: Booze, Broads, and Bullets	9781593072988	$15.00	Dark Horse	High circulation volume (3–4)
Sin City, v. 7: Hell and Back	9781593072995	$28.00	Dark Horse	High circulation volume (3–4)
Spider Man: Back in Black	0785129960	$24.99	Marvel	Continues DVD-ROM series
Spider-Girl, v. 4: Turning Point	0785118713	$7.99	Marvel	Continues series starring young female hero
Spider-Girl, v. 5: Endgame	0785120343	$7.99	Marvel	Continues series starring young female hero
Spider-Girl, v. 6: Too Many Spiders!	0785121560	$7.99	Marvel	Continues series starring young female hero
Spider-Girl, v. 7: Betrayed	0785121579	$7.99	Marvel	Continues series starring young female hero
Spider-Girl, v. 8: Duty Calls	0785124950	$7.99	Marvel	Continues series starring young female hero
Spider-Girl, v. 9: Secret Lives	0785126023	$7.99	Marvel	Continues series starring young female hero
Spider-Man: Brand New Day, v. 1	9780785128434	$24.99	Marvel	Continues DVD-ROM series
Spider-Man: Brand New Day, v. 2	9780785128441	$24.99	Marvel	Continues DVD-ROM series
Spider-Man: Brand New Day, v. 3	9780785132158	$19.99	Marvel	Continues DVD-ROM series
Spider-Man: Kraven's First Hunt	9780785132165	$19.99	Marvel	Continues DVD-ROM series
Spider-Man: One More Day	0785126333	$24.99	Marvel	Continues DVD-ROM series
Strangers in Paradise, v. 2: I Dream of You	1892597012	$16.95	Abstract	Has circulated
Strangers in Paradise, v. 3: It's a Good Life	1892597306	$17.95	Abstract	Has circulated

(continued)

(continued)

Title	ISBN	Price (2009)	Publisher	Why included on list
Strangers in Paradise, v. 4: Love Me Tender	1892597039	$12.95	Abstract	Has circulated
Strangers in Paradise, v. 5: Immortal Enemies	1892597381	$17.95	Abstract	Has circulated
Strangers in Paradise, v. 6: High School!	1892597071	$8.95	Abstract	Has circulated
Strangers in Paradise, v. 7: Sanctuary	1892597098	$15.95	Abstract	Has circulated
Strangers in Paradise, v. 8: My Other Life	189259711X	$14.95	Abstract	Has circulated
Supergirl: Candor	1401212263	$14.99	DC	Continues series starring female superhero
Supergirl: Identity	1401214843	$19.99	DC	Continues series starring female superhero
Superman Chronicles, v. 4	9781401216580	$14.99	DC	Continues series; has circulated two times
Superman Chronicles, v. 5	9781401218515	$14.99	DC	Continues series; has circulated two times
Superman Chronicles, v. 6	9781401221874	$14.99	DC	Continues series; has circulated two times
Ultimate X-Men, v. 14: Phoenix?	078512019X	$10.19	Marvel	Continues DVD-ROM series
Ultimate X-Men, v. 15: Magical	0785120203	$11.99	Marvel	Continues DVD-ROM series
Ultimate X-Men, v. 16: Cable	0785125485	$14.99	Marvel	Continues DVD-ROM series
Ultimate X-Men, v. 17: Sentinels	0785125493	$17.99	Marvel	Continues DVD-ROM series
Ultimate X-Men, v. 18: Apocalypse	9780785125501	$13.99	Marvel	Continues DVD-ROM series

Title	ISBN	Price (2009)	Publisher	Why included on list
Ultimate X-Men, v. 19: Absolute Power	9780785129448	$12.99	Marvel	Continues DVD-ROM series
Uncanny X-Men: Divided We Stand	9780785119838	$12.99	Marvel	Continues DVD-ROM series
Uncanny X-Men: Extremists	9780785119821	$13.99	Marvel	Continues DVD-ROM series
Uncanny X-Men: New Age, v. 3: On Ice	0785116494	$15.99	Marvel	Continues DVD-ROM series
Uncanny X-Men: New Age, v. 4: End of Greys	9780785116646	$14.99	Marvel	Continues DVD-ROM series
Uncanny X-Men: New Age, v. 5: First Foursaken	0785123237	$11.99	Marvel	Continues DVD-ROM series
Uncanny X-Men: The Rise & Fall of the Shi'ar Empire	0785118004	$29.99	Marvel	Continues DVD-ROM series
Usagi Yojimbo, v. 10	9781595822802	$15.95	Dark Horse	Continues high-value series
Wonder Woman, v. 3: Beauty and the Beasts	1401204848	$19.95	DC	Continues series; has circulated
Wonder Woman, v. 4: Destiny Calling	1401209432	$19.99	DC	Continues series; has circulated
Wonder Woman: The Circle	9781401219321	$24.99	DC	Continues series; has circulated
Wonder Woman: The Ends of the Earth	9781401221362	$24.99	DC	Continues series; has circulated
Wonder Woman: Who Is Wonder Woman?	1401212336	$19.99	DC	Continues series; has circulated
X-Men: Messiah CompleX	9780785123200	$29.99	Marvel	Continues DVD-ROM series

Appendix B

Comic Book Characters and Their Titles

Note: These lists do not include various spinoffs, miniseries, one shots, annuals, or giant-size comics

MARVEL

Avengers: *Avengers* (1963–2004, 2010–), *West Coast Avengers* (1984–1994; called *Avengers West Coast* from 1989 to 1994) *Solo Avengers* (1987–91; called *Avengers Spotlight* from 1989 to 1991), *Force Works* (1994–1996), *Avengers Unplugged* (1995–1996), *New Avengers* (2005–), *Mighty Avengers* (2007–2010), *Avengers: The Initiative* (2007–2010), *Avengers Classic* (2007–2008; reprints with original backup stories), *Dark Avengers* (2009 2010), *Avengers Academy* (2010–), *Secret Avengers* (2010–)

Conan: *Conan the Barbarian* (1970–1993), *Savage Tales* (1971–1974), *Savage Sword of Conan* (1974–1995), *Conan the King* (1980–1989; called *King Conan* from 1980 to 1983), *Conan the Adventurer* (1994–1995), *Conan* (1995–1996), *Conan the Savage* (1995–1996), *Conan* (2004–2008; published by Dark Horse), *Conan the Cimmerian* (2008–; published by Dark Horse)

Hulk: *Incredible Hulk* (1962–1963, 1968–1999, 2000–2008, 2009–; called *Incredible Hulks* 2010–2011), *Tales to Astonish* (1964–1968; shared title with Giant Man and the Wasp from 1964 to 1965 and Namor the Sub-Mariner from 1965 to 1968), *Hulk* (1977–1981, 1999–2000, 2008–; called *Rampaging Hulk* from 1977 to 1978)

Iron Man: *Tales of Suspense* (1963–1968; shared title with Captain America from 1964 to 1968), *Iron Man* (1968–2009; called *Iron Man: Director of SHIELD* from 2008 to 2009), *Invincible Iron Man* (2008–)

Punisher: *Punisher* (1987–1995, 1995–1997, 2000–2001, 2001–2004, 2004–2009, 2009–; called *Punisher: Frank Castle* in 2009 and *Franken-Castle* in 2010), *Punisher War Journal* (1988–1995, 2007–2009), *Punisher War Zone* (1992–1995), *PunisherMax* (2010–)

Spider-Man: *Amazing Spider-Man* (1963–), *Marvel Team-Up* (1972–1985, 1997–1998), *Spectacular Spider-Man* (1976–1998, 2003–2005; called *Peter Parker, the Spectacular*

Spider-Man from 1976 to 1987), *Web of Spider-Man* (1985–1995, 2009–2010), *Spider-Man* (1990–1998; called *Peter Parker: Spider-Man* from 1996 to 1998), *Spider-Man Unlimited* (1993–1998, 2004–2006), *Untold Tales of Spider-Man* (1995–1997), *Spider-Man Team-Up* (1995–1997), *Sensational Spider-Man* (1996–1998, 2006–2007), *Peter Parker: Spider-Man* (1999–2003), *Webspinners* (1999–2000), *Tangled Web (of Spider-Man)* (2001–2003), *Marvel Knights Spider-Man* (2004–2006), *Friendly Neighborhood Spider-Man* (2005–2007), *Spider-Man Family* (2007–2008)

Note: *Spider-Man 2099* and *Ultimate Spider-Man* are about different characters from the Marvel Universe Spider-Man.

Wolverine: *Wolverine* (1988–2009, 2010–), *Wolverine: Origins* (2006–2010), *Wolverine: First Class* (2008–2010), *Wolverine: Weapon X* (2009–2010), *Wolverine: The Best There Is* (2010–)

Note: *Dark Wolverine* is about the character's son.

X-Men: *Uncanny X-Men* (1963–; called *X-Men* 1963-1981), *Classic X-Men* (1986–1995; reprints with original backup stories from 1986 to 1990), *X-Men Legacy* (1991–; called *X-Men* from 1991 to 2001 and from 2004 to 2008; called *New X-Men* from 2001 to 2004), *X-Men Unlimited* (1993–2003, 2004–2006), *X-Men: The Hidden Years* (1999–2001), *X-Treme X-Men* (2001–2004), *Astonishing X-Men* (2004–), *X-Men: First Class* (2006–2009), *Uncanny X-Men: First Class* (2009–2010), *X-Men Forever* (2009–2011)

Note: *X-Men 2099* and *Ultimate X-Men* are about different characters from the Marvel Universe X-Men

DC

Atom: *Atom* (1962–1969; called *Atom and Hawkman* from 1968 to 1969), *Power of the Atom* (1988–1989), *All-New Atom* (2006–2008)

Batman: *Detective Comics* (1938–), *Batman* (1940–), *World's Finest Comics* (1941–1986), *Brave and the Bold* (1966–1983), *Batman and the Outsiders* (1983–1986, 2007–2009), *Batman: Shadow of the Bat* (1992–2000), *Batman Chronicles* (1995–2001), *Batman: Legends of the Dark Knight* (1989–2007; called *Legends of the Dark Knight* from 1989 to 1992), *Batman: Gotham Knights* (2000–2006), *All Star Batman and Robin, the Boy Wonder* (2005–2011; called *Dark Knight: Boy Wonder* in 2011), *Batman Confidential* (2007–), *Trinity* (2008–2009), *Batman & Robin* (2009–), *Batman: Streets of Gotham* (2009–), *Batman, Inc.* (2010–)

Black Canary: *Black Canary* (1993), *Birds of Prey* (1999–2006, 2010–), *Green Arrow/Black Canary* (2007–2010)

Catwoman: *Catwoman* (1993–2001, 2002–2008), *Gotham City Sirens* (2009–)

Green Arrow: *Green Lantern* (1970–1972), *Green Arrow* (1988–1998, 2001–2007), *Green Arrow/Black Canary* (2007–2010)

Green Lantern: *Green Lantern* (1941–1949, 1960–1972, 1976–1986, 1990–2004, 2005–), *Green Lantern Corps* (1986–1988, 2006–), *Green Lantern Corps Quarterly* (1992–1994), *Green Lantern: Mosaic* (1992–1993), *Green Lantern: Emerald Warriors* (2010–)

Justice League: *Justice League of America* (1960–1987, 2006–), *Justice League America* (1987–1996; called *Justice League* in 1987; called *Justice League International* from 1987 to 1989), *Justice League Europe* (1989–1994), *Justice League International* (1993–1994), *Justice League Quarterly* (1990–1994), *Justice League Task Force* (1993–1996), *JLA* (1997–2006), *JLA Secret Files* (1997–2004), *Justice League Elite* (2004–2005), *JLA Classified* (2005–2008), *Justice League: Cry for Justice* (2009–2010)

Legion of Super-Heroes: *Adventure Comics* (1958–1969), *Legion of Super-Heroes* (1973, 1980–1984, 1984–1989, 1989–2000, 2005–2006, 2008–2009), *Tales of the Legion of Super-Heroes*

(1984–1987; also called *Tales of the Legion*), *Legionnaires* (1993–2000), *Legion Secret Files* (1998–2004), *Legion* (2001–2004), *Supergirl and the Legion of Super-Heroes* (2006–2009)

Superman: *Action Comics* (1938–), *Superman* (1939–1986, 1987–2006, 2006–), *World's Finest Comics* (1941–1986), *DC Comics Presents* (1978–1986), *Adventures of Superman* (1987–2006), *Superman: The Man of Steel* (1991–2003), *Superman: The Man of Tomorrow* (1995–1999), *All-Star Superman* (2006–2008), *Trinity* (2008–2009)

Teen Titans: *Teen Titans* (1966–1973, 1976–1978, 1996–1998, 2003–), *New Teen Titans* (1980–1984), *New Titans* (1984–1996; called *New Teen Titans* from 1984 to 1988), *Tales of the Teen Titans* (1984–1988), *Teen Titans Spotlight* (1986–1988), *Team Titans* (1992–1994), *Titans* (1999–2003, 2008–)

Appendix C

Further Readings on Comics, Graphic Novels, Manga, and Anime

READING COMICS

Eisner, Will. *Comics and Sequential Art: Principles and Practices from the Legendary Cartoonist.* New York: W. W. Norton, 2008.

McCloud, Scott. *Understanding Comics: The Invisible Art.* Northampton, MA: Kitchen Sink Press, 1993.

Wolk, Douglas. *Reading Comics: How Graphic Novels Work and What They Mean.* Cambridge, MA: Da Capo Press, 2007.

COMICS HISTORY AND BACKGROUND

Cornog, Martha, and Timothy Perper, eds. *Graphic Novels: Beyond the Basics.* Santa Barbara, CA: Libraries Unlimited, 2009.

Goulart, Ron. *Comic Book Encyclopedia: The Ultimate Guide to Characters, Graphic Novels, Writers, and Artists in the Comic Book Universe.* New York: HarperEntertainment, 2004.

Misoroglu, Gina, ed., with David A. Roach. *The Superhero Book: The Ultimate Encyclopedia of Comic-Book Icons and Hollywood Heroes.* Detroit, MI: Visible Ink, 2004.

Pilcher, Tim, and Brad Brooks. *The Essential Guide to World Comics.* London: Collins & Brown, 2005.

Robbins, Trina. *From Girls to Grrrlz: A History of Women's Comics from Teens to Zines.* San Francisco: Chronicle, 1999.

Sabin, Roger. *Comics, Comix and Graphic Novels.* London: Phaidon Press, 2008.

Weiner, Stephen. *Faster than a Speeding Bullet: The Rise of the Graphic Novel.* New York: NBM, 2003.

GENRE/SELECTION GUIDES

Gravett, Paul. *Graphic Novels: Everything You Need to Know.* New York: Collins Design, 2005.

Kannenberg, Gene, Jr. *500 Essential Graphic Novels: The Ultimate Guide.* New York: Collins Design, 2008.

Pawuk, Michael. *Graphic Novels: A Genre Guide to Comic Books, Manga, and More.* Westport, CT: Libraries Unlimited, 2007.

Weiner, Stephen. *The 101 Best Graphic Novels.* New York: NBM, 2005.

MANGA AND ANIME

Brenner, Robin E. *Understanding Manga and Anime.* Westport, CT: Libraries Unlimited, 2007.

Clements, Jonathan, and Helen McCarthy. *The Anime Encyclopedia: A Guide to Japanese Animation Since 1917.* Revised and expanded ed. Berkeley, CA: Stone Bridge Press, 2007.

Drazen, Patrick. *Anime Explosion: The What? Why? and Wow! of Japanese Animation.* Berkeley, CA: Stone Bridge Press, 2002.

Gravett, Paul. *Manga: Sixty Years of Japanese Comics.* London: Lawrence King, 2004.

Lehman, Timothy R. *Manga: Masters of the Art.* New York: Collins Design, 2005.

Poitras, Gilles. *Anime Essentials: Everything a Fan Needs to Know.* Berkeley, CA: Stone Bridge Press, 2001.

Schodt, Frederik L. *Dreamland Japan: Readings on Modern Manga.* Berkeley, CA: Stone Bridge Press, 1996.

Thompson, Jason. *Manga: The Complete Guide.* New York: Ballantine, 2007.

MAGAZINES

Alter Ego. http://twomorrows.com/index.php?main_page=index&cPath=55. TwoMorrows Publishing, 10407 Bedfordtown Dr., Raleigh, NC 27614.

Comic Art Magazine. http://www.comicartmagazine.com. Buenaventura Press, P.O. Box 23661, Oakland, CA 94623.

The Comics Journal. http://www.tcj.com. Fantagraphic Books, 7563 Lake City Way NE, Seattle WA 98115.

ICv2's Internal Correspondence. http://www.icv2.com/articles/news/9922.html. ICv2, 448 W. Washington Ave., Madison, WI 53703.

Otaku USA Magazine. http://www.otakuusamagazine.com. Otaku USA, 1000 Commerce Park Drive, Suite 300, Williamsport, PA 17701.

Wizard. http://www.wizarduniverse.com. Wizard Entertainment, 1010 Avenue of the Americas 3rd Floor, New York, NY 10018.

Index

About the Authors

BRYAN D. FAGAN has an MLS from the University of Maryland and is a freelance writer. He reviews comic book trade paperbacks at his blog, Trade Talks (http://tradetalks .blogspot.com).

JODY CONDIT FAGAN is an associate professor and the content interfaces coordinator at James Madison University Libraries and Educational Technologies in Harrisonburg, Virginia. Ms. Fagan has written numerous peer-reviewed articles, and her first book, *Web Project Management for Academic Libraries*, was published with Jennifer A. Keach in 2009.

Together they created and now maintain a popular comic book collection at James Madison University.